Mysterious Chicago

History At Its Coolest

ADAM SELZER

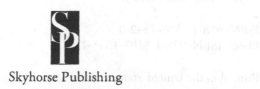

Skyhorse Publishing

Skyhorse Publishing books may be purchased in bulk at special discounts for sales promotion, corporate gifts, fund-raising, or educational purposes. Special editions can also be created to specifications. For details, contact the Special Sales Department, Skyhorse Publishing, 307 West 36th Street, 11th Floor, New York, NY 10018 or info@skyhorsepublishing.com.

Skyhorse® and Skyhorse Publishing® are registered trademarks of Skyhorse Publishing, Inc.®, a Delaware corporation.

Visit our website at www.skyhorsepublishing.com.

10 9 8 7 6 5 4

Library of Congress Cataloging-in-Publication Data is available on file.

Cover design by Rain Saukas
Cover photo credit: iStock

ISBN: 978-1-5107-1342-0
Ebook ISBN: 978-1-5107-1345-1

Printed in the United States of America

CONTENTS

INTRODUCTION

I worked in the ghost tour biz for a decade, and I never saw anything that I'd swear in front of a panel of scientists was really a dead person up and floating around. But I kept going on ghost hunts, because a ghost is the least of what you can find when you go poking around an old Chicago building; in old theaters, hotels, and skyscrapers across the city, I found hidden staircases, secret passages, nooks and crannies, and occasionally even tunnels. At one theater we moved a sign on the wall and found four lip-prints behind it, signed and dated on December 15, 1939. A scan of the newspaper archives from the date indicated that the prints were probably left by a vaudeville troupe called The Dancing Sweethearts.

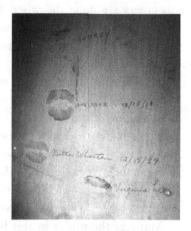

This was the kind of research that really hooked me. Books on Chicago history can be a good starting place, but if you *really* want to investigate, they're just a start. There's a near-endless supply of fantastic stories that occupied a lot of space in newspapers

The lip-prints in the Oriental Theater.

in their time, but somehow never made it into our collective history.

In searching for material for my books, blogs, and tour stories, I've spent many happy days poring over microfilm reels of defunct newspapers, reading through crumbling paperwork in the legal archives, and tracking down surviving witnesses. I could probably spend the rest of my life just finding all of the primary data on H. H. Holmes, perhaps the most fasincating of our antique murderers (and about whom almost nothing accurate has ever been written). But there's always a new story to look into, and every new story comes with new mysteries to solve.

Chicago history is full of questions that no one expects will ever be answered. Among the more famous: What really started the Great Chicago Fire? What was the St. Valentine's Day Massacre really all about, and who were the shooters? Was Marshall Field, Jr., really shot at the Everleigh Club, not in his living room? Who killed the Grimes Sisters? Beyond those are several lesser-known mysteries. Was there really a near-successful attempt to revive Nick "The Choir Singer" Viana after he was hanged? And what was the deal with the submarine wreck that was found in the Chicago River in 1915?

Looking for the answers to these questions can be a real treasure hunt. When I'm working on new stories to tell on my tours, I realize that I don't need *every* piece of data; plenty of tour guides get by on reading a few pulp retellings of a story, then making up the rest, and customers are none the wiser. But Indiana Jones—an authority on these things—once said, "Archaeology is the search for facts, not truth. We cannot afford to take mythology at face value." That's my motto about history, too.

Also, people can fact-check me on their phones nowadays; I'm too paranoid to lie. So I roll up my sleeves and try to find out everything I can about every story I tell.

Though I've tried to focus on lesser-known stories that have never really been retold for this volume, I've also naturally included several of the more famous stories. In those cases, I've at least tried to research them enough that I feel like I'm including data that you won't find in countless other books that have told the same story.

Many of the stories in this book I've researched in depth. Others I don't know *quite* as well, particularly the ones that happened too recently for me to be flippant about them on tours. In a lot of cases, I've probably missed a clue or two. The solution to some of these mysteries could still be out there someplace, maybe not even that deeply buried.

I'll race you to it!

Adam Selzer
Mysterious Chicago Tours
mysteriouschicago.com

The author in the basement of the Sixty-Third Street post office, in the small portion that overlaps with the site of the H.H. Holmes "Murder Castle," 2016.

Does the Historical
Society Have the Bones
of an Early Settler?

If you want to see a dead body, cemeteries aren't going to help you. They're in the business of keeping the dead hidden beneath the sod and behind marble slabs. But plenty of corpses can be seen in Chicago's museums. The Field Museum has its mummies. The Museum of Science and Industry recently hosted Body Worlds, an exibit with over 200 preserved human specimens. The Museum of Surgical Sciences has all kinds of wonderful stuff. The Chicago History Museum isn't *quite* as morbid as some of them, but it does have the bed on which Abraham Lincoln died on display.

And, someplace in storage, they have a box containing the skeleton of one of Chicago's pioneers.

Or, anyway, they *think* it's him.

In 1896, the Chicago Historical Society opened their first museum in a new space on Dearborn Street, a hulking gothic mansion (now a nightclub) featuring displays of weapons from the Haymarket Affair, items that belonged to George Washington, and a fireplace that had survived the Great Chicago Fire in 1871, among other curios. In the corner of the south room on the second floor were the bones of Jean LaLime, one of the city's earliest non-native settlers, and possibly the city's first murder victim.[1]

Back when the eighteenth century was drawing to a close, the land that would one day be Chicago sat right about on the edge of the frontier; you could hunt big game where Chicago Avenue is now, and wolves were common in the woods where Halsted Street now sits. Further west was the sort of wilderness we can barely imagine today.

Though a Potowatomie tribe lived nearby, the first non-native settler to live in what is now downtown Chicago is generally agreed to have been Jean Baptiste Point du Sable, who arrived in the late 1700s and set up an impressive house for himself.

Little about du Sable or his background is really known; some say he was a Haitian native who had studied in France and returned to America to sell coffee, and a fictionalized biography in 1953 theorized that he was the son of a pirate and a freed slave. There's not really enough data to establish either of those as true. The commonly seen portrait of him was drawn decades after his death, and may be strictly the result of the artist's imagination. Du Sable is as big a mystery as any in the city. To call him the "founder" of the city, as we sometimes do, is a bit of a misnomer; he was the first non-native to live here, but didn't set out a plan of roads or anything, and abruptly left town around 1800. A couple of nineteenth-century biographies suggest that he left the area because he was angry that the Potowatamie wouldn't make him chief of the tribe, though these stories weren't based on any real data, either.

What we do know comes largely from Augustin Grigoon, a Wisconsin man who heard from his brother that du Sable was "[a] negro . . . my brother visited Chicago about 1794 and told me that Point deSaible [sic] was a large man; . . . he was a trader, pretty wealthy, and drank freely."[2]

For decades, school children were taught that the founder of the city was John Kinzie, who moved into du Sable's old house around the time that Fort Dearborn was built across the river from it. Kinzie, too, was not exactly a *founder*, per se; his social-climbing daughter-in-law, Juliette, just promoted him as such, and no one got around to checking her story for years. Modern historians have generally said that she exaggerated.

Jean LaLime, another early settler, moved to town about 1804, and became something of a rival to Kinzie. Both worked with the soldiers at Fort Dearborn and as traders with the occasional travelers who came through. Since practically no one *did* come through town looking to trade in those days, the rivalry between the two men may have been fierce. It came to a head in June 1812, when Kinzie stabbed LaLime to death.

One pioneer, Gurdon Hubbard, wrote about what he knew about the killing in an 1881 letter to former mayor Long John Wentworth: "Mr. Kinzie," he said, "never, in my hearing, alluded to or spoke of it. He deeply regretted the act. Mrs. Kinzie said that her husband and Lalime [sic] had for several years been on unfriendly terms, and had had frequent altercations; that at the time of the encounter Mr. Kinzie had crossed the river alone, in a canoe, going to the fort, and that Lalime [sic] met him outside the garrison and shot him, the ball cutting the side of his neck . . . Mr. Kinzie, closing with Lalime [sic], stabbed him and returned to the house covered with blood."[3]

Mrs. Victoire Porthier, who claimed to have witnessed the act, wrote her account in 1883, when she was about ten years old:

"It was sunset when they used to shut the gates of the fort. Kinzie and LaLime came out together and soon we heard Lt. Helm call out for Mr. Kinzie to look out for LaLime, as he had a pistol. Quick we saw the men come together; we heard the pistol go off, and saw the smoke. Then they fell down together. I don't know as Lalime [sic] got up at all but Kinzie got home pretty quick. Blood was running from his shoulder where Lalime [sic] had shot him . . . You see Kinzie wasn't to blame at all. He didn't have any pistol nor knife—nothing. After Lalime [sic] shot him and Kinzie got his arms around him, [LaLime] pulled out his dirk and as they fell he was stabbed with his own knife. That is what they all said . . . I don't know what the quarrel was about. It was an old one—business, I guess."[4]

Kinzie hid out in the woods for several days after the brawl, afraid that he'd be arrested for murder and hanged. The officers at Fort Dearborn, who seemed to like LaLime, decided to bury the body right near Kinzie's house, supposedly so that his front porch would always offer a haunting view of the grave. As much as they liked LaLime, though, they eventually ruled that the killing was in self-defense, though whispers suggest that this was only to stop Kinzie himself from telling the authorities some sort of dirt he had on the officers. In any case, Kinzie returned home and kept LaLime's grave in order.

The bones were eventually said to have been exhumed and moved to St. James's churchyard in the 1830s, near the present-day corner of Illinois and Wabash streets; the church burned down in the Great Fire of

1871, and people of the post-
fire city seem to have forgotten
there was ever a grave there.

In April 1891, workers were
digging out the foundation for
a new building at Illinois and
Rush (where the Jazz Record
Mart would stand in the early
twenty-first century). One
turn of the shovel accidentally
uncovered a human skull,
which flew out of the ground
with the rest of the rubbish and
rolled into the gutter, where

St. James Episocopal Church, LaLime's
second burial site.

nearby kids promptly began to use it as a football. Several other bones were
found in a rotten coffin that crumbled as soon as someone touched it.[5]

A man named Robert Fergus heard of the discovery, had an idea
that they might be LaLime's bones, and ran off to collect them. The
workers were inclined to disregard his request and throw them out, but
Fergus brought in the cops. The officers thought the whole thing was
hilarious, but took the skull away and put it in a box with the other
bones in the cellar in the Chicago Avenue police station. In the days
that followed, a few people came forward and agreed with Fergus: the
new foundation workers were digging right about where the yard of St.
James Church had been, and no one except LaLime was ever buried
there, so the bones were presumably his.

A month later, the bones were turned over to the Chicago Historical
Society, which conducted their own investigation. Judge Blodgett testified that he remembered that in 1831 and 1832, when playing with
other boys on the North Side, he used to run past the old Agency
House, which they called "Cobweb Castle."[6] Behind Cobweb Castle
was a maze of brushes, and the boys told him that in the middle of
them was the grave of a man that "Old Man Kinzie" had killed back in
the old days. The brush behind Cobweb Castle was right about where
St. James Church was built a few years later.

None of the old-time members of St. James Church remembered
the yard ever having been used for burials, but a man named John

C. Haines had a "dim recollection" of LaLime's grave being on the grounds. Another man remembered *a* grave on the space, but had no idea whose it was.[7]

The best forensic analysis 1891 could offer determined little more than that the remains were probably about old enough to be LaLime's, but that was enough for the historical society. Without any *better* idea of who the bones could belong to, they agreed to identify them as LaLime and added what was left of the skeleton to their collection of historical memorabilia. Five years later, when the museum opened, they were a prominent exhibit.

Years passed, the museum moved, and the building on Dearborn became a series of nightclubs, perhaps most famously the Excalibur Club. In a stage show there in the early twenty-first century, it was said that the building was now haunted by LaLime's ghost, though in their version of the story, the bones had been in a previous building on the spot that was destroyed in the Great Chicago Fire, skeleton and all. In reality, the remains weren't even dug up until nearly twenty years after the fire.

In fact, not only did the bones not burn in the fire, the Historical Society still has them. They'll admit it when asked, but they seem a bit sheepish about it; the identification was not entirely scientific, and if they're not LaLime's bones, they might be subject to reburial under the Native American Grave Repatriation Act.

But the evidence given by the Historical Society in 1891 is fairly persuasive; the full testimonies they collected from early settlers and scientists were published in 1893 as Appendix F in Joseph Kirkland's *The Chicago Massacre of 1812*.

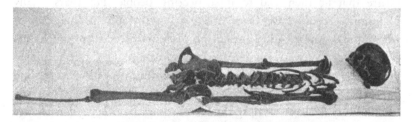

The bones on display in the original museum.

Did George Green Steal the Gallows?

And Is His Wife Still Buried Near the University of Illinois at Chicago Campus?

Just after Lucretia Thompson's dead body was found being swarmed by pigs in 1840, a man named John Stone was caught burning his pants nearby. He said in court that he was burning them because they were dirty, but when asked why he didn't burn his shirt, too, he slipped up and said, "There was no blood on it." That slip of the tongue led Stone to be the first man hanged in Chicago.

A custom-built gallows was set up on the South Side dunes; a noose was prepared by George White, the town crier and local jack-of-all-trades; and Stone was hanged before a small crowd.[8] After a vote on what to do with Stone's remains, his body was turned over to Dr. Dyer, a local physician, for dissection.[9]

Days later, according to later reports, the gallows themselves were stolen by a man named George Green, who used them to make furniture that he then sold to unsuspecting people. For years, many Chicagoans could have been using gallows wood in their homes without even knowing it. It might not have bothered them much; bits of hanging ropes were sought-after relics in those days. But keeping a bit of rope in your drawer was one thing; eating your dinner off of an old gibbet was something else.

The story of Green stealing the wood comes from *Life of the Chicago Banker Geo. W. Green, alias Oliver Gavit, Who Was Found Guilty of Poisoning His Wife,* which is likely Chicago's first "true crime" book. Published in 1855, after Green himself had cheated becoming the *next*

local man to be hanged by committing
suicide in prison, the book portrays
Green as a sort of Dickensian villain
who poisons his neighbors, tortures
animals, and murders babies, laughing
all the while.

In looking over Green's now-forgotten
case, several outstanding mysteries come
up:

George Green, one of
Chicago's first villains.

1. Did he really steal the city's
   first gallows, as the biography
   claimed?
2. Could his wife's body still be
   buried right near the University of Illinois at Chicago campus?
3. Is the photograph of his dead body hanging in his prison cell
   still extant?

George Green was an early settler who made his home near 12th
and Loomis (which would be Roosevelt and Loomis today). Surviving
drawings of the house make it clear that this land was still mostly prairie
in the 1830s, with lots of space for farming and livestock; being a mile
or so away from the future site of the Loop, now the main downtown
area and then pretty much the whole of the city, was as good as being
out in the country in those days.

It would have been a fairly short walk from Green's house down
to the dunes around 26th Street, where John Stone was hanged in
1840, and it's to be assumed that Green was in the crowd that day. The
authors of the book on Green said that they were hesitant to tell the tale
of him stealing the gallows, but "since we are fully able to corroborate
it on the testimony of some of our most respectable citizens," they put
it right alongside all of the many, many stories they collected of him
torturing animals.

"The gallows had been erected by Mr. Isaac R. Gavin, the Sheriff,
and remained upon the ground for some time subsequent to the execution," they wrote. "Mr. Daniell B. Heartt, commonly known as
Popcorn Heartt, purchased the gallows of the sheriff, and proceeded to
the spot where it stood with his team in order to draw it off. He found,

however, that somebody had been beforehand . . . and subsequently
learned that Green had actually stolen it, and that by that time, it had
probably been worked up into articles of furniture for the use of our
citizens generally!"[10]

Green, according to the authors of the book, spent the next several
years on a veritable crime spree that cost him no more trouble than
making him unpopular with his neighbors and in-laws. But fourteen
years after the hanging, he finally took things too far by murdering his
wife.

Green and his wife had, by all accounts, a stormy relationship.
He would send her off on financial errands knowing that she wasn't
familiar enough with currency to know that she was cheating people;
when she found out and objected, he whipped her.

In September 1854, Mrs. Green was four months pregnant. Green
had one grown son with whom he didn't particularly get along, and
anecdotal evidence strongly held that the early deaths of some of his
other children had been largely due to his neglect, or even that he
actively had a hand in their deaths. It was generally agreed that he
wasn't thrilled to have another baby coming.

One Saturday morning, some friends of Mrs. Green came to visit her
and George casually informed them that she had just died of cholera.
He had already dug a grave in the garden in which he planned to bury
her, in fact.

Cholera was a common enough killer at the time for it to be a plausible story, and it killed people fast, so the fact that she'd been fine
the day before didn't necessarily indicate any foul play. But her friends
were suspicious all the same; Green said that she'd been dead for only
a few hours, but from what they could smell from the porch, she'd had
time to decompose. Soon, a casual investigation found that Green's
young son had been showing off a bottle of "medicine" that his father
had given his mother and had demonstrated how far he could throw
it. The broken bottle was rounded up, and appeared to have contained
strychnine.[11]

Green's brother-in-law, S. J. Noble, had heard Green say many times
that he wished to God his wife was dead, and that then he would get rid
of her whole damned family. When word got around that his sister was
now being buried in the garden, Noble charged into the house.

"Green," he said, "I knew you would kill my sister some time; you have done it, and now I hope you are satisfied." Green walked away, muttering that she'd died of cholera, then chatted with neighbors about the price of lots and horses, seemingly unconcerned that his wife was dead.

The next day, Noble came back with the sheriff. Green met them at the door with a loaded gun, threatening to shoot, but the sheriff persuaded him to drop the weapon and be taken in peacefully.

After all of his testimony was taken, it was decided that a postmortem examination would be performed. Mrs. Green's body was exhumed from the garden, and three corked jars were used to preserve the stomach, a bit of the intestines, and the undigested food that was found inside of them.

The resulting trial became something of a landmark case in the history of forensic chemistry. Dr. James Blaney (who would one day be among the founders of Rosehill Cemetery) made a careful analysis of the remains and presented his findings to the jury in great detail. The testimony was transcribed in medical journals worldwide; a portion went:

> *The etherial residue was dissolved in alcohol, in which it dissolved without residue, and the alcoholic solution set aside to evaporate spontaneously. The residue left by evaporation of the alcohol exhibited a great number of exceedingly minute crystals, contaminated with a delinquent animal matter. . . . On inclining slightly the small glass capsule with contained the crystals, the aqueous solution drained to the lower side, leaving the most of the crystals in a tolerable state of purity. The aqueous solution drained from the crystals had an intensely bitter taste.*[12]

One can only hope that he didn't actually *taste* them, but how else would he know about the intensely bitter taste?

From there, Blaney went on at length describing tests made on the crystals to show the presence of strychnine. It's nearly impossible to imagine that jurors would have understood the tiniest bit of what he was talking about, but the testimony persuaded them: Green was found guilty.

No source I've seen mentions what was done with the body of Mrs. Green after it was exhumed; it may have been taken to the City Cemetery that was then in operation on the North Side (where Lincoln Park is now), but it may have also simply been taken back to the grave Green had dug for her. If so, it's entirely possible that it's *still* under the ground someplace along Roosevelt and Loomis. Despite being famous enough to be the subject of a book in his own day, Green was forgotten quickly enough that if a skeleton had been dug up near Loomis Street just twenty years later, it's possible that no one would have even remembered that Green used to live there.

Back in his prison cell, Green took the quilt from his bed, tied one end to the bars of the window, and hanged himself by the neck, saving the city the trouble of executing him.

Not much seems to be known about the final disposition of *his* remains, either; they may have ended up in another grave beside those of his wife, though it's more likely that upon his own death his remains would have been given over to the doctors for dissection (Dr. Dyer was still in town), if they weren't taken straight to City Cemetery. But we do know a great deal about what happened to the body in the first hours after it was found.

After cutting the remains down and lying them on a slab, the sheriff allowed a number of spectators in to have a look, including the authors of the book on Green that was published shortly thereafter. "The appearance of the corpse," they wrote, "showed the terrible determination of the man when living. The lower jaw projected, and there was a look upon the face which almost said, 'I am defeated but not entirely conquered.'"[13]

Even *before* he was cut down, the sheriff let photographer E. M. Strong into the cell to take a photograph of him hanging from the bars. It was the only photograph ever known to have been taken of Green, and the *Tribune* informed the public that Strong would be selling dageuerrotype copies at "[t]he portable daguerrean saloon, corner of Randolph and La Salle Streets."[14]

The drawing reproduced here, taken from the biography, may be all that survives of the photo.

No one's found a copy of the daguerrotype, but with Green's story all but forgotten for over a century, it's likely that no one's been looking for one, either. For all anyone knows, a genuine copy could still be sitting in an archive, a ghastly relic of early Chicago waiting to be rediscovered.

A drawing based on the daguerrotype of Green's suicide. Is a copy of the original still out there someplace?

Who's Buried in
Ira Couch's Tomb?

Though most early settlers were buried in family plots, a few official burial grounds were set up in the city early on. There was a section of graves of soldiers who died of cholera at Fort Dearborn somewhere around the grounds where Wabash Street meets the south banks of the Chicago River, and in the 1830s, two proper cemeteries were founded on the north and south edges of the city, at what is now Cermak and Michigan on the south, and near the site Chicago Avenue on the north, near the spot where the Water Tower would be built a few decades later.

At the time, it was thought that these two spaces were far enough from the city that no one would have to live near a burial ground, which in those days were prone to overcrowding, noxious odors, and bodies that declined to stay buried. People who died in urban areas in previous centuries had generally been buried in churchyards, where bodies tended to be stacked one on top of the other, with the top layer of coffins only inches below ground. If you want a really entertaining afternoon, and don't mind spoiling your appetite, look up *Gatherings from Graveyards*, a sanitary commission's report on the conditions of London churchyards in the 1840s, on archive.org. The commission found open pits of rotting effluvia, bones sticking out of the ground, and smells beyond description at one churchyard after another.

As these north- and south-side graveyards became too close to the expanding city, a one-hundred-acre site further north was set aside to become City Cemetery, which was in business for about twenty years, holding the remains of everyone from the city's elite to the thousands of Confederate prisoners of war who died at Camp Douglas. It was an early attempt to create a "garden cemetery," a then-novel concept in which cemeteries would be pleasant places with lovely monuments, green grass, and no fumes capable of killing anyone who inhaled them. But the area around Clark Street and North Avenue wasn't the outskirts for long, either, and burying bodies so near the waterworks, in moist ground, wasn't the most forward-thinking idea the city ever had. The cemetery was barely a decade old when Rosehill, Graceland, and Oak Woods cemeteries were founded further from downtown.

City Cemetery quickly became fertile ground for grave robbers. Medical schools were always in need of bodies, and when Martin Quinlan, the city sexton, was caught helping "resurrection men" from a local school load bodies from recent interments onto a cart in 1856, it was found that nine of the last ten graves dug there had been disturbed. The *Chicago Tribune* and *Chicago Times* spent a few weeks sniping at each other over a mystery that's never exactly been cleared up: whether Martin Quinlan was a Republican, like the *Tribune* editors, or a Democrat, like the people at the *Times*. Each paper tried hard to pin him to the other side.

One of the bodies he'd been caught robbing was that of a man who'd died after having his leg amputated, and in the midst of the subsequent arguments in the press, the medical schools made a pretty good point: if the doctor performing the operation had had more bodies to practice on, the man might not have died in the first place. Schools *needed* bodies.

Dr. A. J. Baxter reminisced about those days in 1890, in a way that gives us some idea of what the City Cemetery was like in the 1860s: "Cadavers were frightfully scarce," he said. "The hospitals were very small and awfully unaccomadating, and, anyway, people were not dying just then with any praiseworthy rapidity; probably they were too busy or the doctors were not thick enough. . . . Science could not be allowed to suffer, [so] I was perforce compelled to become a bold and burking resurrectionist. I made weekly or even more frequent visits to the cemeteries. My favorite hunting field was the [City] Cemetery then at the lake shore and Schiller Street; right out in the country, for Chicago Avenue was the city limits at that time. It was a dismal, neglected place, and the burial ground was usual[ly] ankle deep with sand."[15]

With rising worries that the dead bodies in the moist ground were being mixed into the drinking water, and with better-planned cemeteries like Graceland and Rosehill now in existence, the decision was made to close down City Cemetery, move the bodies, and convert the place into Lincoln Park.

No one ever believed they moved everyone, and that many bodies were left behind was clear to anyone who came to check out the new park in its early days. Louid de Koven Bowen, an early settler who grew up with the city, remembered being horrified when her father took her to see the brand-new park. "As we drove through," she wrote, "we saw countless open graves with a piece here nad there of a decayed coffin, and every now and then on a pile of dirt a bone . . . the whole place looked exactly as if Judgement Day had come, the trumpets had sounded and everyone had arisen from their graves, dropping now and then a little piece of their anatomy. . . . I remember coming away from the park thinking that never would I be tempted to seek it for pleasure purposes. . . . Years later, when the house in which I now live (on the south end of the grounds) was built I can remember bones cropping up from the ground when the foundation was being dug . . . the first maids who came to me in that house said they were very doubtful about coming lest the people who had been buried in the basement would rise and haunt them."[16]

News stories of bodies being found in Lincoln Park even *now* are not particularly uncommon, and anecdotes from employees at the Lincoln

The Couch Tomb in Lincoln Park.

Park Zoo indicate that news reports only cover a small portion of the incidents when coffins and bones are found in the grounds. In 1998, excavations for a parking lot on the south end of the park uncovered all or part of eighty-one bodies.

And standing right on the south end of the grounds is the Couch Family mausoleum, a little stone tomb which people pass by every day and never notice. At a casual glance, without knowing the history of the grounds, one would think it was simply a stone tool shed or something.

But, in fact, it was a tomb that the *Tribune* announced as a "splendid vault" that was being built for the late Ira Couch, who had died in Cuba in 1857. "It required eight horses for its movement," they marveled. "The vault is to be of sufficient size to contain eleven bodies, which will be placed in niches in the wall, ranged in a semi-circle opening into the center, which will be closed with a marble slab, on which may be engraved the proper inscriptions. It will cost, when completed, $7,000, and is a generous testimonial of the esteem of the living for the departed."[17] Ira had been the owner of the Tremont House, one of the fanciest local hotels of the day and site of the city's first pool table. His brother, James, would continue to run it for years; a month before the tomb was built, Abraham Lincoln gave a version of his "House Divided" speech from the balcony. Later, John Wilkes Booth would stay there for a few weeks while performing at McVicker's Theater, and Senator Douglas, Lincoln's debate rival, would die there. Post-fire versions of the hotel lasted through the end of the nineteenth century.

When the old cemetery was being moved, the Couch Vault was allowed to remain. Exactly *why* is up to debate; some say that the Couch family sued, and the court ruled that "the graves belong to the dead, not the living." Other sources indicate that one monument was allowed to be left behind as a reminder that the grounds had once been a cemetery. Though no legal paperwork has been found in recent searches, the auctioneer who sold the first lots further north when the City Cemetery became overcrowded in 1855, said in 1892 that he distinctly remembered that the Couch family had made a deal with the park (though he also said that Ira had already built the tomb by 1855, which is incorrect).[18]

The most direct evidence of the reasons for leaving it, though, comes from an 1877 article in the *Tribune*, from the time when the grounds were being landscaped into a park. "Masons have examined the structure," the reporter said, "and say it will cost nearly $3,000 to remove it to Rosehill, and the Commissioners have determined to let it remain and plant trees thickly around it."[19] The first burial in the new Couch family plot in Rosehill took place the next year.

It was likely a combination of more than one factor. With some people pushing to leave at least one monument, James Couch threatening to make a stink, and rising costs of moving the old tomb, the city probably just decided that the easiest thing would be to simply let the damn thing stay. And so the tomb remained in place, and today a mystery remains: How many bodies are in there, and whose are they?

The question first came into the news in 1892, when Ira's brother, James Couch, tried to jump on a street car, fell into the road, and was hit by a truck. He was taken to the Tremont House, where he died of his injuries at the age of ninety-two (though you've got to give a man his age credit for even trying to jump onto a moving street car). Rumors went around that the family wanted to put the remains in the old family vault, and this, according to the *Chicago Evening Journal*, "created considerable disturbance at the health department." Burial of human remains in city grounds that weren't specifically designated for the purpose was illegal by then, and whether that included the old tomb or not was the subject of a great deal of argument. The city's chief sanitary officer, Mr. Hayte, told the press that, "I don't see how the family could be prevented . . . I think that if an undertaker should come here with a death certificate, properly signed, and demand a permit to put the body in the vault at Lincoln Park I should grant it, unless restrained by a court order." He noted that, after all, the city *was* still putting aside $500 a year "for the maintenance of the city cemetery."[20]

William H. Wood, an old friend of the family, was asked at the time how many bodies were in there, and said, "Let me see. There is Ira Couch and his father and mother and his wife, and two children, I think. They were placed there long before the cemetery was converted into a park."[21] Another man in the same article, though, said that he'd peeked inside the tomb once and seen only one coffin, that of Ira himself. And Ira's wife, Caroline, wasn't even dead when the article came out, let alone interred anywhere.

But for one reason or another, James Couch was eventually buried in the new family plot in Rosehill, and Ira's wife was buried there a few years later. The monument on the Couch family plot there now lists Ira's name among the dead, as well as Ira's parents, James and Mahitable Couch, whose names are on the back. But records showing that they were ever truly moved there remain elusive.

In fact, the lot card on file at Rosehill doesn't list them at all. The earliest burial on the lot card is that of an unnamed child in 1878, followed by Abigail Wells (James's sister-in-law) in 1885 and Caroline Couch, Ira's daughter, the same year. The next name on the card is James in 1892; nothing indicates that Ira or his parents were ever moved. Still, this doesn't mean they weren't.

Stories about the monument continued to pop up in the news from time to time after James's death, perhaps most notably in 1911, when a locksmith received a prank order to open the tomb. The order made the press, and the park had to control the crowds who came to see it opened.

At the time, Ira Johnson Couch, the original Ira's grandson, said, "My grandfather, his father and mother, and two of my brothers are buried in the tomb. I have heard, also, that four other people are buried there. The bodies have never been removed. We hold the title to the vault and can open it if we want to, but we do not want to."[22]

This data was a little puzzling for modern researchers when it was first discovered in newspaper archives; so far as anyone knew, Ira Johnson Couch didn't *have* any brothers. But a proof of heirship testimony in his grandmother's probate file indicates that he had a couple who were stillborn and buried without names.

In response to the 1911 rumors, A. S. Lewis, secretary of the Lincoln Park Commissioners, said that the bodies were removed in 1880, the last time the tomb was opened.[23] But John Lindroth, a civil engineer who worked for the Lincoln Park board, said he'd been in there himself in 1901. He told the *Daily News* that the tomb was empty. "Ten years ago I was in the tomb," he said. "We were laying out a road and it was necessary to open it. At that time there were no bodies there. They were probably moved with other bodies in what was then a cemetery."[24]

"It is absurd for any one to say that the bodies were removed," Couch countered. "No one had the right to do any such thing."[25]

The statement of Lindroth is the closest thing to a firsthand account that the tomb is now empty, but it *could* simply be taken as the city's attempt to hush the crowds—after all, in a previous article, Lindroth had admitted that he'd removed a few surviving tombstones to obscure the locations of bodies from people who might want to dig them up to sell the metal coffins. Few people have ever felt that the word of a Chicago city official was something that should be trusted without question, after all. The talk of the Couch family in 1892 strongly indicated that none of them believed that the bodies had been moved at the time.

As of 2016, the tomb has still not been reopened, even when it was re-tuckpointed and spruced up in the 1990s. The door on the front of it today is not a *door*, exactly. There is no keyhole, no locking mechanism, and no hinges; it's simply a metal slab with a handle that's strictly ornamental, added at some point to replace an iron grate that was there before.

But there is a crack beneath the door. And by sliding small cameras under the crack, one can see that behind the door is . . . another door. Behind the current metal slab is a larger, somewhat more elaborate door, possibly the "marble slab" alluded to in early articles. But if names were ever inscribed on the inner door, none currently remain.

The interior door, as photographed by The Tomb Snooper 500 (an iPhone taped to a wire hanger and slid beneath the crack under the outer door).

Most coffins that were ever interred in the vault would probably have rotted away to nothing by now, but there's a very good chance that Ira might have been interred in a Fisk metallic burial case, a very ornate type of metal casket with a viewing window over the face. They were all the rage when Ira died, and were among the only caskets on the market that would have been good enough to ship his body from Cuba, where he died, and keep it preserved long enough for him to be interred in the tomb the next year, when it was finally built. City Cemetery expert Pamela Bannos told me there was no doubt in her mind that he would have been interred in one of them. Fisk cases, which have a bit of a cult following today, are dug up from time to time; in fact, one of the eighty-one bodies found in the parking lot in 1998 was in one of them. The bodies inside them seem to be in good shape roughly half the time, so there's not only a chance that Ira is still in the tomb, but even a slim chance that he might be recognizable inside of it.

The tomb has been a regular stop on many of my tours for years; it comes up on my Lincoln Park ghost tour (it was rumored to be haunted in the 1880s), on my Grave Robbing 101 tour, and even many of my bus tours. One time, very recently, I noticed a bit of charcoal around the base, almost as though it was spilling out from inside. I got excited for a second; sometimes when they open up old tombs they find that the coffins have all rotted away, but there's still a pile of charcoal in the nooks that was apparently put over the coffins to absorb the odors. But I could find no place from which the charcoal could have leaked out. It must have just been litterbugs.

I once recorded a podcast in which I interviewed Ira's third great-granddaughter, Rachel Williams, who had a whole stack of old articles and ephemera related to the Tremont House.

"You know," I told her, "sometimes I wonder if it will just take all the fun out of it if they ever open it up."

"Yeah," she said. "It will."

So I'm of two minds as to whether I want the city to finally open the door and have a look. On the one hand, it *will* take a lot of the fun out of it.

But on the other, I'm dying to know what's in there.

Caroline Couch, Ira's widow, outlived him by four decades. A few years before her death, the family considered interring Ira's brother, James, in the old tomb, but decided to put him in the new family plot in Rosehill; Caroline was interred there, too. These are the undertakers' expenses from her probate file.

Is There a Revolutionary War Soldier at Rosehill Cemetery?

Near the front entrance of Graceland Cemetery sits the modest grave of Elizabeth Ely Gridley-Butler, who died in 1921 at the age of ninety-five. A Daughters of the American Revolution plaque on the headstone identifies her as a "Real Daughter," meaning that her father fought in the Revolution.

Seeing that someone who only died in 1921 had a father who fought in a war nearly 150 years before sparked my curiosity; for a veteran of the war still to be having children in 1825, when Elizabeth was born, would have been unusual, though by no means unheard of. After some checking, I found that her father, Theodore Gridley, joined the army as young man in 1777. He married Amy Ely when he was about sixty and she was forty-one, and fathered Elizabeth at the age of sixty-eight. He died a few months before she was born.

Looking up his wife, Amy Ely-Gridley, turned up a fascinating story. Born the same year her future husband joined the revolution, Amy gave birth to her only child at the age of fifty, and first came to Chicago to visit Elizabeth in the 1850s, eventually coming to stay for good after losing most of her own fortune in the panic of 1857. In 1871, she was perhaps the only person who saw the Great Chicago Fire and remembered colonial America. In 1875, she was still said to be lively and a good conversationalist at ninety-eight, though the *Tribune* noted that "her only occupation for the past year has been rumpling hand-kerchiefs, from which she seems to derive considerable amusement." Though she was now thought to be the oldest person in town, they also noted that "[u]nlike the conventional old lady, she does not smoke a pipe."[26] When she passed away ten months later, just short of her one hundredth birthday, her obituary said, "She had lived long and been useful, and she gladly stretched out her hands when the cloudy arms came to bear her to the invisible country far away."[27]

Perhaps she was waiting in the faraway country when her great-great-grandson, President Gerald Ford, left this plane for the next.

Records on her at Graceland Cemetery aren't particularly detailed, but they indicate that she's buried right next to her daughter, Elizabeth, in an unmarked plot. This is just the sort of story that makes digging through historical archives so interesting and rewarding: That a Revolutionary War widow is buried in an unmarked grave in the city is a story worth finding. After all, I don't know any other Revolutionary widows in town, and it may be that there are no Revolutionary War soldiers buried in town at all.

Chicago is a fairly young town. The oldest house in town (by most metrics) is the old Clarke House, an 1836 cottage currently standing on South Prairie Avenue; when I point it out as the oldest house in town to tourists from the U.K., where they might well have wallpaper older than that, they think it's hilarious. But it's as old as we get. We have none of the eighteenth-century graveyards that one sees in New England towns, and in our cemeteries, birth dates from the 1700s aren't common. People buried in the vicinity who are even old enough to have fought in the American Revolution are few and far between. Even War of 1812 veterans are fairly rare.

There are two *supposed* graves of Revolutionary soldiers in the city, though.

In the 1840s, an elderly Chicagoan named David Kennison claimed that he was now the last surviving veteran of the Boston Tea Party, as well as any number of battles in both the Revolutionary War and the War of 1812, and became a bit of a local celebrity.

Kennison was not above using his stories to make money. When he became manager of Mooney's Museum on Lake Street in 1848, he took out an ad saying that if he lived to his 112th birthday, he would have a "donation party" there. "I have fought in several battles for my country," he wrote. "All I ask from the generous public is to call at the museum on the seventeenth of November, which is my birthday, and donate to me what they think I deserve."[28]

Kennison was really about forty years younger than he said, and I've always imagined that the Chicagoans of the 1840s must have known that he wasn't *quite* telling the truth, but no one questioned his claims; perhaps they simply liked having a hero in their midst. And his Revolutionary pedigree gave his occasional anti-slavery speeches a bit more weight. When he died in 1852, he was buried with full military honors in City Cemetery.

A couple of decades later, when City Cemetery became Lincoln Park, his was among the bodies that never got moved. That there were hundreds—perhaps thousands—of dead bodies in the new park doesn't seem to have bothered most people much, but an April 4, 1880, letter to the editor of the *Tribune* lamented the fact that Kennison was never moved. "Now, here is one of the members of the famous 'Boston Tea Party' who is interred in the old cemetery," he wrote, "and the question is, can anyone who is now living identify the spot where he is buried? Or are there any records or maps of the old cemetery still in existence, so that the grave can be found? It is certainly wrong for a people as patriotic as the citizens of Chicago certainly are to neglect to mark the spot where he is buried in some suitable manner."[29]

By 1880, only a small fraction of Chicagoans could have remembered the old man; the city had grown from about thirty thousand inhabitants in Kennison's day to half a million, and it would double again by the end of the decade. The movement to memorialize the man grew slowly, and in 1896 a group of Chicago "pioneers" finally compared notes on their memories of Kennison's funeral, pinpointed the patch of ground where they thought he was buried, and set up a memorial. Today, a boulder stands on the spot, still adorned with a plaque marking it as the burial place of the last surviving veteran of the Boston Tea Party, even though it's pretty well established that he was no such thing. His stories about being a Revolutionary vet were almost certainly fiction.

And, according to City Cemetery expert Pamela Bannos, the boulder isn't even particularly close to the actual burial site. It's just on the spot where the funeral service was held; Kennison was probably buried in a plot about two blocks south.[30]

The other supposed Revolutionary vet in Chicago is more of a mystery. In Rosehill Cemetery, there is a small, modest headstone marking the resting place of William DuVol, with an epitaph reading "Continental Line, Rev War."

The current gravestone of William Duvol at Rosehill. Ebenezer Peck, in whose house Lincoln decided who would be in his cabinet, is right behind him.

The current marker has been in place only since 2005. Previously, a worn-out marker on the spot identified Duvol as being a "Soldier of the Revolution" who died at the age of seventy-five.[31]

No one has ever succeeded in digging up any information on who William DuVol was, whether he was really a soldier of the American Revolution, or even when, exactly, he died at the age of seventy-five. Rosehill has never found paperwork on him. The "continental line" identification on the new stone is entirely guesswork, and likely the result of confusing him with the William Duvol of Henrico, Virginia, who fought in the war and went on to be the first civilian governor of Florida. *That* William Duvol died in Virginia in 1842, and is buried there, not in Chicago.

If our DuVol was only seventy-five when he died, and was a Revolutionary War vet, he must have been a very, very early Chicagoan. Even if we assume he fought at the age of thirteen at the very end of the war in 1783, he would have come to town no later than 1845. And if he had died here in those early days, he likely would have been buried in one of the earliest cemeteries from the 1830s, then moved to City Cemetery (Lincoln Park) before being moved Rosehill. Only a handful of people made the move twice.

And early historians of Chicago were awfully meticulous; careful track was kept of all of the early citizens of any note. A Revolutionary War vet would surely have attracted *some* attention.

According to a 1959 report in the *Chicago Tribune*, Rosehill officials had no record of the man at all, and any records that may have existed before were wiped out in the Great Chicago Fire. The Chicago Historical society knew nothing of him, and neither did the Daughters of the American Revolution. Even modern checks into military rolls (much easier to do now than in 1959) haven't cleared things up.

It may be that DuVol was a veteran of some *other* revolution. Some suggest the Civil War, but that wasn't usually referred to as "The Revolution" on gravestones in Union states. I would suggest, given the French origins of his surname, that perhaps he was in the French Revolutionary Army, which lasted until about twenty years after the American Revolution. But until a new record is discovered, DuVol will simply remain a mystery.

There are a couple of Revolutionary Soldiers buried in the Chicago metro area; Eli Skinner and Aaron Miner are buried in Elk Grove Cemetery in suburban Arlington Heights. But it seems likely that no true veteran of the Revolution lies within the city limits today.

Can You Find the Huck
Tunnels in the Gold Coast?

When John Lennon apologized for his infamous "Bigger than Jesus" remark at the Astor Tower Hotel, it's quite likely that he was sitting several floors atop a network of lost pre-Fire tunnels.

It's hard to get rid of a tunnel. You can fill it with damp sand, like the LaSalle Tunnel under the river, or block it off, like the one connecting the Congress Hotel to the Auditorium Theater, but unless you tear it all away to make room for a new basement or something, the tunnel will still be there. In most cases, workers know where the tunnels are. But the John A. Huck Brewery Tunnels of the Gold Coast remain a mystery.

For some background, John A. Huck was a Chicago brewer; I first became aware of him by running into his nifty tombstone at Graceland, which features a bas-relief portrait of him. Every time I find a neat one with a name I don't recognize, I look up the name. It's amazing how often they turn out to be brewers.

In the 1840s, Huck opened the first lager brewery in Chicago at Chicago and Rush, back when the area was still practically the wilderness. In the 1850s, he moved to a new location at Banks and Astor, just south of the Catholic portion of City Cemetery (now Lincoln Park), which started at Schiller. The area seems to have been bounded by State and Astor at the west and east, and from Banks to Goethe from the north to south—a full square block, across the corner from the future Playboy mansion, though one source says that it went clear north to Schiller. In what was then quite an innovation, the brewery featured a whole network of subterranean tunnels and vaults for brewing the beer at low temperatures year-round. A 1901 book about brewing history says there were two full miles of them in total.

The brewery was destroyed in the Great Chicago Fire in 1871, but the tunnels remained.

They first seem to have made the news in again in 1910 when vandals broke into the mansion of Charles Plamondon, 1344 N. State, and spent a day stealing and destroying things, having what seemed to be a hell of a food fight, destroying priceless art and furniture, and generally trashing the place. Though a burglary on a grand scale, the food fight led police to believe that it was simply the work of neighborhood boys, who then abandoned much of the loot in the old brewery vaults nearby.

"Three deep caverns at this corner (Banks and Astor)," wrote the *Tribune*, "have been known for years among the boys in the neighborhood as the 'robbers' dens.' They were formerly the underground vaults of a brewery and are covered with the exception of three entrances facing Astor Street."[32]

The robbers went through all of Miss Marie Plamendon's wardrobe, breaking one of her old dolls and throwing letters and ribbons and photos everywhere. More than half a century later, Miss Plamendon, now in her eighties, was reached by the *Tribune* when they first heard the story of the tunnels in 1963.

"Certainly I remember the tunnels!" she said. "When we were kids we played in them all the time, and believe me, we got many a scolding and spanking for going into them. We thought they were our discovery, and tried to keep them a secret from the adults, but it didn't work. There were tunnels underneath a lot of the property on Banks Street, near Astor . . . I remember once when our house was burglarized while we were in the country, we found all kinds of stolen things—ribbons, odds and ends—down in the tunnels. We always wondered if the robbers were lurking down there."

The *Tribune* had contacted Miss Plamendon while following up on a letter sent to them by Gilbert Amberg, who thought of them when the Ambassador prepared to tear down some brownstones nearby. "The entire half block on State between what is now Goethe and Banks was the site of a brewery," he wrote. "The area was honeycombed with tunnels that were used as storage areas for aging the brew. Some of them were dug up for the Ambassador East hotel foundations in 1927, but you're going to see a lot more of them when the old brownstones come down."

Reached by phone for a follow-up, Amberg laughed and said, "I was pretty young then, and I don't know if I can trust my memory on this, [but] I do remember walking through the tunnels; they were probably well over six feet high. My guess is that they were made of either brick or stone. There were two connected tunnels that ran under our yard, and they had high arched roofs. I suppose they were perhaps thirty feet underground, because we only discovered them after the lot had been excavated . . . it's quite possible that the tunnels weren't discovered when the brownstones were built, because the foundations for those homes only went down about six feet below the basements."[33]

Amberg's brother John, a minister, added to his account. "There was a solid brick wall along our property line," he said, "and when the excavation for the hotel had been made, the construction workers found a doorway in the wall about four feet under the surface of the yard. This was the entrance to the tunnels, which sloped down under our yard and ran for some distance. They were caved in a little to the north. It explained something that had always puzzled us. There was a vacant lot next to our house where we children used to dig. We could never get very deep without hitting a solid stone-like surface. We must have been hitting the roofs of the tunnels, of course."[34]

The *Tribune* also tracked down Walter Fisher, who remembered playing in the tunnels around 1900 (but probably declined to ask if he was one of the burglars). "We boys used to make candle lanterns out of tin cracker boxes; in those days crackers came in shiny tin boxes that made wonderful toys," he said. We would explore the tunnels, which we were strictly forbidden to do, because our parents suspected that tramps slept there . . . they were perhaps ten or fifteen feet deep, and filled with rubble, but they were wide enough for several boys to walk abreast. They were made of brick, I think, and the roofs were arched; they were more like vaults than tunnels."[35]

Joseph Cremin had lived on State as well, and noted that when they "had the devil's own time" trying to lay foundations for the hotel because of the tunnels, it cleared up an old puzzle for him. "For years, we had tried to freeze our back yard for skating, but the water would soak right into the ground and disappear. We even had the fire chief out to inspect the yard, and damned if he knew what was wrong, either. We found out later that the water had been draining into the tunnels."[36]

In a particularly enterprising bit of reporting, the *Tribune* even tracked down Joseph Beuttas, president of the construction company that had built the Ambassador East decades before, who was away on a Norwegian cruise. "I saw [the tunnels]," he said. "I walked in them. They were about eight to ten feet high, built of stone, and were about twenty feet below ground. They extended to the east and to the south. We destroyed the ones where we were building, [but] no doubt more tunnels will be found when they start excavating for the addition to the Ambassador East."[37]

Newer construction has probably resulted in basements now occupying some of the space where the tunnels used to be, and it's worth noting that the memories of just how deep they went seem a bit fuzzy and conflicting. But James Jardine, water commissioner as of 1963, told the *Tribune* that it was hard to tell. Since they were private property, there might not have been a record of their construction to start with (not to mention the loss of records in the Fire). "Of course," he said, "when the public utilities were installed, the engineers might have run into these tunnels, and undoubtedly they would have made a note in their log books. But the log books aren't part of the public record, and they're probably buried deep in some warehouse."[38]

Given the sheer scope that the tunnels seem to have covered, it's unlikely that *all* of them have been destroyed. There may be no way to access them without some heavy-duty equipment by now, but who knows? Perhaps some basement or manhole still leads right into the old caverns today.

Was Walter Newberry
Buried in a Barrel?

I've tried to refrain from letting these early chapters be nothing but cemetery mysteries. But there are just so many of them!

The last "private" burial grounds allowed in the city were at Sacred Heart, a school and convent near Taylor and Racine streets. The semi-cloistered nuns were not allowed to leave the grounds for something so frivolous as a funeral, so the nuns who died there were buried on the grounds. When the convent moved to the north suburbs in the early twentieth century, and the bodies of the nuns were transported to Calvary Cemetery, two of them, Mother Galway and Mother Gauthreaux, were said to have turned to stone: the coffins contained more than a thousand pounds of what looked like white marble, according to newspaper accounts.

And then there's the similar tale of Julia Buccola-Petta, the "Italian Bride" of Mt. Carmel Cemetery in Hillside. Julia died in her Ukranian village home during childbirth in the early 1920s, and her mother began to have nightmares that her daughter wanted to be exhumed. Six years later, the body *was* exhumed (after Julia's mother guilted her son, then a successful tailor and designer in L.A., into paying for it, against his objections), and found to be in good-enough shape that a photo was fired onto the new monument that her brother paid for (also to his chagrin, according to Buccola family lore).[39] The haunting statue and morbid photo on her grave, across the cemetery from the grave of Al Capone, have inspired a lot of urban legends over the years.

There are a number of scientific explanations for how Julia and the two Mothers Superior could have been so well preserved, but, given the scant data currently known about the circumstances of the exhumations, the only thing that could help clear it up would be to exhume the remains again—which probably isn't worth doing just for the sake of curiosity.

There's one more cemetery mystery, though, that we wouldn't have to go so far as to dig the man up. We'd just have to dig a few feet down and see what sort of coffin he had. If the wood hasn't rotted by now, digging a few feet down could clear up the Legend of Pickled Walt.

The January 9, 1886, issue of the *National Police Gazette* featured an interesting item:

BURIED IN A BARREL

Mr. Walter Newberry, a Chicago millionaire, died at sea, and his body was sent home in a cask of Medford rum. When the cask arrived it was received by Mr. Tinkham and a few friends who were let into the secret. They opened it to satisfy themselves as to its contents. The cask was loaded upon a dray, which was driven to Graceland Cemetery, followed by Mr. Tinkham and his companions, where without religious services the cask was rolled into a grave dug in a lot owned by Mr. Newberry, and there the remains lie to this day in pickle, with no stone to mark the spot.[40]

This was accompanied by a delightful illustration, not unlike a "Phiz" sketch in a Dickens novel, showing three men rolling a barrel toward a grave that was being dug out by a man with a small shovel.

The *Police Gazette* was officially a "sporting journal," not an official law enforcement publication, and it was certainly at least a little bit off in its details (Newberry did, in fact, have a headstone at Graceland,

BURIED IN A BARREL.
HOW MILLIONAIRE NEWBERRY OF CHICAGO, WHO DIED AT SEA, WAS INTERRED IN GRACELAND CEMETERY.

The illustration of Newberry's burial from the *Police Gazette*, nearly two decades after the burial took place.

and a rather large one at that), but quite a lot of the story *was* correct. Newberry did die at sea, and there were definitely stories about him being preserved in a barrel of liquor. And, though it seems unlikely that a millionaire wouldn't be transferred to a coffin after going to all that trouble to get the body home, hard evidence that he *wasn't* buried in the barrel is a bit lacking.

Newberry came to Chicago in 1833, having invested in real estate at a time when there were serious bargains to be had. Men like early tavern owner Mark Beaubien, who "kept his tavern like hell and played the fiddle like the devil," were selling large lots in what is now the Loop for about twenty-five bucks, later only to shrug their shoulders and say, "Didn't expect no town." Newberry became president of the first railroad built from Chicago, and between that and his land holdings, he became very rich indeed. In his will, he left behind a large sum to fund the creation of a public library in Chicago after the deaths of his heirs, but by the time last of them died in 1885, there was already a public library in town, so the money was used to fund the Newberry Library, a non-circulating reference library. It's still in operation today; among its treasures is a copy of the *First Folio*, the 1623 collection of Shakespeare's plays that sells for millions when copies come up at auction. And it's not kept in a glass display, either. If you're a member they'll bring it right out to your table and let you read it and touch it and smell it. It smells like bowling shoes.

But is the library's namesake really lying pickled in a barrel under the soil at Graceland?

In 1868, Walter Newberry went traveling abroad to join his wife and daughters in France. But he wasn't feeling well; while dining with other passengers he spoke at length with a priest from Notre Dame about his failing health. When he didn't come to breakfast the next morning, a check of his room was made, and it was found that he'd died overnight.

The officers of the ship began to make preparations for following the usual procedure when a passenger died during an ocean voyage: committing the body to the deep in a burial at sea. But the priest, with whom Newberry had a number of mutual friends, intervened. The widow and daughters of the dead man were eager for his arrival in Europe, and were sure to take the news of his death badly. The shock, he said, would be almost too much for human nature to endure. They *had* to preserve the body enough that his family could look on the face of their beloved patriarch one more time.

The captain said that burial at sea was standard protocol, but offered to accede to the request if a physician could be found on board who would agree. A doctor was rounded up in due course, and he offered to personally deliver the body to Mrs. Newberry.[41]

Or so went the story seventeen years later, in a letter to the editor of the *Inter Ocean,* after the story of Newberry's burial was appearing all over the country. The article didn't go into detail about how the body was kept in shape, but as the story spread, many sources specified that they'd kept him preserved in a cask of Medford rum. Putting him in *some* sort of alcohol was about all that they could have done in order to get the body across the ocean in decent shape. Ice was hard to get in those days.

The *Tribune* looked into the story and found that on January 9, 1869, a permit was issued to L. W. Morris to transfer the body of Walter L. Newberry from the dock of the French Line to Chicago. But shipping the body in a barrel would probably not have been legal, according to everyone contacted. Morris himself was located and said he was quite certain that he hadn't taken any bodies in liquor barrels in 1868. Another passenger from the ship was found who said that the body was placed in the port quarter boat and covered in canvas until the voyage was complete.[42]

But just putting the remains in a quarter boat would not have preserved him enough to let the family see him again; it would only have spared the other passengers from the sight of a decomposing body.

E. L. Tinkham, the man generally credited as the source of the tale (and the man who buried the barrel), had been in charge of the Chicago Clearing House at the time of Newberry's death. But by the time the story spread in 1885, he was long dead himself.

W. A. Booth, then president of the First National Bank in New York, was also located by reporters in 1886, and claimed to be the man who made sure that the body was preserved. He gave a detailed account of the events that *still* didn't clear things up, exactly: "I had known Mr. Newberry's family, but had never met him," he said. "He was pointed out to me, however, as soon as he came on board . . . He occupied the state room next [to] mine. After two or three days he died. The steamer's doctor pronounced the cause of death to have been old age . . . The body was kept in ice or spirits, I am not positive which, but I think the latter."[43]

It's worth noting that when the story spread, Newberry's widow had died in Paris only days before. Her remains were sent home to Chicago and buried in the Newberry plot only weeks after the barrel story first spread nationwide. If anyone thought to check the grounds for a barrel while they were down there, just a couple of feet to the side, no one seems to have written it down.

Probate files from 1868 were lost in the Great Chicago Fire, which is a shame, as they might clear matters up a little (often they'll include a receipt for the coffin and itemized lists of undertakers' services). But even if we had those, it's likely that most of arrangements, such as embalming, would have been done overseas, unless they *did* just keep him in a barrel. *Something* must have been done to preserve the body for a trip back across the ocean and then across the continent, though.

Today, it's generally said that Newberry likely *was* preserved in alcohol, though sources differ as to whether he's still in a barrel (it's generally agreed that he's not).

There's only one way left to find out. . . .

The Lonesome Death of Barton Edsall

The sheer number of unsolved murders in Chicago history nearly boggles the mind. Open up a newspaper from any date in the archives, and you're likely to find an article about a murder case that no one remembers anymore, and that no one ever solved. Some of the stories were in the paper for a day or two, then gone. Others, like George Green's murder of his wife, occupied papers for weeks and were written about for years before falling through the cracks, waiting for ghouls like me to dig them back up.

Others could have been a lot more famous if other events hadn't pushed them out of the news. One of these was the strange death of Barton Edsall.

In 1871, Edsall was one of the city's best-known wholesale druggists, a partner in the firm of Hurlbut & Edsall on Lake Street. He lived in a handsome home on the corner of Clark and Washington Place (now Delaware Street), right across the street from the leafy square of Washington Park.

On October 5, 1871, Mr. and Mrs. Edsall were both in bed before ten o'clock, but at some point in the night Barton wandered out of bed to take some hydrate of chloral, a sedative that would help him sleep through a toothache, and to give his young son a glass of water.

Later, he got out of bed again at a little before four in the morning on October 6, and minutes later Mrs. Edsall was awakened by the sound of a gunshot. Rushing out of bed and down the stairs, she found her husband lying just inside the open front door, bleeding from a pistol shot to the head. A Smith and Wesson Model 1 revolver lay at his side. Four dirty fingerprints were found on the door, and another bullet was lodged in the wood. She held his dying body in her arms as a small crowd of servants gathered around.

At once, the neighbors came out of their homes and made their way through the foggy morning streets. By the time Dr. Bogue arrived, Barton Edsall was beyond help, and he died minutes later.

Before the body was even removed, neighbors had begun to argue among themselves as to whether it had been a murder or a suicide. There had just been a burglary next door at General Strong's house, and one of the burglars had been caught. Perhaps his fellow burglars had come to get revenge on General Strong for pressing charges and broken into the wrong house.

A servant swore the door had been locked, but there was no sign of forced entry. A house on the other side had been vacant, though, and someone suggested that perhaps the burglars could have snuck in across second-story windows. But the cobwebs hadn't been disturbed.

So, with no real signs of a burglary, and no one able to think of a compelling reason Edsall would have been out of bed to begin with, they had to consider that perhaps the death was a suicide. His health hadn't been good lately; the toothache had reportedly been the least of his problems. That he'd wandered down and shot himself seemed more likely than the idea that he'd wandered down and been randomly shot by a man who then dropped the gun and left.[44]

And yet, at the coroner's inquest, the suicide theory was unanimously dismissed at once.

The inquest began at ten o'clock in the morning, only six hours after the gunshot was fired, and went on for a full two days. It's interesting to read the transcript in the newspapers now; one can imagine that now we would be able to check the fingerprints on the door and see if they matched to Edsall or a servant, and to check the ballistics on the gun and the bullet, or the way the blood had pooled, or any number of things. But that sort of analysis hadn't come into its own yet.

Mrs. Belle Edsall couldn't say whether the revolver was her husband's or not. Mr. Edsall's head was still moving when she found him, but he wasn't able to talk well enough to explain what had happened; her first impression was that he had been shot by a burglar.

Margaret Green, a servant in the house, testified that both of the front doors were open when she came down upon hearing the shot, and she was positive the doors had been shut when everyone went to bed. But she'd heard no one running away. She noted that Mr. Edsall had recently shot at a rat with a pistol, but she couldn't say whether it had been the pistol found at his feet or not.

Sergeant Hathaway of the police testified that he'd combed the neighborhood and heard about a couple of unknown people walking around Washington Park, but that there hadn't been anything suspicious about them. He then examined the gun and found two charges exploded.

Officer Maloney spoke about handprints and fingerprints, but it would be decades before those could be used as evidence in court.

Edsall's partner in the drug firm, Horace Hurlbut, was probably also his oldest friend; they'd been boys together and had come "out west" to grow up with the country together more than twenty years before. He'd even married Edsall's sister. At the inquest, he testified that he'd never noticed the slightest "mental derangement" in his friend, and didn't think his use of painkillers was frequent. He thought Edsall had been in good health, but he'd been out of town for his brother's wedding, so he couldn't swear that it hadn't taken a turn for the worse. The letters he'd received had been cheerful, though, and Mr. Edsall had "a remarkably even temperament—too much so for my disposition. I am excitable—he was not."[45]

A doctor said the dose of hydrate of chloral Edsall had taken would not cause "mental derangement," though there was considerable debate about this. One of the doctors testifying was A.J. Baxter, the same old City Cemetery grave robber who would recount his experiences as a "bold and burking resurrectionist" twenty years later.

Mr. A. Abbey, a gun dealer who had been in business "since [he] could handle a tool,"[46] gave his opinion about the powder burns and how far away a distance Edsall must have been shot from. Edsall's gun, he said, could not have been fired recently; the spring was broken, so it couldn't be cocked. But the next witness, a neighbor, said that with a broken spring, it would have been very easy to shoot the gun off accidentally if it were dropped.

The coroner, for his part, said that he'd gone to a jeweler to have the bullets found in evidence weighed, and found that the bullet taken from Edsall's head was "less than one grain lighter"[47] than the bullet taken from the door.

In the end, the jury was split. While it was unanimously agreed that Mr. Edsall had come to his death from a gunshot wound to the head, half believed that it had been the work of a burglar, and half believed that Edsall had accidentally shot himself. Neither theory was entirely convincing, though.

To further complicate things, a physician wrote a statement that chloral hydrate could occasionally have a "crazing" effect on subjects, and that he'd even spoken about it with Mr. Edsall, who, as a druggist himself, felt that it could be very dangerous in unskilled hands.[48]

After two days of testimonies, the *Tribune* could only say that the death was "still shrouded in mystery."

"It is to be hoped that the case will not rest here," they wrote. "Probably the empanelling of another Coroner's jury, if that were practicable, would not result in throwing any more light upon the affair; but a sufficient reward should be offered for the detection and arrest of the possible assassin, to secure the services of the best talent in ferreting out the awful mystery."[49]

But in between the two days of testimonies, on the night of October 7, as Edsall reposed at an undertaking parlor, a fire swept through the West Side, destroying an acre of buildings—a whole neighborhood—and claiming thirty lives. The next morning, October 8, the *Chicago Times* wrote that, "The city had not recovered from the terrible shock occasioned by the murder of Mr. Edsall, aggravated by its midnight gloom and mystery, when on last evening a great conflagration, such as has not ravaged the city since the great West Lake Street fire in 1860, raged in a perfect ocean of flame from Van Buren Street to Adams on Canal."[50]

While Chicagoans were reading that article, Barton Edsall was being buried in the Hurlbut family plot at Graceland; records there list his death as "accidental."

That evening, the Great Chicago Fire broke out, completely dwarfing the West Division fire of the night before. If the October 7 fire had made people start to worry about other things besides Barton Edsall's cause of death, the fire on the day he was buried took him off their minds completely. The fire burned the entire business district of the city, cutting a swath of destruction from the area southwest of the loop all the way to Lincoln Park, a few miles north, decimating nearly

An illustration from *Harper's* of crowds forgetting all about the news of the day before as they fled into the old City Cemetery, then in the early stages of being converted into Lincoln Park.

everything in its path, including Edsall's home and most of the rest of his neighborhood, not to mention the Edsall & Hurlbut business. Any chance of further investigations was wiped out.

It was later reported, but never exactly confirmed, that Belle Edsall, in a state of "semi-madness," had been taken to a building that was thought to be safer as the flames came to the North Side, but it wasn't far enough, and she perished when the building they took her to went down in the fire.[51] From a brief search of records, I couldn't establish for sure whether she died in the fire or not; she's not buried with her husband at Graceland, which could mean that her body was never recovered, or perhaps her remains couldn't be positively identified, which would mean that she was probably buried in the new Potter's Field at Dunning on the Northwest Side. But it could also mean that she moved away after her husband's death and died someplace else. Records are still being searched.

With so many other questions after the fire, investigations simply fell by the wayside, and the story disappeared into history, leaving only a small marker for Barton in Graceland Cemetery with a date of

death that the observant may notice was only two days before the Great
Chicago Fire.

The plot where Edsall was buried mere hours before the Great Chicago
Fire broke out.

What Started the Great Chicago Fire?

Right after the Great Chicago Fire wrecked the city on October 8–10, 1871, a Philadelphia publisher rushed out a book on the event. The melodramatic tome featured a *delightful* drawing of a looter being hung upside-down and brained, with such prose as this nugget:

> *On the morning of the 10th, the telegraph wires flashed the words throughout the world: "The city of Chicago is in flames." Thrilling news indeed. Those words chilled the heart of man. We stood aghast at such terrible news, and could scarcely give it credence. But oh, how sad the next telegram: "No hope; Chicago is completely enveloped in flames. Our firemen and citizens exhausted. Water works and every public building destroyed. Great loss of life." Think of it, oh reader, and realize it if you can! A great city wrapped in flames!*[52]

Even when the book was written, only weeks after the fire, anyone paying attention knew that Mrs. Catherine O'Leary and her cow were not really to blame.

It's more and more commonly known today that the old story about careless Mrs. O'Leary leaving flammables in between a cow and some hay, thus setting the stage for the conflagration that would become the Great Chicago Fire, is not exactly true. No one really knows *how* the fire started—or exactly who made up the story about Mrs. O'Leary, for that matter. Several reporters later tried to take credit for it.

We also don't know quite what Mrs. O'Leary looked like. There are drawings of her, but they all just come out of the artists' imagination, and usually show her as far older than she would have been in

1871. She always refused to let
anyone draw her, and certainly
never let anyone photograph
her. This was her way of getting revenge on the media; she
developed awfully bitter feel-
ings toward reporters, and one
can easily imagine why.

The Great Chicago Fire
began somewhere around Mrs.
O'Leary's cottage, near Taylor
and De Koven streets on the
southwest side, on October 8,
1871. By the time it was fin-

The O'Leary Property (library of
congress).

ished, it had burned up a four-mile patch from the cottage to what was then
the City Cemetery, destroying over seventeen thousand buildings, leaving
one hundred thousand people homeless, and killing around three hundred
(a surprisingly low number of casualties, given the size of the blaze).

Naturally, the city wanted someone to blame, and within a week or
so many had landed on Catherine O'Leary, based partly on the fact
that the fire did begin in her barn, but mainly on newspaper stories that
were complete fiction.

It's often said that reporter Michael Ahern took credit for the story
of Mrs. O'Leary in 1911, as though it was something to be proud of.
A close reading of his article from that year, though, actually says the
opposite. He admitted that the story was fiction, but didn't really claim
it as his own.

"I knew Mrs. O'Leary well," wrote Ahern. "She was a truthful
woman. A few days after the fire I interviewed her regarding the
story of the cow and the lamp. She branded it as a fabrication. . . .
I have my reason for believing that someone went there to pilfer
milk from one of the cows. There was a social gathering that night
in honor of the arrival of a young man from Ireland. One of those
present told me in after years that two women of the party went to
the O'Leary shed to get some milk for punch. One woman held the
lighted lamp while the other milked the cow. They thought they
heard someone coming, and in their haste to escape, the lamp was

dropped, setting fire to the place. That, I believe, is the true cause of the fire."[53]

According to this fortieth-anniversary article, Ahern was working for the *Chicago Republic* in 1871, and covered the fire along with Johnny English of the *Tribune* and Jim Haynie of the *Chicago Times*. All three had gone to investigate what appeared to be a small fire, much smaller than one that had hit the loop the night before, down on De Koven. Ahern hadn't bothered taking notes, since it was just a small conflagration, but remembered that a fireman named Musham told him it had started in Patrick O'Leary's barn at 137 De Koven. It was only firefighters initially going to the wrong place—while still exhausted from the West Division fire the night before—that allowed the fire to grow as it did.

So, if Ahern never even claimed it, who *did* make the story up? His own articles from the *Republic* aren't available to check, and the *Tribune* didn't mention Mrs. O'Leary until she was brought in to testify along with her husband. Of the papers Ahern mentioned, that just leaves the *Chicago Times*, a far more likely culprit. Wilbur F. Storey's *Times* loved railing against the Irish almost as much as it loved railing against black people, which is saying something. Though Haynie was the one on the scene, Storey is probably the man to blame for pinning the destruction of an entire city on an innocent woman.

In their October 18 issue, a week after the fire, the *Times* referred to Mrs. O'Leary as a seventy-year-old woman who was "ragged and dirty in the extreme," who was angry because the city had found out that she was making money off of selling milk from her cows and was cutting off her pension. "The old hag swore she would be revenged on a city that would deny her a bit of wood or a pound of bacon," they wrote. "How well she kept her word is not known, but there are those who insist the woman set the barn on fire and instigated the most terrible calamity in the history of nations."[54]

The *Times* reporter said that he'd found Mrs. O'Leary the morning after the fire, rocking back and forth and saying, "My poor cow, my poor cow. She is gone and I have nothing left in the world." "On Sunday night, about 9 1/2 o'clock," he wrote, purporting to quote O'Leary's own account of the story, "she took a lamp in her hands and went out to have a look at her pet. Then she took a notion the cow must have some salt, and she sat down the lamp and went in the house for some. In a moment the cow had accidentally kicked over the lamp, an explosion followed, and in an instant the structure was enveloped in flames."[55]

A notary public who took the O'Learys' affidavits took exception to the *Times*, saying in a letter to the editor of the *Tribune* that he had known the O'Learys for years, and they were of "irreproachable character." Mrs. O'Leary, he noted, was "neither haggard nor dirty."[56] He also noted that the *Times* had just about doubled her age when they said she was seventy.

The *Chicago Journal* landed an interview with Mrs. O'Leary for their October 21 issue, and were already highly skeptical of the story about her, which they attributed to "Mistress Rumor." "Mrs. [O']Leary has made a sworn statement in refutation of the charge, and it is backed by other affidavits," they wrote, "but to little purpose. She is in for it, and no mistake. Fame has seized her and appropriated her name, barn, cows, and all."[57] They described her as "a stout Irish woman, some thirty-five years of age," and had a frank conversation with her on her porch.

"We all knocked our living out of those five blessed cows," she told the reporter. "I never had a cent from the parish in all my life, and the dirty *Times* had no business to say it, bad cess to it. There is not a word of truth in the whole story. I always milked my cows by daylight, and never had a lamp of any kind, or a candle about the barn. It must have been set afire . . . I hope to die if this isn't every word of it true. If you was a priest, I wouldn't tell it any different."[58]

The reporter wasn't entirely sure that he *believed* Mrs. O'Leary, but he was sympathetic. "It was pretty rough on you, anyway," he said.

"Rough!" said Mrs. O'Leary. "Why, my God, man, it was a terror to the world!"[59]

By the end of the month, nearly every paper was saying that the rumor about the O'Learys had been thoroughly debunked. A witness had even testified that the fire began in the hay in the loft, on the second level of the barn, not down by the cows.

But on October 22, the *Times* sent John Hay to visit O'Leary, whom they now described as "Our Lady of the Lamp and the Calamitous Bovine." Hay said that De Koven Street was nearly impossible to find at all, and, when he managed to stumble on it, he found a "mean little street of shabby wooden houses with dirty soot yards and unpainted fences falling to pieces. It had no look of Chicago about it." He spoke a bit with Patrick O'Leary, and seemed quite sure that he was only *saying* he didn't know how the fire started.[60]

The *Journal* had noted that Mrs. O'Leary blamed a "strange man" that neighbors had seen around the area, and who might have set fire to the barn for purposes of his own. That someone, or some group, had set the fire on purpose was a common theory in the early days of the fire.

The same day they ran Hay's story, October 23, the *Times* also published a lengthy "confession" said to be written by an exiled member of the Societe Internationale, a communist organization, stating that he and several other local radicals had deliberately started the fire as an act of terrorism. But he couldn't give his name, or he would "die a death more horrible than that which met any of the victims of the inquisition."[61]

"The organization in Chicago was formed," the anonymous author wrote, "under the direction of two communists who had fled from Paris, and myself. As elsewhere, none but the most daring and trustworthy were admitted. The avowed purposes of the society were harmless in themselves. They were to endeavor to elevate the workingmen to the level of the rich . . . Plan after plan was suggested and abandoned as impracticable. Finally, the burning of the business portion of the city was suggested. Appalled by the thought of working such desolation in the fairest city on the continent, I at first shrank from participation in the transaction. But all the others were firm, and, weakly, I yielded."[62]

The Societe Internationale was a real group, but functioned more in the press and the public mind as a sort of a boogeyman organizaiton along the lines of the modern "Illuminati," an easy scapegoat for conspiracy theorists. At one point, the anonymous author named celebrity speaker and businessman George Francis Train as a member, and said that the night before the fire, he'd given a speech in Chicago, predicting that the audience was listening to the last speech that would ever be given in the hall, because some great disaster was about to strike the city.

Few outside of a fringe of conspiracy theorists seemed to believe that the "confession" was legit even then (even the *Times* made a point of saying that they didn't vouch for it), and it may be that editor Wilbur F. Storey simply made it up to make radicals look bad. That's just the sort of thing he *would* have done.

But for several days, the idea that the fire was deliberately set by some group or another held a lot of sway, and rumors were strong that a number of people were caught setting fires in the course of the evening, and had been shot or hanged from the nearest lamppost on the spot. For a time it was even said that one of the "incendiaries" was Barney Aaron, a New York bare-knuckle boxer, and that *he* had been shot in the aftermath. Aaron was soon found alive in New York; he admitted he'd been gambling in Chicago the night of the fire, but, the *Nashville Union* reported, "denied that he was either shot or hung."[63]

A charming illustration of an "incendiary" being brained from *The Great Fire of Chicago*, published weeks after the fire.

One bit of evidence that may work in favor of the "incendiary" theory is the fact that the Great Chicago Fire wasn't the only major midwestern fire that day. There was an even bigger one, in fact, in Pesthigo, Wisconsin. Several smaller Wisconsin towns burned as well. This could be a sign that there was a coordinated attack planned that night.

More common today, though, is the theory that the multiple fires are evidence that what *really* started the fire was a meteor. As early as a decade after the fire, it was suggested that a meteor shower that night had started the assorted blazes, and in 2004, physicist Robert Wood revived a theory that the real culprit for starting the fire was Biela's Comet, which Victorian prophets of doom had been fond of claiming was on a collison course with the earth in the 1860s.

The earliest account of the theory that Biela's Comet started the Chicago Fire dates to 1883, when Ignatius Donnelly wrote of it in his book *Ragnarok: The Age of Fire and Gravel*. To support his theory that the fire came from outer space, he noted some of the strange characteristics of the fire itself. "They absolutely *melted* the hardest building-stone, which had previously been considered fire-proof . . . Athens marble burned like coal!" He quoted a book on the fire that stated that "strange, fantastic fires of blue, red, and green played along the cornices" of the buildings, and quoted William Ogden as saying that there was a tornado of winds in the city during the fire. All of these, he said, were evidence of a fire from the cosmos.

His explanation for the fire was all part of his larger theory that there was once a far more advanced civilization on Earth that was wiped out by another comet twelve thousand years ago; *Ragnarok* was a companion to his book popularizing the theory that Plato's story of Atlantis was literally true, not just a fable (a novel concept at the time). *Ragnarok* is entertaining as hell, really, though one gets the impression that if Donelly were alive in the twenty-first century, he'd be eager to corner you at parties to tell you that Beyonce's hand gestures in her latest video indicate that she knows more about UFOs than she's telling.

But the idea that meteors can really start fires at all holds no more sway with most modern scientists than theories about ancient advanced civilizations do.

Perhaps the most persuasive theory as to the origin of the fire is that it didn't come from above the Earth, just from above the cow. Mrs. O'Leary's son James grew up to to be "Big Jim" O'Leary, a local gambling kingpin. And in 1909, he offered 1,000:1 odds that he could prove his own origin story for the fire: that it had started when a load of hay spontaneously combusted.

At the time, O'Leary had just heard the theory that one of the O'Leary cows had started the fire by kicking over a lantern in resentment when three boys snuck into the barn to milk it to make whisky punch. The story had come from a local minister, who heard it from a local man, who heard it from the O'Neill brothers, two of the kids involved, years before, but kept it to himself so the brothers wouldn't get in trouble (though he did give them a lecture about their attempts to become whiskey drinkers, which he apparently thought was far worse than burning the city down).

"I don't care what anybody else says about the fire," O'Leary told a reporter in response. "My parents are dead and can't defend themselves against the latest fake as to the origin of the fire, but I'll speak out, and plainly, too. That story about the cow kicking over the lamp was the monumental fake of the last century. I know what I'm talking about when I say that the fire was caused by spontaneous combustion in the hayloft."[64]

According to O'Leary, his father had just put a load of green hay into the loft above the barn (where at least one eyewitness said that the fire started in the early investigations), and that hay had caught fire all on its own. Blaming spontaneous combustion sounds like even shakier science than the meteor theory at a glance, but spontaneous combustion of wet hay, in particular, is not only real, but a great danger for farmers. Scientists don't seem to agree entirely on *why* hay sometimes spontaneously combusts, but most theories revolve around microbial organisms growing on the wet hay, producing heat as they grow. A load of brand new hay wouldn't generally be a risk for combustion, but it wouldn't be out of the question, either.

"The popular belief has always been that my mother was milking a cow when the beast kicked over a lamp," O'Leary lamented. "Nothing is farther from the truth than that musty old fake. Both my father and mother went to their graves sad at heart over the worldwide notoriety given them in the printed accounts of the burning of Chicago. I wish to make it as emphatic as possible that the O'Leary cow did not kick over a lamp."[65]

Did George Francis Train Predict the Great Chicago Fire?

A few years before the Great Fire, lecturer George Francis Train was invited to speak in the Chicago Opera House as part of an evening featuring several presentations on the subject of votes for women, and the *Tribune*'s summary of the event could just about sum up Train's entire career: "George Francis Train, Mrs. Elizabeth Cady Stanton, and Miss Susan B. Anthonty spoke," they wrote. "The latter two on woman suffrage, the former on G.F. Train."[66]

In late 1871, they would be writing about a rumor that he'd predicted the Great Chicago Fire the night before it happened.

Even some of the more reputable books on the Great Chicago Fire refer

George Francis Train as photographed by Matthew Brady.

to George Francis Train's prediction that Chicago would soon be destroyed as a matter of fact. Onstage at Farwell Hall on October 7, 1871, he is quoted as saying, "This is the last public address that will be delivered within these walls! A terrible calamity is impending over the city of Chicago. More I cannot say; more I dare not utter!"[67] Twenty-four hours later, the Great Chicago Fire began, wiping out Farwell Hall, just as predicted.

The earliest known source of the quote comes from the "confession" of the anonymous writer to the *Chicago Times* who said that the fire was a terrorist act perpetrated by the Societe Interanionale, of which, it said, Mr. Train was a member. The histories that recount the tale generally say that the topic of Train's speech that night is now lost, but that he was a speaker on "moral topics."

The truth of the speech, or what we know of it, is *way* more interesting than that. George Francis Train was not exactly a speaker on moral topics. Rather, he was one of history's great cranks.

Train, who is thought to be the inspiration for Phineas Fogg, the main character in *Around the World in 80 Days*, was a businessman, traveler, and revolutionary with an ego the size of all outdoors and a tendency to make an ass of himself. The *Tribune* called him "that singular lunatic" in 1862, but when he ran for president as a third-party candidate in 1872, he called himself "The Man of Destiny," and his book of campaign speeches featured a tagline calling it "the most remarkable book of speeches in the world."

Ahead of his time on some issues (women's rights), and a product of his times, at best, on others (race), Train was certainly in Chicago on October 7, 1871, making a speech at Farwell Hall. Though the contents of the speech do seem to be lost, it's to be assumed that the subject of his speech was George Francis Train. Specifically, it would have been one of the speeches to kick of his independent campaign for the presidency. Months later, after the "confession" was published, he would note "accused of burning Chicago" among his many accomplishments in his book.

From classified ads in days leading up to the fire, Farwell Hall looks like it was quite the hub of revolutionary presidential candidates. Victoria Woodhull, a free love-promoting radical who ran for president in 1872 with Frederick Douglass as her running mate, was scheduled to speak there on October 18 (though the lecture was probably cancelled after the fire). Train would be jailed briefly for defending her a few years later.

But in the same paper that advertised her upcoming lecture in the *Chicago Journal* are two ads for Train's talk the night before the fire. The first reads:

George Francis
TRAIN
Will deliver his New Lecture in Farwell Hall
TO-NIGHT
Tickts 75, 50 and 25 cents.[68]

Just beneath that is another ad:

TREASON!

It has been ascertained that George Francis Train will seek to influence the minds of the people to-night. Loyal citizens are notified to be vigilant.[69]

Ads for Train's Oct 7, 1871, appearance at Farwell Hall.

Exactly what he said in the lecture is not really recorded, so far as I could find. A few books have said that the *Chicago Times* printed his prediction the next morning, with a few choice words for Train himself in response, and I traced that story down with due dilligence. The microfilm of the October 1871 *Times* at the Harold Washington Library was missing October 7–17, but there was a paper copy of the October 8 issue, the morning of the fire and the day after the Train lecture, in Special Collections at the University of Chicago. Examining it, I found no mention of Train at all. The closest was a tidbit about the upcoming Victoria Woodhull lecture: "Nothing, it seems, can intimidate this strange woman. With a wonderful pertinacity she pursues her way, apparently defying any who may presume to question her motives or her principles."[70]

Neither the *Times* nor any of the other October 8–9, 1871, newspapers I consulted had a thing about what Train had said onstage at Farwell Hall, which is a little odd, because papers usually had something snarky to say after his speeches. Lacking a firsthand account or transcript, the best remaining way to piece it together is probably to look through his other speeches of the era, many of which were collected in his *Man of Destiny* book.

Going by those, it's safe to assume that the speech was probably a mixture of populism, socialism, racism, conspiracy theories, and a lot of grade A bullshit dotted with jokes and "impromptu epigrams," little goofy poems he was fond of composing and performing in the middle of speeches. To stop in the middle of a lecture and predict that the city he was in would soon be laid waste *does* sound like the sort of thing he would have done, and one realizes right away from his speeches that Train *hated* Chicago. In his campaign book, he promotes St. Louis and Omaha as rising continental cities (no surprise, given that he owned five thousand lots of land in Omaha), and said that Chicago was a flash in the pan.

Title page of a book of Train's campaign speeches, *Man of Destiny.*

In the early days after the fire, Train even criticized the spirit and vigor with which the city set about rebuilding. "It is a sad thing," he roared, "to see a man whistling at a funeral—it looks heartless to see a man smoking a cigar while sitting on a corpse."[71] In November 1871, as relief money poured into city, he suggested organizing a ring to steal the cash. "Chicago is a gigantic fraud," he told a St. Louis crowd. "And there never was a city that lived on other people's thunder as it does."[72]

Even predicting Chicago's imminent doom wouldn't have been unlikely in his October 7 speech; prophesizing the city's destruction was, in fact, a regular part of his act. Critical partly of the speed with which Chicago had been built the first time around, he believed that one day the polar ice caps would melt, the water level in the Great Lakes would rise, and the city would be washed away. It's quite likely that he would have brought this up in his 1871 Chicago speech, as it was a common topic for him in those days.

But did he really pause, seem to have an epiphany, and claim that no other speech would ever be made in Farwell Hall, as the story goes? Telling his potential voters that they were all about to die would have been a hell of a way to kick off a campaign. But, again, not one totally out of character for Train.

Train, at the very least, was more than happy to take *credit* for the prophecy. Speaking in Louisville the month after the fire, a moderater asked if he really foretold Chicago's doom, and Train not only said that he did, but practically claimed psychic powers. "Who accounts for this power of fortelling events?" he asked. "This marking out the future. For ten years the papers of the world have had in their columns my predictions fortelling the great events that started mankind. The building of the Pacific railroad, the saving of the Union, the downfall of McClellan, the assassination of Lincoln . . . two hundred American audiences have seen me map out of a black board the destruction of the 'Doomed City of Sin' by the melting of the mountains of ice overflowing the Lake Superior into Lake Michigan and sinking Chicago . . . Omaha will be the new Chicago."[73]

Really, his precognitive powers were not all that he claimed. In September 1864, he confidently predicted that Lincoln would be crushed in the coming election, and even wrote an impromptu epigram that would seem particularly unfortunate months later:

> *Not a tear was shed, not a funeral note*
> *as his corpse to Chicago we hurried*
> *Not a white man was there to throw in a vote*
> *in the grave where Abe Lincoln we buried.*[74]

And Train's prediction of the "downfall of McClellan," Lincoln's rival for the presidency that year, came only *after* he was booed off the stage and kicked out of the Democratic National Convention in Chicago at which McClellan was nominated. At the time, Train was predicting the downfall of both Lincoln *and* McCellan, which was like going to a Bears game and predicting that both of the teams would lose. You'd at least end up half-right.

And his grandiose response to the prediction question doesn't *quite* answer the question of whether he uttered the line attributed to him. It doesn't seem that he ever predicted it would *burn*, exactly. His prediction was always that the city would be destroyed by water, and nothing but the phony "confession" of a supposed co-conspirator credits him with saying the destruction would come before another speech could be made in Farwell Hall.

As of December 1871, the *Tribune* was already calling the tale of Train's prophecy an "old story." "While we would not strip Mr. Train of any of his laurels," the reporter wrote with a sarcastic grin you can see right through the microfilm, "for we all know that he is the founder of the Internationale; that he fought bravely at the head of the Communists; that he is the lineal successor of Brian Born, King of all the Irelands; that he is the next President of these United States; and that some angel, dragging him through space like Habakkuk, has given him glimpses of what has been, is, and is to be—while we would not do anything to wound the sensitive nature of Mr. Train . . . It was not a vision of fire that he saw, but, with him, as with Ophelia, it was too much water. If he is to be apprehended and examined at all, we shall insist upon it that he shows he did not carry out his glacial theory, ex post facto, by fetching on his water and putting out the fire."[75]

So, predicting Chicago's doom had been part of Train's stock in trade for some time, but that he truly said it would happen so soon that no other speech would ever be made at Farwell Hall on October 7, 1871, has still only been sourced to the anonymous terrorist confession in the *Chicago Times*. No source from the two weeks between the speech and the confession seems to have quoted it. But, on the other hand, no one who was at Farwell Hall that night ever stood up and said, "Hey, that's not what he said!"

Even if they *did*, though, it's just as likely that someone *else* who was there might have countered by saying that *they* were there, too, and that Train had made the prediction exactly as he quoted. After all, if you read the dozens of accounts from people who'd been in Ford's Theater the fateful night six years earlier when Lincoln was shot, there's no real consensus on what John Wilkes Booth shouted from the stage (if anything), whether Booth broke his leg jumping from the president's box, whether an actress came and cradled Lincoln in her arms, exactly who carried Lincoln across the street, or whether Lincoln's guest, Major Rathbone, was wearing civilian clothes or military clothes.

Two decades after the fire, Train was still predicting Chicago's imminent demise. In an 1893 speech at the Palmer House, he said, "Chicago's doomed. It's built on a salt stratum. The waters of the lake are dissolving the salt. The town's sinking. I'm going to get out."

So whether George Francis Train was really struck with a premonition live on stage will have to remain a mystery. But I'm sure he'd love that anyone's still talking about it.

The Missing Mansion
of Old Man Storey

When you read a lot of nineteenth-century newspapers, you come across numerous sociological attitudes that make you uncomfortable. Even more progressive writers of the day often said things about race, gender, and class that inspire a cringe today. Usually, you can put them in context; people in those days lived in a different world and were taught different things. We can't expect them to have all the same attitudes about things like race and gender that we do today.

But then there's Wilbur F. Storey, editor of the *Chicago Times*. Even for his time, that guy was awful.

A few years before his paper called Mrs. O'Leary "an Irish hag," he was so violently anti-Lincoln that General Ambrose Burnside tried to shut the paper down for a while in 1863 (Lincoln personally intervened and let him go back to press). Storey was not against the war effort because of anything to do with "state's rights," either. He was a slavery man. While in the early days Lincoln pushed the battle as one to save the union (which was less controversial than ending slavery, which still didn't even seem like a plausible goal to begin with), Storey never believed it for a second. He believed from the start that Lincoln was fighting to end slavery, and that didn't sit well with him. He was a Northerner, but he thought slavery was pretty keen.

Many anti-slavery crusaders of the day were underwhelmed by the narrow reach of Lincoln's Emancipation Proclamation when it was announced in 1862, but Storey did not think it was any sort of half-measure. "History does not make us acquainted with so deplorable a failure as this administration," he wrote on the day before it was to take effect. "Do we longer present the grand heroic spectacle of a people striving for the perpetuity of their nationality? On the contrary, have we not dwarfed the war to the pitiful dimensions of a contest as to what shall be the status of the debased and irreclaimably barbarous negro amongst us?"[76] When midnight passed and Lincoln hadn't changed his mind, he wrote another article stating that the proclamation "[w]ill be known in all history as the most wicked, atrocious, and revolting deed recorded in the annals of civilization."[77]

Storey's rancor wasn't just reserved for people of other races and nationalities. He also picked every fight he could with other editors. While most of the city adopted a sort of "we're all in this together" attitude after the Great Chicago Fire, Storey specifically declined to congratulate the *Evening Journal* on getting back up and running two weeks later. "The *Times*," he wrote, "is a truthful journal and can't do it. We absolutely fail to discern any merit in the resucitation of so imbecile an institution."[78]

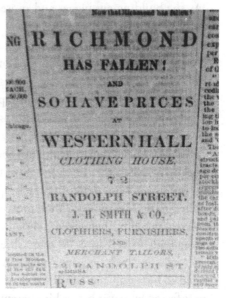

When it looked as though the Union was winning the war, Storey softened his position on Lincoln just slightly. At least enough to run this ad, which is probably the finest ad ever run in any newspaper ever.

But his papers sold well; in fact, Storey's probate file indicates that he was a millionaire. Among his real estate holdings, Storey owned more than four acres of land along 43rd Street, east of what was then known as Grand Boulevard, and in 1879 he began construction of an incredible mansion at the southwest corner of 43rd and Vincennes. Made of sparking white Vermont marble, and towering far higher than most buildings downtown at the time, people called it the Storey Castle or Storey's Palace.

Or, anyway, that's what they called it to his face. Behind his back, the horrifically expensive dwelling was known as "Storey's Folly."

Construction on the "palace" continued in fits and starts over the next couple of years. The main portion of the mansion was four stories of white marble, with multiple towers that stretched a couple of stories further. It was rigged so that it could be lit at night with electric lights, a rarity in an early-1880s house. Out-of-town papers called it "the most showy residence in this country."[79]

As the building got bigger and more unwieldy, rumors began to go around that the inside was a complete mess, a maze of twisting halls and oddly shaped rooms. At one point Storey came inside to examine the work in progress and announced that everything inside had to be torn up and redone, because it was infested with snakes.

The "snakes," it seems, were the pipes. Storey had completely lost his mind at this point and was building the house on the direction of "spirits." During the war he'd gleefully printed rumors about Lincoln getting advice from the dead, and now he was getting it himself. Indeed, it's been suggested that he might have been for some time, and it had been the spirits who told him to pick fights with other editors.

The "spirits" he spoke to were mostly broad ethnic stereotypes, and all were said to be belligerent, though they apparently liked Wilbur well enough to call him "White Chief." The one he spoke of most was "Little Squaw," a Native American princess who told him that he needed to hurry up and finish his marble mansion because he was getting infected by sewer gas in his current home.

One can't help but think of the Winchester Mystery House in California, where the widow of Mr. Winchester built a house full of secret passages and blind alleys, believing she was acting on the instructions of the spirits of people killed with Winchester Rifles. It's a huge draw for tourists, and perhaps Storey's would be, too, if it survived.

Before Storey's mansion was even half complete, it was fairly apparent that his physical health was slipping along with his mental health, and people began to wonder just what would be done with the place, as it probably wouldn't be finished in his lifetime. Indeed, after his death in 1884, it sat unfinished and abandoned while heirs fought over his estate. The lower stories were boarded up, but windows were left open on the second, allowing birds to make their nests inside freely. Neighbors, perhaps inevitably, told stories that it was haunted.

Arguments over Storey's estate went on for ages before anyone could decide what to do with the place; before anything could be determined, his heirs had to argue about whether his most recent will was written after his insanity had taken hold; newspaper accounts of the various trials and lawsuits are so interesting that I hoped some of the letters in which he wrote about his "spirits" might be included in the probate file, or maybe, just maybe, even a photograph of the mansion. You don't *usually* see that sort of thing in a probate file from those days, but sometimes some random bit of evidence will be included and marked "Exhibit A."

Nothing like that was in the file, but the documents included were quite a ride. The Storey Probate docket included a twenty-page inventory of everything they had in the *Chicago Times* office, which is an interesting glimpse at a world gone by, as well as an inventory of Storey's lands, and the various encumbrances on them, which are amusing to see because of all the references to people who appeared in earlier chapters of this book. He owed money to the estate of Walter Newberry, and to the Hurlbut family from the Barton Edsall story.

It also contains two versions of Storey's will. The first is a regular, formal sort of will. The other was made later, and was the subject of the dispute in court: it consists of several small pieces of paper with the words "My Will" scrawled on the top. It's written in pencil, and leaves everything to his "beloved wife," Eureka Storey.

According to a testimony as to whether this will was legal, Storey wrote that one out at his desk one afternoon, then called a couple of witnesses into his office to have them sign it. It wouldn't *seem* legal at a glance, but it's a fairly basic

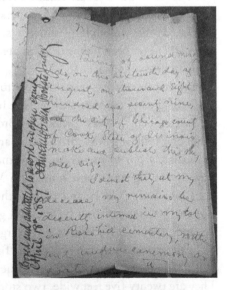

Title page of Storey's second will, written in pencil on scrap paper but lacking any telltale signs of dementia.

will, with no hints of insanity in the contents. He didn't leave anything to Little Squaw.

The probate file only gives one hint of what the "palace" was like: an inventory of his estate says the property at 43rd is "improved by a white marble dwelling about one hundred by one hundred feet in course of erection . . . (with) a conservatory, mainly iron and glass, (and a) white marble porter's lodge."

Eureka Storey herself gave up all claims on the estate (presumably because she was planning to remarry, which in those days sometimes kept you from being able to inherit an estate; some years later she married another newspaper editor), and the details of who got what were finally worked out around 1890. But no one had a good idea what to do with the unfinished mansion. No buyer for such an immense and unwieldy structure could be found, and in 1892 the "old Storey castle" was being advertised for sale as a tear-down. It was razed the next year, and the last of the foundation was finally carted away in 1906.[80]

Whether there's a photograph of it out there is a mystery I've never solved. 1892 is late enough that someone *probably* took a photograph of it at one point, but it would still be a few more years before photographs started to be reproduced in newspapers; the only images of it that were published were a couple of drawings. If any photos survive, they've likely *still* never been published and are instead just sitting unidentified in an archive someplace.

Another interesting question still to be answered is just how many pieces of the building are still present in the neighborhood to this day. The acres of land Storey owned on 43rd were broken into smaller plots when the building was torn down, and pieces of the mansion were immediately put to use as building materials for other houses in the area, including seven new homes on Vernon Avenue, which was cut right into Storey's land, and at least three on Vincennes. The marble, and the 400 tons of iron beams and girders, were said to be enough material to build fifty houses, each large enough for a family of five.

In the *Tribune*'s description of the first houses built in 1893, it said: "All are built on practically the same plan of interior arrangement. They are twenty-five feet wide, two stories high, and contain ten rooms each, all finished in hardwood and handsomely fitted. The fronts of the houses differ. Some have swell fronts. Others have square windows and others have four small windows in a row on the upper story. There are window casings of rounded marble, pediments, and ornaments such as are generally seen on houses of the highest class. All of these ornaments were carved years ago. The plans of the new houses were so drawn as to use the ornamental carved marble of the Storey House just as it appeared in that edifice."[81]

At the time, developers were still in the early stages of building houses from the material, and planned for many more. Looking around the neighborhood now, most of the houses currently standing are clearly of more recent vintage, but others *do* appear to be about the right age to have been made out of the missing mansion, and quite a few appear to have some marble features. Could these be leftover bits of the Storey Castle?

The site of the mansion, and the area where most of its pieces were said to be used for new houses, is now right in the heart of historically black Bronzeville, and Grand Boulevard is now South Martin Luther King Drive. It's nice to think of how Old Man Storey would hate that. King's grave is visited by countless pilgrims every year, while Storey is forgotten by all but a few Civil War trivia buffs who remember him as the copperhead fool who called the Gettysburg address "[s]illy, flat, and dishwatery utterances," and his attractive headstone at Rosehill visited only by people who come on my tours, on which I invite people to stomp on the old bastard's grave.

Storey's tombstone at Rosehill.

THE STOREY PALACE.

The best illustration available of the Storey Palace. No photograph
has ever been found.

Did Thomas Neill Cream Kill Alice Montgomery?

Chicago's reputation as a murderous town is not new. As early as 1858, the *Chicago Times* spoke of a seventh murderer being added to the prison population, and asked, "What are we coming to?" "Scarcely has the death-shriek of the fifth murdered victim ceased to startle the public," they wrote, "ere the weapon of death again descends, and the blood of a sixth cries to heaven from the ground for vengeance upon the murderer. Another murder! The word has become so familiar in the ears of our citizens that it would seem scarcely adequate to excite their

Thomas Neill Cream. Should an unsolved 1882 murder be added to his list of crimes?

wonder. Murder is growing common in Chicago!"[82]

These murders were usually crimes of passion, drunken one-off killings, and people killing their spouses. They had not yet conceived of the idea of the serial murderer.

We tend to advertise H. H. Holmes as "America's first serial killer," but that isn't really accurate. That Holmes fit the psychological profile of what we now call a "serial killer" is only one theory about what was going on in his head, and recent research indicates that it's not likely to be an accurate one. Holmes probably killed quite a few people, but he doesn't seem to have killed because he felt a psychological need to; there was usually a financial motive to his crimes, which makes him more of a "multiple murderer" than a "serial killer."

The difference between a serial killer and a multiple murderer is often just a question of semantics, really, but if we use a broad enough definition of "serial killer" that Holmes counts, he wasn't even the first one in Chicago, let alone the United States.

The title of "Chicago's first serial killer" could go to any number of people, really—lots of criminals are said to have killed quite a few people over the course of their careers. If half of the stories about George Green were true, he'd fit the definition at least as well as Holmes did. But perhaps our earliest murderer to fit the model of the "serial killer" is Dr. Thomas Neill Cream, a doctor who seemed to delight in giving his patients painkillers that contained *way* too much strychnine.

With his high-crowned top hat and curly mustache, Cream looked just as you'd expect a Victorian murderer to look. Born in Scotland, he came to Chicago in the 1870s and opened a clinic on Madison Street, near Throop, where he gained a quiet reputation for being the man to see if you wanted an abortion. In 1880, he was arrested for murder after one of his patients died; the press was quick to convict him (the *Chicago Times* couldn't resist using "Cream a Tartar" as a headline), but the jury was unconvinced of his guilt, and he was back at work in 1881.

That same year, he began an affair with a woman named Julia Stott, a young woman from far out beyond the west suburbs who sent her much-older husband, Daniel Stott, into the city to see Dr. Cream for treatment. Daniel kept getting sicker and sicker. Finally, Cream wrote two prescriptions for Mrs. Stott to have filled at at a nearby drugstore, one of which involved a tiny amount of strychnine. He then mixed up the powders the stores gave her into

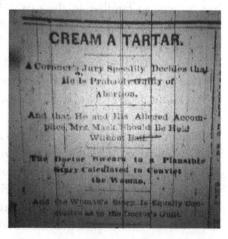

Papers couldn't resist puns on Cream.

pills himself, quietly adding much more strychnine. Daniel Stott died forty-five minutes after taking the capsules.

Cream wasn't just out to kill Mr. Stott and take his wife. He was apparently also out to blackmail Buck & Rayner, the drug store where Mrs. Stott had the prescriptions filled. Once he blamed them for putting in too much strychnine, he planned to use Stott's widow to sue them for $5,000. To this end, he sent a telegram to the coroner of the county where the Stotts lived and told him he suspected foul play in Stott's death. After looking into the drug store's record, and into Cream's, the police figured out what had really happened right away.

There was a break in Cream's relations with Mrs. Stott at that point. Rather than going along with his scheme, she admitted her suspicions that Cream had tampered with the capsules she gave to her husband. He responded by telling reporters that Mrs. Stott was "the biggest liar unhung . . . I knew her to be a bad woman, and dangerous," he said. "And I kept her away as far as I could." [83]

This time, the jury didn't believe him. He was sentenced to spend the rest of his life in prison in Joliet for the murder of Daniel Stott.

He served only nine years in prison before his brother managed to get him an early release, at which point he returned to the United Kingdom and got right back to work poisoning women with strychnine after performing abortions on them, then trying to blackmail druggists whose medicines he'd tampered with. All told, he poisoned at least four more women before July 1892, and reportedly attempted to kill another, but she turned down his offer of an "American drink" by saying she was too patriotic to drink something that wasn't British.

When he was questioned by the police at one point during his London years, he went right to Scotland Yard and complained in person that their accusations were hurting his reputation, and noted that the police had even connected him with the deaths of two young women named Alice Marsh and Emma Shrivell.

This was news to the police. They hadn't connected him with the recent murders of the Marsh or Shrivell girls at all. He knew more about the crimes than they did, which made them suspect him at once. He was soon brought to trial in London and sentenced to hang.

According to one enduring legend, Cream's last words on the gallows were, "I was Jack the. . . ." Contemporary accounts of the execution don't mention it, though, and it's been conclusively shown that Cream was in Joliet Prison during fall 1888, when the Jack the Ripper murders took place (strangely, though many have suggested that he wasn't really in jail, no one thought to track down his extensive prison records until author Amanda Griffiths used them as a source for her 2015 novel, *Prisoner 4374*).

Still, though Cream may not have been the Ripper, on a recent scan through newspaper archives looking for something completely different, I stumbled onto an unsolved Chicago murder story that seems too much like his work to ignore.

In spring 1881, between Cream's two Illinois trials, a young woman named Alice Montgomery checked into the Sheldon House, a Chicago hotel that was so close to Dr. Cream's office that you could probably have seen it out of the second-story window. After dinner, she asked for a glass of water and a teaspoon, which she took to the "ladies' private closet." When she stepped out of the closet later, she was writhing in agony, screaming and convulsing as she fell to the floor.[84]

Dr. Seymour Knox was brought to the scene to give her ether, but it was too late. Alice died in the hotel, and Dr. Knox believed that her death was the result of strychnine poisoning. An investigation showed that she had been, in the words of the *Daily News*, "in the way of becoming a mother."[85]

Dr. Byron Griffin told the authorities that Alice had recently been to his office attempting to procure an abortion, which he'd refused. A quick examination of Alice's remains, though, showed that she'd found another doctor who was more willing to step around the law. And that someone had apparently tampered with the drugs she'd been given.[86]

The medicine was traced to another West Madison Street drug store, and the prescription paper was found to have been signed by one Dr. Fraser. Fraser was found, examined the prescription, and confirmed that she'd probably used the drugs to induce an abortion, but he denied that he'd written the prescription himself. It wasn't in his handwriting, and the spelling was not up to his own standards. Also, it was written in English. He always wrote his prescriptions in Latin. This was a forgery.

Fraser assisted at the post-mortem examination of Alice's body and confirmed that she had died of strychnine poisoning from the medicine; the druggist professed ignorance. He *had* strychnine in his store, of course, but it was in a sealed bottle with a skull and crossbones on it. He couldn't have accidentally slipped it into her medicine.

Though letters from Alice to a friend strongly indicated that Fraser himself had performed the operation, he fiercely denied it. "If I desired to produce an abortion," he said, "I had the necessary drugs at my own office, and need not have sent the patient to the drug store."[87]

The coroner's jury believed both Fraser and the druggist, so the two were exonerated and the matter became a cold case. The press still believed Fraser had probably been the guilty party, at least of performing the abortion, and spoke no more about it.

Examing the case today, it certainly *sounds* like Dr. Thomas Neill Cream's handiwork: adding strychnine to medicine in order to murder an abortion patient, while implicating another doctor in the crime, was *exactly* the sort of thing he was known to do. And he was in practice on Madison Street at the time, barely a block away from the Sheldon House and the drug store. Just how many strychnine-happy abortionists could there have been around Madison and Loomis in 1881?

Dr. Cream's connection to the case seems so obvious that the biggest mystery, really, is the mystery of why no one connected him with the case at the time. Cream was arrested for the murder of Daniel Stott barely four months after Alice's death; given the use of strychnine and the attempt to frame another doctor in that case, the press and authorities should have remembered the recent Alice Montgomery case and noticed the similarities.

Part of the reason for the oversight was surely the fact that Stott had died clear out in Boone country, far beyond the edge of Chicagoland. Another may be that he wouldn't become known for murdering abortion patients until far later, if you don't count the case for which he was acquitted in 1880. But examining the newspapers of the era brings up one major factor as to how the authorities let it slip by them: they were distracted.

In 1880, while Cream was dealing with his previous murder charge, James Garfield was elected president after a surprise nomination during the Republican National Convention in Chicago (they were all contested conventions in those days; Garfield was nominated after thirty-six ballots). He was only six months into his term when Charles Guiteau, a Chicagoan himself, shot him in a train station.

Guiteau was a crank's own crank. After growing up in Illinois, he'd drifted to New York, where the Oneida Colony, a free love sect, found him unlovable and kicked him out. Making his way back to Chicago, he cheated his way through the bar exam, then failed to make a living as a fake lawyer, a fake preacher, and a wannabe politician before deciding to kill the president. He would have failed at *that*, too, but for the fact that Garfield had rather incompetent doctors whose attempts to remove the bullet with their bare hands only made things worse. The president lingered for weeks before dying.

These news stories—the president being shot, the slow uncovering of Guiteau's long history, and the president dying—happened to neatly coincide with the return of Thomas Neill Cream to the news. When Cream was first captured and brought back to Illinois for the murder of Daniel Stott, everyone was too busy talking about Garfield having been shot to think much about Cream or about another unsolved murder from months before; an interview with him aboard the train to Chicago was buried on page eight of the *Tribune*. The next month, Cream went to trial just as the presi-

dent succumbed to his wounds and died. When newspapers mentioned Cream's trial and conviction at all, the coverage was buried deep under all of the Garfield news. By the time his London trial brought him back into the Chicago papers, years later, the story of Alice Montgomery was forgotten.

Alice Montgomery lies buried in Illiopolis, her murder never officially solved.

Daniel Stott tombstone in Garden Prairie Cemetery, a very rare example of a grave marker with a murder mystery carved right into the stone. *Photo by author.*

Daniel Stott lies in Grand Prairie, sixty miles out of Chicago in a lonely, out-of-the way cemetery, surrounded by farmland and worn out roads. His is one of few older stones that is still legible at all; the epitaph reads, "Poisoned by his wife and Dr. Cream."

Charles Volney Dyer and the Vampire of Chicago

One of the great unsung treasures of the Chicago Historical Society is a gold-headed hickory cane that was presented to Dr. Charles Volney Dyer to replace one that he broke in 1846. Or, anyway, it should be. It's not currently on display, and doesn't come up when you search for it. Dyer himself was the sort of person you come across now and then in history: a once-prominent citizen, a great hero, and a really fascinating character who comes up again and again in local history, but who has been almost totally forgotten today.

The story behind the cane is an exciting one. Dr. Dyer had been harboring a fugitive slave in his home, as he did with hundreds of escaping slaves over the years. When the enslaver recaptured the fugitive and took him to the Mansion House hotel, Dyer broke into the room, helped the young slave get out the window to safety, then calmly walked out to the street. Moments later, the furious slave owner came up to Dr. Dyer with a bowie knife, and Dyer broke his cane over the man's head. The new gold-headed one was presented to him by admiring friends.

Dr. Dyer was one of Chicago's pioneers, settling in the city in 1835; before he reached the age of thirty he had been elected town clerk. He was the city's first prominent abolititionist, active in the underground railroad and friends with Abraham Lincoln. He was also the physician who dissected the body of John Stone, the first man hanged in Chicago, and was remembered as a man who loved a joke so well that he would have used his last breath on a pun.[88] He's one of those individuals you can start researching, and then find yourself down a rabbit hole hours later. A few good anecdotes of his rapier wit and daring were recorded in obituaries, and I hope that there are more out there to be discovered.

Charles Volney Dyer, a well-
known wit and pioneer, dissected
the first man hanged in Chicago,
broke his cane over a slave-owner's
head, helped hundreds of fugitive
slaves, and is the only source of
information on Chicago's only
known vampire exhumation. One of
the city's heroes who deserves to be
better remembered than he is.

A few stories about him come up in recaps of his career and remi-
nisces of him at the pioneer reunions that were common in the late
nineteenth century, and in the many tributes to him that were written
later, but one thing that none of those tributes mentioned was that
Dr. Dyer was also the sole source for the tale of Chicago's only known
vampire slaying.

"Vampirism" is a term given to the Old World practice of digging up
dead bodies and mutilating them to cure tuberculosis in the living. It
wasn't exactly *common* anywhere, but it survived its early European origins and continued to be reported in the States into the late nineteenth
century. "Consumption," as they called tuberculosis in those days, was
one of the Victorian era's biggest killers, and was little understood as a
disease, particularly in rural areas. In New England, in particular, there
existed a folk belief that when a person died of consumption, and then
other family members began to suffer from the same disease, the first
to die might be sucking the life out of the living. The exact protocol
for how to *stop* the "vampire" varied from locality to locality, but the
usual method was to disinter the body and burn the heart and perhaps
the lungs, sometimes with great ceremony (now and then the heart-
burning would attract a large crowd), and sometimes with sick family
members inhaling the fumes, or even consuming the organs.[89]

Though the tales often sound more like psuedo-science than a fear
of the supernatural, a great many instances are only known today
because some newspaper wrote about them in articles that, almost uni-
versally, expressed astonishment and disgust at the "horrible supersti-
tion." Even many of the people doing the exhumations made a point
of saying that they had no faith in it. But when your whole family is

dying, you're ready to try anything. "People find themselves in dire situations," explains folklorist Michael Bell, "where there's no recourse through regular channels. The folk system offers an alternative, a choice. Sometimes, superstitions represent the only hope."[90]

The bulk of these "vampire" exhumations in the United States took place in New England, the most famous being that of a woman named Mercy Brown. Bell's excellent book, *Food for the Dead*, cataloged a great many of the known instances. One Chicago case he discovered survives only as a tiny reference from *Demonology and Devil Lore*, an 1879 tome by Moncure Conway.

Conway was an interesting guy himself; a prominent abolitionist who traveled and lectured on the evils of slavery, it was presumably through abolitionist circles that he met Dr. Charles Volney Dyer. After slavery was abolished, Conway needed a new lecture topic and started speaking on demonology (from the point of view of an atheist, another topic on which he frequently lectured). Ten years after the end of slavery, he had a conversation with Dr. Dyer revealing the only known case of Chicago vampirism.

"Dr. Dyer, an eminent physician of Chicago," Conway wrote, "told me [in 1875] that a case occurred within that city

Conway, the lecturer who spoke to Dyer about the vampire exhumation.

within his personal knowledge, where the body of a woman who had died of consumption was taken out of the grave and the lungs burned, under a belief that she was drawing after her into the grave some of her surviving relatives."[91]

So, when and where did this Chicago vampire exhumation take place? No contemporary references to it have been found; all that we can really assume from what Dyer told Conway is that it happened some time between 1836, when the doctor first came to town, and 1875.

One clue may be that Dr. Dyer was a charter member of the Rosehill Cemetery Company in 1859 (the president was Dr. Blaney, who did the chemical analysis on the body of George Green's wife four years before). In his capacity as as a founder, he would have presumably been in a position to hear about anything unusual that went on there. And perhaps hearing about such goings-on is what made him decide he'd rather be buried at Oak Woods, where he ended up.

But Rosehill was not the sort of place where such things would likely have been allowed—as what was then thought of as an endlessly modern cemetery, with great attention paid to landscaping, there were highly detailed by-laws governing visitor etiquette. Exhumations were rare, and usually only in cases when a body was being moved or foul play had been suspected. Certainly the cemetery management would not have allowed anyone to dig up a corpse to burn the lungs.[92]

It's more probable that the exhumation took place in the old City Cemetery, at the present site of Lincoln Park. Perhaps it was stories like this that made Dyer think that a better-regulated burial ground was needed and got him involved in plans to create Rosehill.

Exactly what Dyer *thought* of the exhumation was not recorded, but one biographical sketch of him makes it seem as though he would not have approved. "He is an honest hater of shams and imposters," the sketch claimed, "and never spares the lash when specious hypocrites cross his pathway. Woe to the luckless wight who invites upon his unfortunate head the vials of his wrath. When he opens his magazine of ridicule, sarcasm, and invective, nothing but absolute stupidity or the epidermis of a rhinoceros can survive the onslaught."[93]

Lincoln Park was not only the likely grounds of the exhumation, it was also beyond a doubt the grounds of the only vampire hunt in Chicago that was ever big enough to make the news.

You'd think it must have been a slow news day for a vampire hunt to make the papers, but the day of the Vampire Scare of 1888 happened to be the same day as a presidential election. As ballots were being counted that handed the presidency to Benjamin Harrison, a small posse of vampire hunters was tearing through Lincoln Park, looking for the vampire that was rumored to have spirited a local man away after years of tormenting another local man, Samuel Patton.

Patton had been making the news off and on for a number of years by then, first in 1882 for claiming that he'd been held prisoner in an insane asylum for several years. A doctor who'd cared for him there was obliged to write to the *Chicago Daily Inter-Ocean* and say that while Patton *had* been in the facility, he had not been a prisoner, just a patient. While there, Patton had claimed that the spirit of the biblical Ezekiel had been speaking through him to prophesize the destruction of Chicago by an earthquake in 1883.[94]

By 1888, Patton was out of the institution, and he and one Judge Thalstrom were giving talks about vampires on Paulina Street. Thalstrom cited a few recent vampire exhumations, including the case of Horace Ray of Grisworld, Connecticut, who had died of consumption and was disinterred so his heart could be burned when the rest of the family got sick (in recent years, a "vampire" coffin was exhumed in Griswold, with the skeleton rearranged inside to resemble a skull and cross-bones; that it was Horace Ray seems likely, except that tacks on the coffin spelled out the initials J.B.). Thalstrom was ready with a long list of other examples, and Patton told tales of a vampire he said had been following him since the Civil War.

The main purpose of these meetings seems to have been for Patton to sell a book he had written called *The Spirit World as it Is,* as well as something he'd invented called Patton's Clairvoyic Varnish for Glass, some sort of goop that, when rubbed on one's glasses, would enable the wearer to see the vampire that had been plaguing him. "[It looks] nothing like a bat," he said. "It sucked at my mouth and nostrils. It followed me to my children's graves. It dogged me to the only place on earth that I felt was sacred."[95]

Most people seem to have thought the whole thing was a joke, but not everyone: When a local man named Claus Larson went missing, his wife suspected it was the work of the vampire, and a posse of vampire hunters went running through Lincoln Park trying to find it (Larson turned up alive and well, admitting that he'd just been off on a bender).[96]

Of course, most of this posse, if not all of them, were children. And the *Tribune*'s report on the whole affair is so jocular that whether it even took place is a bit questionable.

Patton, for his part, died a few years later. Of tuberculosis.

No copy of his book has ever turned up.

581

Samuel Patton 171⅗

MILITARY HISTORY.

Time and Place of each Enlistment.	Rank.	Company and Regiment.	Time and Place of Discharge.	Cause of Discharge.	Kind and degree of Disability.	When and Where Contracted.
July 17, 1862. Fairbury, Ills.	Pvt. M.	1. Ill. Art'y	July 24. 65. Chicago, Ills.	Close of war	Gen'l disability old age.	Since the war.

DOMESTIC HISTORY.

WHERE BORN.	Age.	Height.	Complexion.	Color of Eyes.	Color of Hair.	OCCUPATION.	Residence Subsequent to Discharge.	Married or Single.	P. O. Address of Nearest Relative.
Virginia	58	5'10"	Light			Blacksmith Protestant	Chicago, Ill	Married	Mr. E. Ammens Rogers Park Chicago, Ill.

HOME HISTORY.

Rate of Pension.	Date of Admission and Re-Admission.	Condition of Re-Admission.	Date of Discharge.	Cause of Discharge.	Date of Death.	Cause of Death.
8⁵	November 6. 91. To N.H.S. Oct 1 - 03 Re-adm Nov. Nov 21. 05				Feb. 3, 1912	

GENERAL REMARKS.

PAPERS.

Admission Paper. Gen'l Jno. C. O'Black

Army Discharge. One

Certificate of Service. none

Pension Certificate. 1,048,182

Died in G.H.S. Washington D.C.

EFFECTS.

Labor Money, $

Pension Money, $

Personal, Appraised at $ sold for $

Total, $

How Disposed of,

Military records for Samuel Patton.

Where Was Zanzic's Ultimate Spiritualistic Studio?

When the World's Fair came to Chicago in 1893, everyone in town expected to get rich. The fair organizers were counting on millions of paid admissions, and they got them; there would eventually be something like twenty-seven million tickets sold, roughly the equivalent of half the country's population at the time. And the millions who were coming were ready to spend money all over town, not just in the fairgrounds.

Perhaps no one had a more interesting idea for how to make a fortune during the fair than a magician named Zanzic.

Zanzic is thought to be the alias of one Mr. Brenner, of New Orleans, but even his real identity is a bit of a mystery; there were other Zanzics on the magic circuit, including a mentalist in Chicago named Jules Zanzic, which muddies the waters considerably. This Zanzic was apparently a stage magician in the early vaudeville era, at a time when magicians often performed in dime museums, or alongside elocutionists and jugglers in traveling shows. From what anecdotes survive of him (most of which come from an article Harry Houdini wrote for the Society of American Magicians in 1923), he once went onstage and did a show less than two hours after having one of his eyes removed.

When the World's Fair was announced, he went to work with a bold scheme that ended up working a little too well.

Houdini, who performed at the World's Fair in between gigs at a dime museum on Clark Street himself, probably learned of Zanzic's great 1893 scheme through his own interest in spiritualism, the then-popular practice of holding seances to contact the dead. Houdini always maintained that he was not a skeptic about spiritualism and sincerely hoped that there might be a real medium out there who could

Scene from a typical phony
seance. Even most of the
true believers in seances
knew that there were a lot
of fakers out there; Houdini
and Arthur Conan Doyle
both spent a lot of energy
exposing fakes (with Doyle
being a lot more suspecitible
to being tricked than
Houdini, who, as a working
magician, may have had a
better instinct for spotting
tricks). Library of Congress.

genuinely contact the departed, but he spent considerable time and
energy exposing the countless frauds who used sleight of hand tricks
to make people *think* they were talking to the dead. Even the most
hardcore believers in spiritualism generally knew that there were a lot
of fakers out there.

Zanzic was one of those. In fact, Houdini referred to him, with no
small amount of admiration, as the "Charlatan Supreme."[97]

When the World's Fair arrived, Zanzic/Brenner changed his name
to "Professor Slater" and invested $5,000 converting a Michigan
Avenue house into the ultimate "spiritualistic studio." There were
trap doors, secret chambers, hidden telephones, and all of the props
a phony medium could want, from carrier pigeons with pre-written
messages to iced rubber hands that could be dangled onto a customer's
shoulder using a fishing rod. There was even a "materialization room"
where spirits (or people made up to look like them) would actually be
seen, which was the sort of spectacle you only got from really high-end
hucksters.

No expense was spared. A team of private detectives was hired
to follow prospective clients to get information that Zanzic could
say he got from spirits. A lawyer and a physician were hired for
similar purposes. Three professional magicians were hired as full-
time staff; one of them, known as Ziska, was Houdini's main source
of information.

One of the doctors in Zanzic's employ sent him a German widower who was having trouble with his eyes; Zanzic sold him a pail of gutter mud that he represented as a magic charm. The up-front cost was $25, but if he rubbed it on his eyes and they improved, he was to send another $500. Zanzic probably figured that the $25 he made up-front was pretty good money to make for a handful of mud as it was, but two weeks later a check arrived for $1,000. The placebo had worked so well that the man added a 100 percent tip.

When the widower returned to the "studio," Zanzic told him that the mud had been charmed by the spirits, particularly that of his late wife, who had been anxious to help him. Naturally, the man requested a seance in which he could speak to her spirit personally.

Knowing that he had a man who paid well and tipped better on his hands, Zanzic put everything he had into giving the man a memorable seance, including hiring a "beautiful demimonde" made up to look like the man's late wife (based on photographs that he obtained either through the detectives or the legal team). In the seance, the man was overcome with emotion as his "astral wife" materialized, then disappeared (by means of a series of veils being placed in front of her, making her appear to fade away in the dark room).

When the session came to an end, the widower asked Zanzic if it would maybe, just maybe, be possible to arrange a conjugal visit.

Like any professional con artist would, Zanzic said it would certainly be possible—for a price.

How much the man paid is not recorded, but one can assume that it was a fabulous sum. The risks Zanzic was taking were high; materialization tricks generally relied on distant views in dark rooms to be convincing, and Zanzic was going to let the man get as close to the "spirit" as humanly possible. The widower would be in a fine position to figure out the trick, and with all the money he'd already paid, it would be disastrous for Zanzic if the mark found out it was all a hoax.

But Zanzic took his fee and made sure everything would be perfect when the man arrived to have sex with his dead wife. He fixed up one of the rooms in the Michigan Avenue house to look like a bridal chamber, and hired chefs to prepare a wedding feast (which presumably involved a lot of booze). The widower feasted while a woman was again made up; whether they used the same woman from the last time or had to hire another one who was willing to do a lot more than materialize across a room is not recorded. While the man ate and drank, Zanzic gave him a little pre-game talk: when he was done eating and drinking, he would be taken to the bridal chamber, where he could spend roughly an hour with his wife's spirit. Spending longer would be dangerous; within an hour she would have to "dematerialize," and it would be terribly dangerous for him if he were near her when the dematerialization took place.

The man agreed to the rules, and was led to his honeymoon suite. The door was shut behind him, Zanzic retreated, the hired woman took her position, and the magicians congratulated themselves on a successful caper.

Until they heard the ghastly shriek from the bridal chamber.

Fearing they'd been found out, the magicians rushed into the suite, and found that the trick had worked too well: the man was lying naked on the floor, lifeless. He'd become so excited that he'd actually *died* when the conjugal visit began.

Now in crisis mode, the team put the man's clothing back on his body and tried to lay him out just outside of the side door, as though he were simply a drunk who died in the alley. But for once they weren't sneaky enough: the man's servant had been waiting outside, saw the body being removed, and informed the police.

How Zanic avoided going to prison, Houdini didn't know. One assumes that money changed hands. Lots of it.

The account Houdini based on Ziska's information, thirty years after the fact, may be all the data that exists on Zanzic and his studio. No advertisements for Professor Slater's "Spiritual Temple" have been found.

So, some unanswered questions remain. Did Zanzic *really* fix up a Michigan Avenue house to become the ultimate spiritualistic studio? If so, was the story of what went on there true? And where was the place, exactly? Could the building still be standing?

It's generally been assumed that the house was on the north side, in what would now be the Magnificent Mile, but that section of Michigan Avenue was still a small road called Pine Street in those days. There were mansions around there at one time, but they were torn down ages ago to make room for some highrise or another. But as you travel south on Michigan Avenue, beyond the South Loop, you do start to see more nineteenth-century houses that have survived. By the time you reach Hyde Park, closer to the old World's Fair grounds, you see a number of turreted old graystones that you can imagine having served as the head-quarters of the ultimate spiritual huckster. Perhaps someone is living in one of them right now, wondering why there's an open compart-ment underneath the kitchen, what all the extra closets are for, and why there's a trap door in the bathroom . . . .

H. H. Holmes and the Vanishing Skeletons (and Other Outstanding Holmes Mysteries)

One could go on for days about the mysteries related to H. H. Holmes, currently the most famous—and intriguing—of our antique murderers. How many people did he kill in his "castle" on Sixty-Third Street, the block of retail and residential spaces that he filled with hidden rooms and secret passages? How did he kill them? And what did he do with the bodies? Theories abound, but none were ever proven, and yellow journalism and urban legends make it hard to sort fact from fiction. Nearly everything written on the man today is based

Holmes at the time of his 1894 arrest.

far more on myth than fact. Though setting up a "murder castle" to prey on World's Fair patrons is the story everyone starts with on the man, the number of fairgoers he can reasonably be suspected of murdering is exactly one. The idea that many more missing fairgoers could be traced there was invented by a New York tabloid and was little noticed for nearly fifty years, when pulps began to fold the idea into the story.

When Herman Webster Mudgett, alias H. H. Holmes, was first captured in November 1894, he was arrested simply as a swindler who had passed off a random body as that of Benjamin Pitezel, a friend of his, in order to cash in on Pitezel's $10,000 insurance policy. Reporters in Chicago soon found out just how many swindles he'd pulled in Chicago—paperwork for about sixty lawsuits involving him are on file—and for a week the story of his life and crimes was front page news all over the country. His various swindles alone were enough for newspapers to give him terms like "The King of Crime" and "The Arch-Fiend of the Century" before he was even suspected of more than two or three murders, tops.

At the time, Holmes was admitting that he'd defrauded the insurance company and claimed that Pitezel and three of his children were now in hiding in South America. The next month, however, he changed his story. Now he said that body *had* been Pitezel's own, but it was a suicide, and the children he'd said were with Pitezel were really with Minnie Williams, an old friend of his, in Europe.

Minnie and her sister had both come in summer 1893 to Chicago, where Minnie said that she was about to marry Holmes. Both had disappeared right around the fourth of July, and attempts to locate Minnie, Nannie, or the Pitezel children in London were unsuccessful.

Months went by while Holmes awaited trial, and six months later, when he pleaded guilty to conspiracy to defraud Fidelity Mutual, the children still hadn't been heard from. Detective Frank Geyer traced Holmes's footsteps around North America and eventually found Alice and Nellie, daughters of Pitezel, buried in a shallow grave in the basement of a house Holmes had rented in Toronto. Howard, Pitezel's son, was eventually found in the flue beneath a stove outside of Indianapolis; a half-empty bottle of cyanide was found nearby.

When those bodies were found, and it became clear that Holmes was up to a lot more than just swindling, people remembered the block he'd owned in Englewood—the one that was known to be full of secret passages.

The city knew about this building already. Originally built as a two-story retail/residential block in 1887, Holmes had added a third story in late 1892, ostensibly to use as hotel rooms during the upcoming World's Fair.

By all available evidence, though, the building never functioned as a hotel. The third-floor hotel space that Holmes constructed was little more than a facade used to swindle investors and furnishers out of thousands of dollars worth of startup funds, building materials, and supplies. When several creditors, including the Tobey Furntiture Company, tried to repossess the goods Holmes had bought and never paid for, they found them hidden in secret compartments, which inspired a lengthy article in the *Tribune* in March 1893.[98] Holmes also took out four insurance policies on the place, all of which he tried to cash in when the building caught fire in August 1893. None of them paid him off in the end. Reports of the fire indicate that only half a dozen or so people were in the building that night, mostly long-term residents and employees. If it was a hotel, it wasn't a busy one.

But when the police decided the time had come to comb the place for more bodies, the press began to call it the Castle.

Three men wound up in charge of the investigation: Chief John J. Badenoch, Inspector John E. Fitzpatrick, and Detective Sergeant John W. Norton. The 1890s was an era when police work was not exactly professional, though; there was no police academy

Sample of the Holmes cases on file in the legal archives in Chicago.

or any real training requirements. Badenoch himself was a political appointee whose background was in selling flour and feed; he'd been on the job all of two months and was in no way qualified for it. He saw the Castle as a chance to prove himself, and the press saw it as a chance to sell papers.

The investigation became a worldwide sensation. Bones, some of them apparently human, were found in the cellar. A soundproof vault was discovered near a stove on the third floor. Neighbors told of mysterious trunks being hauled out of the place just after the days when certain women had last been seen alive.

Though evidence was strong that at least three people had been killed there, the stories about the Castle soon got out of hand as both the police and the press indulged in wild theories. The police would find a rope and announce that Holmes must have been hanging people. A fuel tank was advertised as a gas chamber. A bench became known as a dissection table.

Toward the end of July, a man named Myron Chappell told the police that he'd bought several dead bodies from Holmes to turn into articulated skeletons to sell to medical schools. In fact, he still had one of the bodies; most of the bones were in a trunk at his house, and the skull was dangling from a tree in his yard. These bones he turned over to the police, along with a skeleton retrieved from Hahnemann Medical College that he claimed to have sold them. In the castle cellar, Chappell pointed to two spaces and said that if they dug behind the wall, they'd find an acid tank for dissolving flesh in one spot and a bleach pit for bones in the other.

When workers began to dig in the first spot, they found a tank, right where he'd said they would.

But from there, Chappel's story began to fall apart. When the tank was fully uncovered, it contained nothing but a bucket of crude petroleum.[99] In the space where he'd said they would find a bleach tank, nothing was found at all. Hahnemann College showed records indicating that the skeleton they'd turned over was from long before any of Holmes's victims were known to have died, and the Chappell family said the bones in the trunk and the skull in the tree had been in the family for ages. It came out that a neighbor who was obsessed with the Holmes case had thought of the skull and suggested to police that perhaps it was a Holmes victim, and the police had pumped Chappell full of booze and started him talking. His family said he had a habit of making up stories while he was drunk, then forgetting that they were made up when he sobered up. He did seem to know his way around the Castle fairly well, but it's entirely possible that he never worked for Holmes at all, and unlikely that any bones he turned over were actually those of Holmes victims.

The discovery that Chappell's stories were mostly nonsense turned the Chicago press against the police, and even the wildest tabloids began to brush off the Holmes Castle as a whole lot of nothing. The news about Chappell's stories falling apart didn't always make the news outside of Chicago, though. And when the *New York World* published a story on the castle that spoke of the acid tanks, bones, and Mr. Chappell as real discoveries, they became a part of the legend. Even now, nearly every book about Holmes talks of Charles Chappell (the name the press mistakenly gave him the first day) and the acid tank.[100]

In the end, Holmes was convicted of the murder of Ben Pitezel. He famously confessed to twenty-seven murders, but many of the "victims" were still alive at the time. A more realistic figure stands at around nine: the four Pitezels; the Williams sisters; two castle employees, Emeline Cigrand and Julia Conner; and Julia's daughter. A few other "maybes" are fairly convincing, but most of them are just wild theories that were never fully investigated.

But behind the myths the Castle investigation generated were some real finds. Some of the bones in the basement probably *were* the bones of Pearl Conner, who was likely killed in the building on Christmas 1891. The possible blood stains, bones, and other "clues" found in Chicago were never properly analyzed, either, beyond quick investigations in the drug store on the first floor. For every expert who said the substance in the fuel tank was deadly, there was another who would say it was just gasoline.

Modern forensics and DNA testing could likely do much to clear up these questions, which leads to one of the biggest outstanding questions about the Holmes case: What happened to the bones and evidence that the police found in the Castle?

In September 1896, four months after Holmes was hanged in Philadelphia, a city worker was attending to his duties, sorting through items in a dingy, windowless room in City Hall that served as the deposit place for the custodian of stolen property, John D. Hall. It was here that they kept confiscated brass knuckles, opium pipes, and cash-stuffed envelopes recovered as evidence. Among them were trunks belonging to Minnie and Anna Williams, two of Holmes's victims, that had never been claimed at the depot after the sisters disappeared in summer 1893.[101] On that autumn day, a new trunk arrived. Custodian Hall opened the trunk and screamed. Inside was a skeleton, facing upward, a hand outstretched as though it were trying to get out. This was the trunk full of Holmes evidence; police believed the skeleton was that of Emeline Cigrand (even though all evidence suggested it was far too old to be).

Holmes had never been brought to trial in Chicago, but the case was aired in court here in April 1897, when Patrick Quinlan, the castle janitor, and his wife sued Chief Badenoch. The police had become convinced that Quinlan and his wife had been accomplices of Holmes, and kept them in the "sweat box" for nearly three weeks while the press painted them as murderers. Officially, they were only at the station on a voluntary basis, though Badenoch had made it very clear to both of them, again and again, that if they didn't cooperate, they were both going to be hanged for sure. The untrained chief used every dirty trick he could dream up, including telling Mrs. Quinlan that he'd learned that her husband had been cheating on her with one of the now-missing women from the Castle in attempt to get her to give him some dirt on Patrick.[102] But they never learned anything. The Quinlans probably had nothing of value to tell.

The lawsuit became a court case that brought in all the witnesses who'd never had a chance to testify against Holmes in Chicago. Mrs. Pitezel, the children's mother, was present. So was Ned Conner, Pearl's father and Julia's divorced husband. And H. W. Darrow, who'd briefly turned the second floor of the Castle into a museum before a fire wrecked the upper floors in August 1895. Frank Geyer, the detective who'd found the bodies of the Pitezel children, pointed a finger at Quinlan and said that it was a tip from him that led Holmes to know that the detectives were looking for him after the alleged insurance fraud; if it hadn't been for him, Geyer said, the children would still be alive.

To illustrate why the police had felt justified in hauling in the Quinlans, the trunk full of "finds" was brought out into court. Among them were a pearl necklace Geyer said had belonged to Minnie Williams, some photographs of Holmes victims Emeline Cigrand and Julia Conner, Minnie's trunk, several pieces of valuable jewelry, and, of course, the skull and bones recovered from Chappell. There was a letter from Holmes to Quinlan saying, "Everything came off all right in the East."

So, what became of these finds?

Currently, the Chicago Police vault of Evidence and Recovered Property is a facility on Homan Avenue that is sometimes called a "Black Site" where suspects are taken; stories and reports of what goes on there rival the stories of the Holmes castle itself (and, one *hopes*, are just as sensationalized). A 2012 report on the inventory management painted a bleak picture of poor record-keeping and a lack of structure.

Nothing in the facility likely goes nearly so far back as the 1890s; the police keep no records from before the 1920s, so anything they ever had on Holmes is probably long gone now.

But there are several other bits of Holmes data known to have existed at one point that may still be out there, besides the trunk of evidence:

LOST PHOTOGRAPHS

Photographs of Myrta Holmes (his second wife), Georgiana Yoke (his third), and many of his victims are known to have existed once; newspapers in 1895 were a couple of years away from publishing photos, so they published drawings of the photos. The originals of many of these have never surfaced, but may still exist somewhere.

Emeline Cigrand

THE QUINLAN TRANSCRIPTS

Police collected nearly four hundred pages of testimony from the Quinlans. They didn't know anything incriminating, but what they said could not only illumi-

Emeline Cigrand, one of the known victims. This was a photograph of which several newspapers made drawings. No real copy of the photo has ever turned up.

nate many details of Holmes's career, but show a lot about how Chief Badenoch and his force operated in 1895.

THE CORBITT COLLECTION

Amateur detective Robert Corbitt (who had exactly as much train-ing as some of the real detectives on the force at the time) ended up in possession of many of Holmes's letters, his bank book, and even a revolver he once owned. They're probably long gone, but who knows?

THE MACDONALD FILES

Little is really known of Holmes's childhood; most of what we do know comes from Holmes's own autobiography. The autobiography of a chronic liar is not exactly a reliable source (not to mention the strong possibility that the manuscript was heavily altered by the editor for publication). But Arthur MacDonald, a criminologist who is known to have studied Holmes in prison, once claimed to have in his possession over two hundred letters from Holmes's old neighbors and schoolmates. About thirty were published and will be detailed in my upcoming book about Holmes (due April 2017), but the rest are currently lost. The MacDonald papers held by a university library does not seem to include them.

MOYAMENSING RECORDS

Holmes was incarcerated at Moyamensing Prison in Philadelphia for nearly eighteen months before his execution; records may still exist. The Philadelphia City Archives website has not been updated in ages.

And these are just a sample, really. Holmes generated volumes and volumes of paperwork, much of which still exists. And more is being found all the time; many lawsuits related to him and his activities are not under his own name, and are therefore difficult to locate among the files at the archives. The original architect's plan for the first floor of the Castle, for instance, was buried in a lawsuit. Who knows what else is still out there?

Holmes's various letters and writings show that he believed that papers had consistently charged him with the death of Anna Betts. They hadn't, though, and the fact that he seemed to think they *had* is fairly suspicious. He confessed to murdering her in 1896, but only in a confession that admitted to the murders of several people who were known to have died of natural causes, or, in many cases, weren't dead at all.

Did Inspector Shippy Employ a Tell-Tale Corpse?

There are any number of stories about the Chicago police using questionable tactics in order to solve a crime (or at least say they've solved it, so the public will get off their backs), but sometimes you've got to at least give them some credit for being creative. Like in the case of the Selafini Murder of 1904, when the head inspector supposedly tried to turn a cemetery into a house of horrors, hoping that he could scare a suspect into confessing.

In November 1904, the body of an Italian man was found washed up on the shore of Lake Michigan in Rogers Park. The crushed skull could have theoretically been the result of the body being knocked against a rock while being tossed in the waves, but the multiple stab wounds made it clear that the man had died as a result of foul play. In fact, the condition of the body suggested this was no mere robbery that turned violent. This was the sort of brutal murder that pointed to someone satisfying a lust for revenge.

The name Joseph de Leonardy was found on a railroad pass in the dead man's pocket, and de Leonardy was soon located and brought into the city morgue, where he identified the dead man as Latone Scalsani, a laborer. Records and papers could never agree on what the man's name was, exactly; within a couple of days the press were calling him a number of different things, though perhaps most commonly Natoli Selafani (the name I'll use here).

The detectives got to work, and somehow determined that the body had been hauled to the lake in a carriage driven by a horse named Guiseppe. Inspector Shippy tried to take the horse to the spot in the lake where the body was found, hoping it would somehow lead them to the killer, but it worked about as well as one would expect. Guiseppe was no detective.

It was just the sort of weird attempt to solve a case that Shippy was known for, really. George M. Shippy had joined the police force in 1887, had been made a captain in 1898, and in 1904 was appointed Inspector. In between appointments, he claimed to have been hired and fired more than any officer in the city. For a year he worked as the supervisor of an otherwise-all-black company of firefighters, and for the rest of his life told amusing anecdotes that wouldn't have been out of place in a minstrel show. A few years later, while serving as chief of police, he'd shot and killed a man who came to his house one night. Exactly what the man was doing became the subject of some debate, but it was fairly clear that Shippy had shot the man at least partly because he simply looked like a radical.

And yet, Shippy was fairly progressive, for the time; he believed that criminals could be reformed and was generally said to treat criminals under his supervision with consideration.[103]

Most of the time, anyway.

Stories of him that paint him in a less-flattering light are not uncommon.

Even though using a horse to sniff out the murderer failed, several suspects were soon arrested for Selafani's murder, including the owner of the Clark Street lodging house[104] where Selafani (who happened to be Guiseppe's owner) was living, several of his other lodgers, and one of the porters. But evidence was lacking against all of them, and with no one ready to confess, all the police could do was keep them all in the holding cell.

On November 20, a bloody hatchet was found in the saloon on the first floor of the lodging house, and the coroner's physician matched it to the gash in the dead man's head. A porter in the lodging house told of hearing the struggle and of seeing one of the suspects waving a large roll of bills around in the saloon.

Some of the papers—particularly the *Evening American*—believed that it had been the work of not one killer, but a whole gang of "Black Hand" criminals. If a wealthy man in an Italian community bought a new piece of property, he could almost expect to receive a letter from the Black Hand demanding that he place a large sum of money in a secret location, or his building would be bombed. Bombings and reprisals became common, and since extortion via the mail was not yet a federal offense, the perpetrators were almost never caught. Both the police and the community tended to imagine that one shadowy organization was behind all of the Black Hand letters, but it was probably several of them.

One of the Selafani suspects, Joseph Lombardo, was rumored to be a Black Hander who told the police that he couldn't have been the killer, because at the time of the murder he was bringing three trunks to Mrs. Gatto's grocery store. The detectives brought Lombardo to the store, and Mrs. Gatto not only denied that he'd brought any trunks that night, but shouted, "You're a bad man, Joe! You lie about things. You have not been here since that man's body was found in the barrel!"[105]

Lombardo had been telling the police he'd only come to Chicago two weeks before the crime, but the body Mrs. Gatto mentioned had been found in a barrel two years earlier. It wasn't enough to convict Lombardo of the Selafani murder, but it was a start.

"I have caught these Italians in a dozen lies since this case came up," said Shippy, "which inclines me more than ever to the belief that we are on the right track."

By November 21st, there were eight suspects in custody. But no amount of putting suspects in the "sweat box" seemed to bring Inspector Shippy any closer to a solution in the case.

And, even though the new clue about Lombardo suddenly reopened as many as five unsolved murders in which Black Hand groups were thought to figure, the media forgot about Selafani almost almost at once.

Moments after the police's encounter with Mrs. Gatto, another murdered body was found slumped over the steering wheel of a car near Lemont. No one had ever been murdered in a car before, and the fact that the only suspect was a shadowy figure who gave his name as "Mr. Dove" made it a case built for the media. The papers and public stopped talking about Selafani almost completely, and police resources for the case were soon to be diverted. If the Selafani murder was going to be solved, it would have to be solved fast before all of the resources were going to the Dove case.

And so, Shippy spent the evening reading detective stories by Edgar Allan Poe and Arthur Conan Doyle and came up with one of the most

creative, yet ludicrous, methods of
ferreting out the guilty party every
devised.

On the morning of November 21,
while he continued "interviewing" the
suspects, he sent four detectives out
to Mt. Caramel Cemetery to exhume
Selafani's body. The press assumed the
police were going to re-examine the
wounds and try to connect the murder
to some of the other recent Black
Hand killings, which was the logical
assumption to make. But Shippy had
more ambitious plans.

Mrs. Gatto.

According to the *Chicago Tribune*, the detectives took the body into
the cemetery's receiving vault and propped it up on a chair. The the
right arm was raised, with a finger outstretched, as though pointing
straight ahead. Anyone brought into the vault would be greeted by
the sight of Selafani's corpse pointing right at them, staring at them
with glaring eyes sunken into his gruesome, decomposing skin. Shippy
believed that perhaps the guilty party would be scared into confessing.

Four of the suspects were brought to Mt. Carmel Cemetery to face
their mute accuser. Joyce Toppin, the porter at the saloon, was brought
into the vault first. He jumped at the sight of the accusing corpse, and
his knees shook violently, but he didn't shout out a confession.

Suspects Charles Renzino and Frank Bell were brought in next, and
neither showed any reaction at all.[106]

Shippy, by now discouraged, ordered that Peter Miro, the last suspect, be brought in. Word of what was set up in the vault seems to have
circulated, and Miro objected violently. Detectives had to quite literally carry him inside. He was visibly terrified when he saw the rotting
corpse silently pointing at him, but made no confession.

The full story was printed in the *Chicago Tribune*, but none of the
others seem to have found room for it. It may simply be that the story
got swept out of the news as the "Mr. Dove" murder became front-page
news, but it makes one wonder if the scene in the vault ever really happened. Would a guy who'd been buried a week, after floating in the

water for a few days, have been in any shape to prop up on a chair like that?

I asked mortician and author Caitlyn Doughty, who was skeptical. She said, "Rigor mortis can last up to seventy-two hours after death, but that's well before the mark stated in this story. If the body wasn't embalmed, or preserved in any way (and had been buried), it would already be well into decomposition, bloating, smelling. Handling a floppy, bloated body would be miserable for the cops, and the smell would be pretty bad. I don't see any way for them to have propped him up with a pointed finger in a natural fashion, unless there were ropes or poles or contraptions involved."[107]

Exactly how the body was treated and prepared for burial after it was found is not terribly clear from contemporary reports; the mentions that it was being exhumed from Mt. Carmel are the first signs I see that it was even interred there. And the use of the phrase "exhumed" is the only sign that it was ever actually buried, not just kept in the vault awaiting burial. Whether it was embalmed is similarly unclear. In any case, it seems unlikely that the story could have happened *exactly* as described.

For the next month, the Dove murder would take up the news, and in January the papers would turn their attention to Johann Hoch, a new "bluebeard" who may have married as many as fifty-five wives, killing about a third of them in the process, and the story would be gone from the news, even as the eight suspects continued to languish in jail. In February, they were finally released on a lack of evidence. The murder was never solved.

Who Was Mr. Dove?

Out beyond the city, and past the last rim of suburbs, there still existed a wide stretch of bucolic countryside between Chicago and Joliet at the turn of the twentieth century. It was in this bucolic country haven that a farmer woke up on November 19, 1904, to see one of those new "automobiles" sitting on the road beside his house. That was probably strange enough at the time, but it was the dead body sitting in the driver's seat that truly startled him.

Slumped over the wheel was the body of a chauffeur, his hand gripping a gear lever. Frozen blood trailed from gaping bullet holes in the back of his head. Like most vehicles of the day, the car was an open model; the victim's collar flapped in the biting winter wind. Other than some footprints in the mud whose trail was soon lost, there was no sign of the killer.

The very idea that you could hire a car and chauffeur in Chicago and have him drive you clear out to Joliet was still brand-new. Only ten years before, when the first professional automobile race had been held in Chicago, the winning car made the trip to Evanston and back in ten and a half hours, and only a third of the cars entered made it all the way. Automobiles that could reliably take you to suburbia were brand-new. And so was the idea of being murdered in a car. As far as anyone knew, it had never happened before.

Newspapers smelled gold. The *Chicago Evening American*'s headline that morning had been about the Black Hand and the Selafani murder, but by the time they published their later edition, the story that had looked like the crime of the century in the morning before was relegated to second place status behind a new headline: MURDERED IN AUTO 270!

The *Evening American* then rushed out new extra editions every couple of hours, well into the night, as new bits of evidence in the "auto murder" came in.

The dead man, J. William Bate, was in his early twenties. The son of a wealthy man, "Will" had been working at Dan Canary's garage, near the Auditorium Theater on Michigan Avenue. The first theory the *Evening American* published was that some farmer, angered by the noise and trespass of a newfangled horseless carriage on his property, had killed the young man, and the passenger had fled or been taken prisoner.

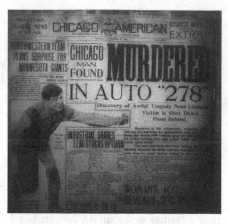

The *Evening American's* first headline of many in its obsessive coverage of the Dove case.

But by the time the next edition was printed, hours later, it had come out that in Bate's pockets were the photograph of a woman and several love letters—most of which were addressed to him, but one of which was to someone else, suggesting a love triangle.

And the killer had thoughtfully set up some dirt behind the tires to keep the car from going into the ditch, which made it seem less like a crime of passion.

By the next extra edition after *that*, reporters had learned that the car and driver had been rented by a dark-complexioned man in a bowler hat. This stranger, presumably the missing murderer, had called Dan Canary's garage from a phone in the Auditorium Annex Hotel (soon to be renamed the Congress), giving his name only as "Mr. Dove." He had expressed indignation over the cost of the rental; had he killed Bate in an argument over the fare?

Publishing photographs in newspapers, not just drawings of them, had finally become practical, and the *Evening American*, William Randolph Hearst's entry into the Chicago market, had been acting like a kid with a new toy. By the late edition that night, they were publishing a photographic re-creation of the crime scene: a young man in a chaffeur's outfit slumped over the wheel of the exact model of car Bate had been driving, out on a lonely country road. You had to read the language very carefully to see that you were looking at a re-creation, not an actual crime scene photo.

The *Evening American* had come upon an interesting strategy in the four years since they'd launched: They would publish photographs of every piece of evidence they could find—marriage certificates, rental slips, murder weapons, crime scene photos, and anything else a detective might want to see. Then, they would exhort their readers to study them carefully, looking for clues. Perhaps some reader might know a critical piece of information that would allow them, and no one else, to see the connection between the items. This not only truly did occasionally lead to breaks in the case, but it also sold papers; people liked the feeling that they were playing a role in solving the crime, and that made them feel less guilty about a tabloid like the *Chicago Evening American*.

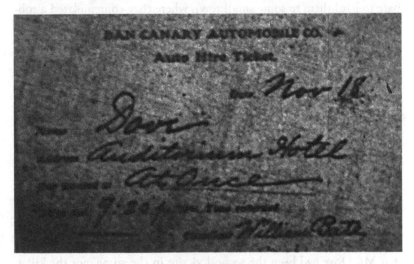

Copy of the rental slip as published in the *American*.

And it *was* a tabloid. They would print any rumor they could dream up, under the most sensational headlines they could imagine, often printed in fonts so large that one word took up a whole line. At peak times, they were known to have new editions, each with a new sensational twist in the case worthy of 480-point font that covered the whole top half of the page, almost hourly. To make sure every new edition had a new twist, they doctored photos, invented interviews, and used every other dirty trick in the book.

But they also dilligently worked to get real scoops. They engaged switchboard operators at all the big hotels to send them scoops. Many reporters never set foot in the "Madhouse on Madison," the main office, but called in their stories by telephone to rewrite men.

And to keep on top of murder news, they had nine out of eleven coroners' deputies working for them. When the coroner held his inquest on the murder of J. William Bate, reporters managed to bring a deputy coroner to a tavern while photographers took pictures of the evidence he was supposed to be guarding.[108]

As the Bate story developed, reporters tracked down everyone they could find to get their theories on what had happened.

"I believe that two men were in the case," said Dan Canary, Bate's boss. "And I think the men were bank robbers and that they employed Bate to haul them to some small town where they contemplated a robbery. From the marks of the machine, I believe they notified Bate of their plans and that he whirled the machine around and started back."[109]

They also brought in Mary E. Holland, whom the press sometimes called "Chicago's Woman Sherlock Holmes." While not a member of the police force, Holland was an accomplished detective in her own right; she had studied fingerprint sciences at Scotland Yard, and was slowly helping U.S. agencies to learn the science using dusting powders of her own invention. Within a decade, she would give testimony at a Chicago trial that would be the first modern instance of fingerprints leading to a murder conviction.

At the time of the Bate murder, she used her deductive skills to examine the blood stains and prints on the car and agreed with Mr. Canary that there had been a third man, but brought in a new idea: that Mr. Dove had been the second victim in the crime, not the killer. Someone had murdered Dove and hidden his body, then killed Bate because he knew too much. The *Evening American,* which did contain some great reporting in the midst of their yellow journalism, published pictures of Holland examining the car and commissioned her to write up her report on the case, an important document that would have been lost to history if they hadn't printed it.

She wrote: "There exists in the blood stains on the automobile the unmistakable evidence that some person or some heavy object has been dragged from the rear seat over the right side of the machine. This was done when the blood was warm. I cannot be mistaken in this. The hands of the person, whose fingerprints still remain on the front portion of the machine and on the brass of the lamps, were dripping with blood. There is evidence that blood was actually dropping from his hands . . . It is my theory that the man known as Dove was the real victim of the murder plot and that the chauffeur was killed mainly to silence his tongue. There seems to be no previous motive for the killing of the chaueffer."[110]

As to why someone would kill Dove, she could only guess, but she could see there was something fishy in the story. "His midnight ride over the lonely country road was peculiar, to say the least," she wrote. "The police have not learned what prompted him to take it, what secret object he had in hiring an automobile to go to Joliet or elsewhere in that direction when seemingly the electric car or railroad train

The *American*'s recreation of the murder.

would have been better . . . [he said] he only wanted it for three hours. The trip to Joliet could not have been secured within a three hours' hire."[111]

More twists in the case kept coming. A letter to Bate from another woman was found, this one hinting of some scandalous affair and containing what sounded like a threat: "When I love I love, and when I hate I hate."

But Bate himself almost couldn't have been intended as the target from the start; Dove would have had no way of knowing who the driver would be when he hired the car.

Some evidence and sightings suggested that perhaps Mr. Dove was a woman in disguise, though this was just the sort of wild theory that the *Evening American* was prone to make up when they needed a new rumor for a new edition—perhaps for the "Indiana Edition" that was timed to hit the streets just as Hoosier commuters came to the train station to go home.

All of these theories, stories, and investigations were circulating in the press when the case was barely forty-eight hours old. On the third day, the *Evening American* published a bulleted list of eleven theories the police were working with, plus four more that they'd discarded, just in case one of them would give someone an idea.

For a time, the press was hot on the story that Dove had been identified as one Joseph Weil, but Weil quickly went to the police and established that he wasn't. Weil, also known as "The Yellow Kid" (named after the same comic strip in Hearst papers that gave "yellow journalism" its name), was one of Chicago's great con artists; practically every trick in *The Sting* can be read about in his autobiography. But now and then, one of his victims would find out that he was a swindler, and, in this case, one had tried to get revenge by fingering Weil as Mr. Dove.[112]

More than a week would pass before the coroner's inquest. Most of the witnesses gave information that the press had leaked days before, but there was one new face: Peter Freehauf, the farmer who lived closest to the crime scene. Freehauf had told his story already, but he had previously told police and reporters that he hadn't heard any gunshots, just the sound of a car going by. He and his wife had feared that if they said more, the killer would come back for them. Now he changed his story a bit. "At 11:45, my wife heard someone rapping on the front door, and she could hear someone say, 'Those people in there cannot hear me.' I awoke when my wife passed through my room to the front door. I did not hear the rapping. We occupy separate bedrooms. I went to the window and looked out. I saw an automobile's lights going toward Lockport from our house. My wife and I retired. Some minutes later I heard a shot. I jumped out of bed and ran into my wife's room. 'Someone is shooting outside,' said I. Just then came the second shot. I looked out the window."[113]

Not seeing anything, he believed that the people in the automobile were shooting for sport. "Not until six o'clock the next morning, when I saw a man sitting as if asleep in the front seat of the machine, did I know exactly what had happened."[114]

Despite Freehauf's testimony and Mrs. Holland's investigations, the coroner's jury ruled that there had only been two men in the car, Bate and Dove. Their ruling was that somewhere near the farm, Dove had announced his refusal to pay the fare. Bate had ordered Dove out of the vehicle, declining to return him to Chicago, and Dove had shot him, then taken his $10 advance rental fee out of the dead man's pockets and run away.[115] That version of events left plenty of unanswered questions (if someone refuses to drive you home, shooting them won't get you home any faster), but was generally considered the last word in the case.

By then, there were several men that police believed might be the mysterious "Dove," but all of them turned out to be false leads, and by Christmas the story was almost gone from the news. New scandals came along, and people forgot all about the strange case of William Bate and Mr. Dove.

In 1913, when Mary E. Holland began writing short stories about her adventures under the name "Mistress of Mysteries," one of them was a fictionalized account of her involvement in the Dove case, "The Problem of the Second Stain."[116] In the nine years since the case, she had revised her theory some; she now believed that the third person in the car was a woman. Perhaps one who was engaged to Mr. Dove. Perhaps Dove had killed her and disposed of the body, then killed Bate to keep him from talking.

But if she was right, the world would never know. A second body was never found, Mr. Dove was never identified, and the first automobile murder in history would remain forever unsolved. In a retrospective in 1929, the *Chicago Tribune* wrote that, "Dove is safe in the port of missing murderers." It was last time they'd ever mention the case at all.

How Many Wives Did Johann Hoch Kill?

In November 1904, the month of the Selafani case and the Dove murder, a man named Johann Hoch rented a cottage at 64th and Union in Chicago. He told the owner that he was a big shot at the Armour and Co. meatpacking company, pulling in a cool $125 a month. Once the keys were in his hand, he spent a small fortune outfitting the cottage with furniture and told the people at the furniture shop that he was about to be married.

Johann Hoch, one of our most fascinating antique murderers.

He left out one crucial piece of information: He hadn't picked out a bride yet.

This was a small matter; Hoch knew he'd have one within weeks. He had done this before many times.

In fact, by some estimates, he'd been married more than fifty times already.

Hoch had apparently been born in Germany under the name of Jacob Schmidt and came to the United States in 1895. He was a stout, wheezy fellow who spoke like a German dialect comedian. With a look one might liken to that of the guy on the Pringles can, he was even less of a typical "ladies man" than H. H. Holmes, whose old "Castle" was still standing a stone's throw from his new home. Instead of young women, as Holmes had usually targeted, Hoch's favorite prey was middle-aged widows who were eager to settle for just about any man who would offer to support them.

In December 1904, he found an ad in the German-language newspaper *Abendpost* from Marie Walker, a North Side widow who owned a candy store and was looking for a husband. Hoch went to visit her in the shop, saying that his wife had recently died after an eighteen-year illness, but he was a rich man who owned a house on Union Avenue and could take care of her. After chatting for half an hour, he reportedly said, "I like you, and you like me. So we can get married, then, ya?"

A week later, Mrs. Walker gave Hoch the $75 she'd made by selling the store and the $80 she'd had hidden in her bed, and the couple adjourned to the court house to get married.

Only two days later, Marie's health began a slow decline.

A month after the wedding, a friend who'd known Marie at the candy store visited the Union Avenue house and found that Marie was deathly ill. Her sisters Bertha and Amelia had been pressed into service giving Marie soap and salt water enemas that Mr. Hoch had prepared (though Bertha insisted on using colder water, which pleased Marie, who said that Mr. Hoch made them too hot), as well as a thick, greenish medicine that Marie said nauseated her. Mr. Hoch himself had taken to sitting in the hall, making a show of feeling sorry for himself. "I thought I had a healthy wife," he said, "but now it's the same trouble."

Marie had told Amelia that every time she took medicine that Johann gave her, she only got worse. She and Amelia had been on bad terms; Amelia had left nine children in Germany, and Marie thought it was a disgrace. The sickness didn't do anything to repair relations between them, and the sick Marie became jealous of the attention her new husband was paying to her sister. While Amelia was downstairs eating, she heard Marie telling Hoch, "Why, go on and marry her; go on and marry her after I am dead." Amelia charged back up and shouted, "Is that the thanks I received for what I do for you?" then ran away to pack her things, vowing never to come back.

"You can take him!" Marie shouted after her.

It was too late to go home, so Amelia said she would stay the night and start in on her vow never to speak to her sister again the next morning.

By morning, though, Marie had died. Blood trickled from her blue lips. The undertaker came and moved the body from the bed, but left it in the house while Amelia helped Hoch clean up, watching as he threw the medicine bottles against a brick wall outdoors, breaking them.

While they cleaned, Hoch proposed to Amelia.

"If you stick to me I will be good to you and your children," he said. "I am worth thirty or forty thousand. We will open a hotel and run it together."

"My sister is not buried yet," Amelia said. "She is still lying in the room next door. It is not the time to talk about a matter like that."

"The dead belong to the dead," said Hoch. "And the living to the living."

While her sister began to decompose in the next room, Hoch promised Amelia, a widow herself, that the youngest of her children in Germany could come to be "Americanized," and he wished she would decide *now,* or at least stay in the house with him, because "it [was] not very nice to lie all alone in the house with the body."

They were married in a courthouse the day after the funeral, and the day after that, Hoch left town. With all of Amelia's money.[117]

When Amelia went to the police, the now-missing Mr. Hoch became a media sensation. By the end of January, it was being reported that he'd married as many as fifty-five women in his career, and murdered roughly a third of them. Nine days after the funeral, Marie's body was exhumed from Oakwoods Cemetery to be checked for arsenic, and papers gave grim accounts of Amelia looking at the remains after the now-frozen coffin was thawed out enough to be pried open in the nearby undertaking parlor: "She looked at the frozen features without apparent feeling."

"Yes, that's my sister," she said.

Bertha, meanwhile, was overcome with emotion.[118]

Arsenic poisoning was, or had been, a perfect crime; arsenic was often used in embalming fluid, so if an undertaker so much as stepped into the room with a body, it was nearly impossible for prosecutors to get a conviction. Hoch, unaware of new advances in the embalming arts and sciences, was quite cheerful and optimistic when he was captured in New York and taken back to Chicago. As reporters peppered him with queries, he spouted witticisms and answered questions with jokes. When asked the names of his last three wives, he said that each was named "Mrs. Johann Hoch." When asked why he'd married so many, papers, possibly exaggerating his dialect, quoted him as saying, "All der vimmen for Johann go crazy, jah?"

And when asked why so many died, he simply said, "Kidney trouble, I suppose."

Meanwhile, it was announced that arsenic had been found in Marie's body.

For a brief time there were rumors that Hoch had been an old accomplice of H. H. Holmes himself. But the main witness confirming his presence there was M. G. Chappell, the man who told the police that he'd bought dead bodies from Holmes to turn into skeletons, and whose stories hadn't held up to any fact-checking at all. Now he told them that Hoch had been a janitor named "Jake" who worked in the Castle, but his new stories didn't come to anything, either. The pictures he claimed to have showing Hoch in the Castle didn't show anyone remotely resembling him, and Dr. Edward H. Robinson, a druggist whose daily presence in the old Castle was beyond doubt, not only denied having seen Hoch, but denied that there was ever anyone named "Jake" to begin with.

Still, Hoch's background was full of enigmas and question marks. Though it's likely that he was then taking the blame for every husband who'd ever deserted a wife, police were fairly confident that quite a number of them had identified him correctly.

And there were *many* dead wives in his history. Though his use of aliases made positive identification difficult, there were about ten now-dead women who could fairly positively be linked to the man. Years later, the coroner's physician gave the following "canonical" list of known wives before Marie and Amelia:

Martha Steinbrecher—Married in Chicago, dead in four months.
Mary Rankin—Married shortly after Martha's death, deserted at once.
Martha Hertzman—Married and deserted in 1896.
Mary Hoch—Married in West Virginia in 1896, soon died of nephritis, the same disease that killed Marie Walker.
Clara Bartell—Married in Cincinnati in 1896, died of nephritis, just like Marie Walker, three months later.

Julia Dose—Married and deserted in 1897.
Marie Goerhke—Married and deserted in late 1901–early 1902.
Mary Becker—Married and deserted in St. Louis, 1902–3.[119]

Those were just the confirmed ones; as of 1936, it was said that police records still in existence at the time implicated him in sixteen more verified marriages, five of them to women who promptly died, plus another eighteen unverified cases, including ten possible murders. If all of the accusations were true, Hoch would have married well over forty women and killed around twenty. Some newspapers in 1905 had put his number of marriages in the fifties.

Of these, only a few cases were really investigated thoroughly. Perhaps the best documented in Chicago was Mary Steinbrecker, whose funeral was held up by the deputy coroner after a furniture delivery man informed police that he'd heard Mary say on her deathbed that she'd been poisoned. But Hoch had been ready with a death certificate stating that Mary died of natural causes, and the funeral and burial went on.

Oddly, Hoch continued to develop a reputation as a ladies' man as he sat in prison in Chicago, and Inspector Shippy brought bundles of valentines from the mail to his cell. He and Shippy had a grand time reading them aloud to the press; one was from Florence Cook, "a girl of forty" living at 1155 Perry Street. She advertised herself as a wealthy woman who would happily help Hoch secure his freedom.

"If she's got all that wealth, I had better answer the letter tomorrow, when I get time," Hoch said with a chuckle.

Shippy read one signed "Carrie Nation." "If you can't come, write us regarding your matrimonial career of the past years. Hoping you will succeed in getting released very soon." "I wish you would answer Carrie," said Shippy, obviously amused.[120] This was *presumably* not the Carrie Nation who'd made a name for herself crusading for temperance by attacking bars with hatchets, but she *was* a older divorcee at the time—exactly Hoch's type.

At the end of his trial, Hoch nearly gave himself away. Shortly after the jury had announced a guilty verdict, he stated, "I did not kill my wife with arsenic!"[121]

Papers made much of the wording. Was he saying that he *did* kill her some other way? Or that he was doing something *other* than killing her with the arsenic he gave her? Some suggested that perhaps he'd killed her some other way, then injected the arsenic into her body in order to make sure he couldn't be convicted, still believing that arsenic was a perfect crime. But the embalming fluid used on Marie was arsenic free, and the jury felt the large quantity found in her body when it was exhumed was a clear sign of murder.

In early 1906, Hoch was hanged for killing Marie Walker-Hoch; the other twenty or so possible murder cases were left uninvestigated.

Even beyond all of the possible murders and desertions that may yet be attributed to him, there are other outstanding mysteries related to Hoch as well.

Seven years after his hanging, an article about him appeared in the *Chicago Record-Herald,* noting that in one of his final statements before his execution, Hoch said, "Let my secret be interred with my bones. When you bury this poor old body of mine, you will also bury the secret of my life. I have never revealed that to anyone, and I prefer to carry that secret locked up in my heart."[122]

The *American* broke out their biggest type when Hoch was hanged—which, for them, was really saying something.

The actual quote is difficult to trace to a reliable source, but a doctor featured in the article said, "Oh yes, there was a secret. Was the secret another crime, a pivotal epochal event in the man's life?" The doctor said that the case had puzzled him for years, and a few people close to Hoch had been in on the secret, including his spiritual advisor, but still weren't talking. His own belief was that Hoch hadn't been killing women for their money; none of his victims were exactly wealthy, after all. Usually, he would only net a few hundred dollars out of them, tops.

Marie-Walker Hoch death certificate.

He believed that the real reason Hoch was marrying women was to perform chemical experiments on them. He was trained as a chemist in Germany, and perhaps he had theories that arsenic could be beneficial to health.

But the "secret" story circulated only much later, and wouldn't explain the many women that Hoch deserted without murdering them. Money really does seem to have been his object; the widows he picked simply seemed like low-hanging fruit for his matrimonial adventures.

How many were brought into his web? Though arsenic poisoning was a perfect crime for much of Hoch's career, it's also a crime for which evidence can last forever. Since it's an element, arsenic doesn't break down. There may still be arsenic in the graves of any number of women who married Hoch over the years . . .

Amelia Fisher-Hoch, Hoch's last wife (who forgave him completely and spent his last months trying to win him back).

Marie Walker-Hoch, the last woman Hoch murdered.

Was Marshall Field, Jr.'s Death Really an Accident?

Marshall Field, Jr.'s death in 1905 was not officially a mystery, but Chicagoans of the day sure thought it was. Almost no one seems to have believed that he'd actually shot himself in his Prairie Avenue mansion. But you wouldn't necessarily know it from reading contemporary documents. Marshall Field, Sr., the department store owner, threatened to pull his advertising from any paper that dared to mention any of the rumors that flew around the city.

This much was known: Marshall Field, Jr.'s butler had reported to the police that he'd found his employer lying on a couch in his wife's boudouir, bleeding from a gunshot wound in his side. The only people in the house were the butler, a few assorted servants, young Marshall Field the III, and Miss Penfield, a nurse who was taking care of the boy.[123] The official version of events was that he'd accidentally shot himself with his own automatic revolver, which he'd been cleaning in preparation for an upcoming hunting trip in Wisconsin. But suicide rumors—as well as more scandalous ones—circulated at once.

Marshall Field, Jr., at the time of his death.

Marshall Field, Jr., lived in oppulence in his mansion at 1919 S. Prairie Avenue, back when the stretch of Prairie between 16th and 22nd was the crown jewel of Gilded Age Chicago. Though in just twenty years the few remaining mansions would look like leftover teeth in a mouth that had just been thoroughly punched, in 1905, it was still one long boulevard of splendid mansions. Marshall Field, Sr., himself lived a few doors down from his son; people were still talking about the extravagent *Mikado*-themed party they'd had nearly twenty years before.[124]

At the time of the shooting, Marshall Field, Sr., was in New York with his wife, but made preparations to return to the city at once. A team of surgeons at Mercy Hospital had performed an operation on Field, Jr., and removed the bullet, but listed his chances of recovery as slight. Field's mile-a-minute race back to the city by train was considered almost as newsworthy as the shooting itself.

Reporters decided that there was something odd about the case right away when they learned that the police only learned of the shooting from the hospital report. And two detectives put on the case found the Field household and the hospital staff so uncommunicative that it was three hours before they could make a report to the chief.

The *Chicago Evening American*, of course, was all set to play up the strange sense of secrecy, and managing editor Moses Koenigsberg prepared a headline for the morning edition: MYSTERY IN SHOOTING OF MARSHALL FIELD, JR.

Fifteen minutes after he called it in, circulation manager Max Annenbert burst into Koenigsburg's office. "I saw the head you ordered," he grumbled. "Koenigsburg, you're murdering the paper."

"First degree, or just manslaughter?" asked Moses.

"This is too serious to kid about," said Max. "You know that we need the Marshall Field business more than anything else; and your head[line] will put the kibosh on our last chance to get it back."

"Do you mean to suggest that the story be suppressed?"

"Of course not, but the mystery angle is suicide."[125]

Koenigsburg put up a fight. "What would be the attitude of other advertisers," he asked, "if they learned that we had omitted important intelligence with the purpose of having one of their competitors accept the omission as a bribe for the renewal of his business?"

He won the argument, and the *Evening American* went with the mystery angle in the end. Field wasn't advertising with them at the moment, anyway, and that the *Evening American* would go with the most sensationalistic view possible could not have surprised anyone.

Outside of Chicago, other cities felt far more free to push the mystery. Why all the secrecy? Had it been an attempted suicide? Something worse? Shouldn't a bullet fired from such close range have left more powder marks? Would it be unusual for a bullet fired under those circumstances to remain in the body, not pass through it?

The *American's* risky coverage.

When Field, Jr., regained consciousness after several hours, access to him was not granted to the press, but reports spread that his first words had been, "How was I shot? How did it happen?"[126]

The *Greensboro Daily News* reported that Marshall Field, Sr., was livid at the suggestion that it was suicide when he was asked about it the minute he arrived in Chicago. "That's a lie. It is impossible," he said. Relatives issued a statement that Field, Jr., had told the butler it was an accident, and Marshall Field, Sr., spent only ten or fifteen minutes examining the scene of the shooting personally.

The suicide theory was not generally popular in the city. It was, in fact, probably impossible for Field to have killed himself under the known circumstances. He had been shot in the side, which is not generally where a man wishing to kill himself would aim. And one man, A. A. Carpenter, said he had just dined with Field a few hours before the fatal shot was fired, and that Field had seemed fine.[127]

And Field, Jr., for his part, was reported to be cheerful in the hospital, despite the grueling pain and grave prognosis the doctors were giving him. Doctors were warning him not to talk, but he reportedly continued to say that the shooting was an accident. If the reports were accurate, the patient didn't seem like a man who'd been suicidal.

A more popular theory around town was that earlier in the afternoon, Field, Jr., had been shot at the Everleigh Club, the fanciest brothel in town. Run by sisters Minna and Ada Everleigh, the Everleigh was the sort of brothel that had its own orchestra, a library, and several full-time decorators on staff. According to the rumor, Field had spent his afternoon at the club and gotten into a fight with either one of the girls or the bouncer, depending on who was telling the story. After being shot, the club had graciously taken him home, so that he wouldn't die in the club and besmirch the good name of the Fields (or the good name of the Everleigh Club, which didn't want to be known as *that* kind of brothel).

The theory that Field had accidentally shot himself while preparing for a hunting trip was further discredited when reporters interviewed August Hirth, the man who'd sold Field, Jr., the pistol, a Colt automatic, a few weeks before. "I do not see how it could have been fired accidentally," he said.[128] It couldn't by fired by dropping it, and a safety catch that was built in had to be slipped back before the trigger was pulled. Furthermore, Field, Jr., had distinctly told him that he wasn't going hunting this year.

Lowe, the butler, had a fairly novel explanation of his own: "If, as I think, he held the weapon upside down in his left hand with the barrel against his side, which would be natural for a person unfamiliar with the gun who wished to take out the magazine, it would be possible for him to shoot himself. While he was trying to pull the magazine out of the handle with his right hand the thumb of the left hand might be against the trigger and the first finger against the safety device in the handle. In working to get the magazine out, he fired the shot."[129]

This convoluted theory would have required Field, Jr., to be incredibly careless and incredibly unlucky at the same time.

Field, Jr., succumbed to his wound on November 27; the coroner's jury ruled that the death had been an accident. For Marshall Field, Sr., to influence a jury would have have been unheard of, and the ruling did nothing to quiet the rumores. Field, Sr., himself died just a couple of months later.

The red mansion on Prairie Avenue was sold, and went in and out of being occupied for years. After several years of being boarded up and abandoned, it was finally converted into a residential building again just over a century after Field, Jr.'s death; what was once a mansion for one Gilded Age family is now six spacious townhouses.

The story of Marshall Field, Jr., and the Everleigh Club far outlasted Prairie Avenue's time as a celebrated thoroughfare; for several decades, it was one of the most famous unsolved mysteries in Chicago, the sort of story everyone had a theory about. And new data came in from time to time over the next several years, keeping the story alive.

In 1913, eight years after the shooting, a woman going by the name of Vera Prosser Scott was jailed in Los Angeles for extorting money from millionaires. While in jail, she told the police that she was the one who shot Marhsall Field, Jr.

According to her confession, she'd met Field at the Auditorium Annex (now the Congress Hotel), and two days after the meeting, he'd asked her to go to a party with him. "I demurred for a time, as I was married to Prosser," she said. "He, however, kept insisting and I finally consented to accompany him. We went to the Everleigh Club, where there was a large party of people. I went under the name of Vera Leroy. For a time we sat around drinking and talking and then Field asked me to go to a room. When we reached the room Field began to annoy me and I began fighting him. Suddenly in the tussle I fell against his clothes, and, finding a revolver in a pocket, I grabbed it and shot him.

"Just as I shot, Emma [sic] Everleigh, one of the sisters, entered the room and was a witness of the affair. I hurriedly left the place, and, after what seemed like ages, got to my room . . . Early the next morning, Marshall Field, the father, came to me and offered $25,000 if I would leave the country and told me that I would never be arrested if I forgot what happened the night before."[130]

She recanted the confession the next day, and her claim that Field, Sr., came to her right after the shooting, when he would have still been on the train from the East, makes it all a bit suspect). One paper said that at least a dozen other women had confessed to being the one who shot Field over the years.

If that was true, though, the other dozen or so confessions didn't make the national news the way Vera's did; when her story hit the papers, reporters began interviewing anyone they could find who could possibly confirm or deny her story. Jack Johnson, a former porter at the club, told a Chicago reporter that he knew of only one person who'd been shot at the Club, and it wasn't Field—but he did say that Field had been a regular customer.[131] But other old-timers in the Red Light district said that Vera really had been one of the "butterflies" at the Everleigh Club. Shortly after her release months later, she married another man, then had him arrested as a "white slaver." The man shot her to death, then committed suicide the night before his trial was to begin.[132]

In 1925, a septuagenarian millionaire named W. E. D. Stokes was in the process of divorcing his wife, Helen, and told a jury that some time before, he'd made a concerted effort to prove that Helen had once been an "inmate" at the Everleigh Club. He'd gone to New York, where the Everleigh sisters now lived, and asked them personally. On the stand, he did an impersonation of Minna Everleigh as he repeated her response: "Our life in Chicago is a closed book. We'll give you no information. Our girls have married into some of the richest families in the United States. They were the pick of the country. If I open the door to you I will be opening the door to hundreds of others."[133]

Back in Chicago, he said, he'd gone to the old Everleigh Club building. It had been shut down in 1911 by order of Mayor Harrison, along with the rest of the old Red Light District, and was now abandoned but for one Etta Wright, a caretaker.

"[Wright] took me to a room at the right of the entrance," Stokes said. "It had a beautifully decorated ceiling. I showed her my pictures and she said, "There's a picture of Helen Underwood. She came [to the club] off and on. See that ermine cape she is wearing in that picture? Well, ermine capes were very rare in those days. And that ermine cape caused more trouble and jealousy than you'd ever guess." Then, Etta Wright pointed over to a vase on the mantel and said, "If that vase could speak it could tell who murdered Marshall Field, Jr. It was in this room that he was murdered."[134]

Stokes bought the vase from Wright for ten bucks and it was used as evidence at the divorce trial. In the run-up to the trial, he'd mentioned having several letters stating that his wife, in her Everleigh days, had been questioned by the police after Field's shooting. One allegedly read, "I know the Chicago situation from every angle and who killed Marshall Field."[135]

Mrs. Stokes, for the record, was cleared of all charges, no evidence was found indicating that she'd really been questioned, and no one felt like reopening the Field case because of anything Mr. Stokes claimed to have discovered. No witnesses brought in for the divorce trial, including the woman who'd managed the club and the club physician, would back her husband's claims, and the vase, well . . . the vase *couldn't* talk. Obviously.

In 1955, journalist Arthur Meeker wrote a book called *Chicago with Love.* Meeker had grown up a few doors down from the Field mansion, and said that he and his sister were among the last to see Field, Jr., before he was shot, when he stopped at their house to speak with the nurse. At the time, he was on the way to the Everleigh Club—or wherever he'd gone that day. "All we can be sure of," Meeker wrote, "is that the version the family gave out and forced papers to print . . . had no truth in it."[136]

In the 1980s, *Chicago* magazine printed an old family legend of the Korr family that Henry Korr, a grandfather of the family, had paid an allowance to the son of one of his clients who used liked to go to the levee district with Field, Jr., On the night of the shooting, the client's son had called Korr from the Everleigh Club and said, "I'm in trouble. There's been a shooting."[137]

It was only a family legend, but a remarkable example of how clues can keep popping up, decades after the fact, keeping a mystery alive.

Hypnotized to the Gallows?

On February 10, 1906, they exhumed Bessie Hollister's brain.

On a secret visit arranged under the direction of Coroner Hoffman of Chicago, a doctor from Rush Medical College and Coroner's Physician Hunter journeyed to a cemetery in Rockford, Illinois, disinterred Mrs. Hollister's body, opened the skull, and took the brain back to Chicago for testing to see if he could prove that she was strangled to death, not frightened to death, in a murder so brutal that no one in the city would have believed that the story would ever drop from public consciousness. It was the sort of case that people imagined would end up in every history book.[138]

Just under a month before, Bessie, a young society woman and church worker, had failed to show up at a funeral at which she was supposed to sing. She had left her home on Fullerton Avenue, just west of Halsted, to buy flowers, and had never returned. The next morning, her body was found in the back of a barn a couple of blocks away, her clothing shredded as if in a fierce struggle, and a coil of copper wire wrapped around her neck.

The *Inter Ocean* published a map of Mrs. Hollister's neighborhood near Lincoln Park, with photos of three other elegant-looking women who had been murdered in the area recently. Their killers had never been caught. All over the city, mass meetings were planned to protest the police's inability to capture criminals and protect women. In response, the police force would eventually be doubled.[139]

This time, though, the police already had their man.

Or, at least, they *said* they did.

When Mrs. Hollister disappeared, they'd spent the evening searching casually around her neighborhood, entertaining theories that perhaps she'd just decided to skip the funeral. In the morning, Edward Ivens alerted them that his son, Richard, had found a body in the back of their barn. The body in the barn was instantly identified as Bessie's, and Richard was arrested at once. After several hours of questioning, he broke down.

"I might as well admit it," he said. "I killed her."

The police had the young man sign a written confession, then brought him to the coroner's inquest. As they did, William Hollister, the dead woman's brother-in-law, ran at him with a revolver drawn. "I'll shoot you now!" he shouted.

Coroner Hoffman jumped in front of the gun, and Ivens ducked behind a desk as other officers pried the gun away from the would-be vigilante. "I couldn't help it," Hollister said. "The loathing for that brute got the better of me."

The *Tribune* said that no one blamed him.[140]

Ivens's full confession was published in the papers the next day. He said that he'd been drinking whiskey and come across Bessie while walking down the street. When she didn't want to go with him, he choked her and forced her down the road the barn, where he raped her on top of a manure pile, then tied a copper wire around her neck (though he didn't know why he'd done so), and attempted to "outrage" her again, but found his own body unwilling. When he was unable to get her to stand back up, he got frightened that he'd gone too far and left the scene, jumping over the fence to get away. In the morning, he read the sporting news and market prices in the newspapers, then went to the barn and fed the horse before checking to see if the woman had gone away. He found her lying on her face, dead.

The confession was read out loud at the inquest, and most of the city considered it an open-and-shut case. Ivens seemed disinterested and bored, perhaps even catatonic, for much of the proceedings.

But as the murder trial approached, Ivens claimed not to have remembered making the confession at all. He remembered being brought in to the station and developing a severe headache, and remembered a lot of fingers being pointed at him, but that was about it. J. Sanderson Christison, a doctor who interviewed him in prison, believed that Ivens was not only innocent, but that the police had hypnotized him into confessing.

Ivens did have multiple alibis placing him somewhere else at the time of the murder. And one Belden Avenue woman testified that she'd been sitting on her porch, looking right at the alley at the time the confession said he'd dragged Mrs. Hollister past, and hadn't seen a thing. Two others who were nearby should have been able to hear the screams if they happened when the confession said they had—and to see Ivens jump the six-foot fence—but heard nothing.

But Ivens's own statements at his trial in an attempt to establish that he'd been influenced by the police to make a false confession were unconvincing; the most damaging thing he could say was that he remembered Inspector Lavin pointing a finger at him and saying, "Ivens, you didn't sleep last night. I can see it by the looks of your eyes."[141]

None of this convinced the jury, and Ivens was sentenced to be hanged.

"I suppose I must have made those statements," he told the *Evening Journal*, "since they all say I did. But I have no knowledge of having made them and I am innocent of that crime. From the time I was arrested I do not believe that I was myself for a moment until after I was over here in the jail. Everything about that time was a blur, a blank to me . . . I know that the very first thing the inspector said to me when I was brought in was, "You did this!"[142]

The confession held up to the jury, as they almost always did in those days, regardless of the circumstances under which the confession had been extracted. Though some continued to doubt that the crime could have possibly happened the way Ivens had confessed, he was eventually hanged in the county prison.

Christison, the doctor who'd met him in prison, believed the execution was the greatest obstruction of justice of the new century, and published an entire book on the case: *The Tragedy of Chicago: How a Young Man was Hypnotized to the Gallows*. Citing all the statements he could get from eminent psychologists and doctors at Ivy League schools, he suggested that the very look on Ivens's face in the photographs of him in newspapers was evidence that the man had been hypnotized.

Today, large portions of Christison's book are difficult to take seriously; his emphasis on hypnosis keeps his allegations firmly rooted in the world of hocus-pocus, and his assertions that Ivens had good parents and came from a good background, so he *couldn't* be a criminal, are the sort of "evidence" that might have seemed a lot more convincing in the olden days. Even the fact that the confession contained swear words seemed like evidence that it was all a fake to Christison, because he didn't believe Ivens swore.

There were, however, some entirely logical reasons to doubt the confession. Could a young man have "wrestled" a well-dressed woman down a busy, well-lit street and into a barn without anyone nearby noticing or hearing anything? Why was there no sign of struggle in the barn itself, or any evidence on the body that the killer had struggled in wrapping the wire around her neck? Why were there so many differences between his spoken statements and the written confessions? Why did he say that he had jumped over the fence, when the fence was six feet high and the gate was opened?

The full confession Ivens didn't write, but signed, and the transcript of the one he gave under questioning, were both included in the book, though Christison omitted a few sections he felt were too explicit (for instance, after a point at which Ivens is asked if he'd had an erection at a certain point in the crime, Christison simply says, "He here, through a series of questions, describes an unmentionable and impossible act, for which he gives absurd reason and then unwittingly contradicts himself.")[143] Contradict himself he does; throughout the confession are a number of changing stories, impossible feats, and unlikely claims. The prosecuting attorney (who pushed for life imprisonment, not the death penalty) believed that Ivens had committed the crime, but that he was "feeble minded" and insane, and that the contradictions in his confession came from his mental disorders. But it was the confession, and the confession alone, that convicted him.

This sort of fishy confession extracted by questionable methods was known to have happened in Chicago before, and would happen again. In 1894, a man named Buff Higgins was hanged based on a confession that police, by most accounts, tricked him into signing. After "sweating" and starving him for several days, they'd gotten him extremely drunk and given him a paper to sign that they told him established his alibi. It was really a confession that sent him to the gallows.

The papers that year began calling for the practice of "sweating" to end. "If a prisoner chooses to plead guilty," wrote the *Inter Ocean*, "that is his priviledge, but to be wheedled or intimidated into a confession to be used in court, contrary to the wish of the accused, is a palpable and gross violation of the constitution of the United States."[144] But juries, the public, and the press in general would be slow to coming around to the idea that a confession wasn't necessarily a gold standard of evidence.

The case would not be such a mystery today, when DNA tests would probably have cleared things up at once, but such things were still a long way off in 1906. Some still believe that the real killer of Bessie Hollister went free while the cops invented a suspect to keep the public off their backs.

George Shippy, chief of police. At the end of his career, he shot and killed a man who came to his house for reasons unclear. Officially, the man was an anarchist and would-be assassin, but there are strong arguments that Shippy simply shot him because he *looked* like a radical.

Richard Ivens. Hypnotized into confessing?

The Strange History of *Eternal Silence*

It may be the most striking image in Graceland Cemetery, and in a burial ground that contains some of architect Louis Sullivan's best work (in addition to his mortal remains), that's saying something. Lorado Taft's *Eternal Silence*, the cryptic hooded figure standing before a black marble obelisk, the bronze covered in a green patina except for the dark face, is unforgettable and aresting. Even the U.S. Department of the Interior described it as "eerie" when the cemetery was given landmark status.

Eternal Silence, Lorado Taft's incredible statue that serves as a monument to the Graves family.

It would be a mark of shame on all Chicagoans if there were no creepy urban legends about it, but, frankly, the ones we have are pretty lousy: some say that it's impossible to take a clear photo of it, and some say that if you look into its face, you'll see your own death. Both can be easily disproven in seconds.

However, there are a few more enduring legends about the statue, as well. One is that it used to face east, not west, but had to be turned around so "L" riders couldn't see it after many of them complained that it freaked them out (which would be hard to verify, but seems plausible enough that one can imagine it was true). Another is that architect Claes Oldenburg tried to have a one-thousand-foot-tall skyscraper that looked just like it built on Michigan Avenue (he drew a design, but never seriously pursued it; it seems more like one of those things architects sometimes design just to keep themselves off the streets and out of trouble).[145]

Digging into the history of the statue, though, reveals a lot more interesting stories—and unanswered questions—than one might imagine. Just reading the plaque on the back could inspire a few. According to the plaque, it was built as a gravestone for Dexter Graves, a man who had been dead for more than twenty years before Graceland Cemetery even existed, and for almost three quarters of a century by the time *Eternal Silence* was in place.

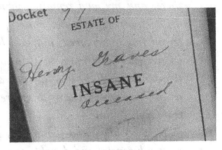

Henry Graves probate cover.

Dexter Graves was an early Chicago settler; he and his son, Henry, arrived in town in 1831 on the schooner *Telegraph*, which was piloted by Captain Naper, the namesake of Naperville. Once in town, Dexter founded the Mansion House, a hotel that hosted, by some measures, the first professional theatrical performance in town.[146] When he died in 1844, he was likely buried in the old City Cemetery, where Lincoln Park now stands, though it's possible that he was in a family plot on his own property before then (it wasn't exactly *legal* to bury a body on private property then, but it still happened). At some point, he was moved to Graceland.

Henry Graves, his son, kept living on the South Side, and wound up living in the middle of Camp Douglas, a Civil War prison camp; he refused to give up his land when the government was turning the area into the prison, so it was built around his land. Maps of the grounds have a section marked "graves" that everyone who checks the map assumes was a burial ground (I sure did), but it was, in reality, just Henry Graves's house.[147]

By the turn of the twentieth century, Henry was being pointed out in newspapers as the man who had lived in Chicago longer than anyone else. It was he who put aside the money for a monument to his father on the family plot in Graceland.

His will included the following:

> *I will and direct that my executors herein mentioned shall*
> *construct build and erect in Graceland Cemetary [sic], where*
> *the remains of my father, Dexter Graves, my mother, OLIVE*
> *GRAVES, my brother LOREN, my sisters Lucy and Emaline,*
> *and my wife Clementine are interred, a building and mon-*
> *ument combined over the remains of those already interred*
> *there, and my own remains, which I desire to have buried*
> *beside those of my wife; none of said remains to be disen-*
> *terred [sic] or removed, but said building and monument to*
> *be erected over the same . . . to cost the sum of two hundred*
> *thousand ($200,000) dollars less a proper sinking fund to be*
> *set aside by my executors to secure its proper care and repair*
> *from time to time.*
>
> *Said building and monument to be built of the best and*
> *most substantial and durable granite and so placed on my lot*
> *as to cover the remains of those hereinbefore mentioned, and*
> *to contain a room with suitable inscriptions stating the name*
> *of the parties buried underneath, their age and date of death,*
> *and the memoranda found in this will, signed by me; and said*
> *monument shall be open for the inspection of the public on the*
> *first Sunday in each of the months of May, June, July, August*
> *and September in each year and on all Public holidays.*
>
> *This monument I desire to be made as substantial and*
> *imposing in appearance as the sum set aside for its erection will*
> *permit.*[148]

Graves also put aside $50,000 for a statue of George Washington to be placed in Washington Park (though when they put up one of their own, he amended the will to add that money to the fund for his own monument), and $40,000 to build a drinking fountain for horses in Washington Park, as well; the fountain was to include a life-size bronze statue of Ike Cook, the first horse to trot a mile in two and a half minutes in the state of Illinois.

When Henry died in 1907, it was the Ike Cook monument that made the news. The plans for the statue survived some legal challenges

I, HENRY GRAVES, of the City of Chicago, State of Illinois, do make, publish and declare the following as a second codicil to my last will and testament which bears date *September* *Second 1898* —

Inasmuch as a monument to George Washington has been erected in Washington Park since the making of my said will, and it is probable that the South Park Commissioners will not consent to the erection of a second monument in said Park, I hereby revoke the bequest of Fifty thousand ($50,000) Dollars made in Clause Three (3) of said will for the purpose of erecting a monument to George Washington in said Park, and direct that said sum of Fifty Thousand ($50,000) Dollars be added to the bequest of Two hundred thousand ($200,000) Dollars in Clause Two (2) of said will therein set apart for the purpose of erecting a building and monument in Graceland Cemetery, as specified in my said will and modified in the former codicil to said will.

Excerpt of Graves's will addendum, adding more money to the fund for his own monument.

and got as far as having a model built, but it seems never to have been constructed.

Graves's probate file is a really interesting one. It's full of enough documents revoking bequeathments, or cutting them in half, that you get the impression that there was some pretty good drama in Henry's life. But it also brings up a few mysteries about the monument:

1. What happened to the idea for the walk-in building that would be open to the public one day a month? There can be no doubt that he got as "substantial and imposing" a monument as he ever could have wanted, but it's not *quite* what he asked for.
2. Where did all the money go? *Eternal Silence* is a landmark statue, and Taft was already a famous sculptor, but it's unlikely that they could have spent $250,000 (in 1907 money) building it. That would be millions today.

The answer may lie in a similar Taft statue on the other side of town.

Designed, planned, and built over the course of several years, starting a few years after *Eternal Silence*, Taft's *Fountain of Time* may be his ultimate masterpiece. A cloaked figure of Father Time (looking almost exactly like the enigmatic figure in *Eternal Silence*) stands before a fountain, facing a parade of over one hundred figures passing by on the other side of the water, representing the progress of humankind. It's an incredible creation, even though it might be the most depressing statue in any public pleasure ground in the country.

In one interesting twist, *Fountain of Time* happens to stand exactly on the spot where the statue of Ike Cook was supposed to go.

Could the two Taft statues be connected in more ways than just thematically? The probate file offers no hints, but given the location and the likelihood of leftover money, one has to wonder. I like to theorize that perhaps the Graves heirs diverted some of the funds from the monument to the funding for the fountain, given the similarity of theme and the location that Graves had already been tied to. Perhaps they threw in some money in exchange for having their own faces added into the parade of figures. Taft's own face is there; it's not impossible that he quietly worked in a few donors as well. But any official connections between the two statues remains strictly theoretical.

15 to be paid for out of my estate, by my said executors hereinafter mention-

16 ed, and to cost the sum of two hundred thousand ($200,000) dollars

17 less a proper sinking fund to be set aside by my executors to secure

18 its proper care and repair from time to time. Said building and monu-

19 ment to be built of the best and most substantial and durable granite

20 and so placed on my lot as to cover the remains of those hereinbefore

21 mentioned, and to contain a room with suitable inscriptions stating the

22 name of the parties buried underneath, their age and date of

23 death, and the memoranda found with this will, signed by me; and said

24 monument shall be open for the inspection of the public on the first

25 Sunday in each of the months of May, June, July, August and September in

26 each year and on all Public holidays. This monument I desire to be

1 made as substantial and imposing in appearance as the sum set aside

2 for its erection will permit, and the following inscription carved upon

3 the outside thereof, viz:, "Erected by Henry Graves, born August 9th, 1821

4 died . The son of Dexter Graves, one of the

5 pioneers of Chicago. Dexter Graves brought the first colony to Chicago

6 consisting of thirteen families, arrived here July 15th, 1831, from Ash-

7 tabula, Ohio, on the schooner Telegraph, and father and son remained

citizens of Chicago till their death."

Excerpts of Graves's will regarding the monument.

Is That Really Belle Gunness in a Forest Park Grave?

Belle Gunness is not generally thought of as a Chicago murderess. She got her *start* here, but the farm where the bodies of numerous victims were found was in La Porte, Indiana. We have plenty of our own multiple murderers, so we tend to let Indiana have this one.

But the most enduring mystery about her was brought home to Chicagoland: is that really her skeleton buried in the grave in Forest Home Cemetery?

It seems like every time an outlaw dies, there are rumors that their death was a hoax. Billy the Kid was said to have escaped. So were Butch Cassidy, John Wilkes Booth, John Dillinger, and Jesse James. Despite roughly eighty witnesses seeing H. H. Holmes make a speech before watching him hanged, including several people who knew him and hated his guts, efforts are underway to exhume him, too. It's certainly worth noting that when these stories get investigated, they almost always turn out to be false; a 1990s exhumation made it quite clear that the body in Jesse James's coffin was really that of Jesse James.

But the facts of Belle Gunness's death seem suspicious indeed. Officially, she was killed in a fire at her farmhouse; her body was found beneath a piano that fell through the burning floor to the floor below, but her head was never found. Where could it have gone? That she lost her head and then managed to hide it seems less likely than the notion that she simply planted a substitute body that couldn't be positively identified before making her escape.

Belle, by most accounts, was born in Norway in 1859, where legend has it that she killed a man who kicked her in the stomach while she was pregnant, causing her to miscarry. According to some 1908 sources, she was the daughter of Petters Paulsen, a "traveling necromancer and magician," and performed as a rope dancer herself as a child (though this is the sort of backstory that comes up in a lot of stories of historical murderers, and seldom turns out to be true). She followed her sister to the United States in 1881, married Mads Sorenson in Chicago, and the two of them opened a candy shop near Grand Avenue and Elizabeth Street in 1886. It may have been a genuine accident when the shop burned down, but when the insurance check came, Belle seems to have decided that she'd hit upon a fine way to make money.

Belle as a young woman; either a very rare photo published in the *American* or a somewhat manipulated version of the other known photo of Belle in her younger days.

Belle, later.

Rumors in 1908 said that her first American murder had been a few years after the candy store fire, when Belle and Mads lived at Grand and Elizabeth with a little girl named "Lucy." Neighbors knew nothing of the girl, including her last name, except that she lived with the Sorensons and was something of a foster daughter. She vanished without a trace in 1893. Some neighbors heard that she'd been taken back by her parents, or sent to an asylum, but no one ever found out a thing about her, really.

Mads Sorenson died very suddenly in 1900, supposedly on the one day when his two insurance policies overlapped.[149]

"Sorenson came home one evening apparently in good health," a neighbor said eight years later. "He ate his supper and threw himself on the couch to have a nap. He never woke up. His wife found him dead at ten o'clock . . . Mrs. Sorenson gave strict orders that the body be embalmed that night, and in a coffin by three o'clock next morning. The process of embalming, of course, made it impossible for an autopsy to determine whether he had died from poison . . . All the neighbors thought at the time Sorenson's death was queer. Their suspicions were not allayed when the Sorenson house caught fire twice soon afterward, and the widow collected insurance on both fires."[150]

Police at the time largely verified the story—no physician had been called until after Sorenson was dead—but declined to investigate further. By the time they decided Sorenson had been murdered, Belle was under suspicion for several more murders at the farm she'd bought in La Porte, Indiana. As would be the city's usual position on Belle, they let Indiana have this one. Belle used insurance money to buy the farm, where she married Peter Gunness in 1902. Both Peter and his infant daughter had died by the end of that year, and over the next half decade, Belle lived with a series of suitors and children, none of whom seemed to survive long. She began to take out ads in the matrimonial sections of newspapers advertising herself as a "comely widow" looking to join fortunes with a "gentleman equally well provided." Just how many of these men she ended up killing is difficult to know; as with H. H. Holmes, the number is often reportedly to be unrealistically high, and it's to be assumed that exaggerations and rumors got folded into the story as fact over the years. But no embellishments are really necessary; her last victim received a love letter saying, "Come prepared to stay forever." A murder mystery writer would hardly dare write something that perfect into a book.

Bodies were buried in the cellar and all over the farm, all while Belle's own children were living there. A teacher at their school recalled that, one day, the two girls had shown up black and blue and said that their mother had beaten them for going near the cellar.[151]

Some suggest that many of the victims could have actually been Chicagoans, perhaps killed at the West Side house Belle still owned as of 1908. A hired man on the farm said, "Some of the bodies, I think now, must have been shipped here. Mrs. Gunness received many trunks. They were all brand-new. They were kept overnight, and then I was ordered to chop them up for kindling."[152] Several were found to have been shipped to Indiana by a company on State Street.

I always love to play "What if?" with Belle. She came to Chicago right about the same time as H. H. Holmes, and was placing her matrimonial ads right around the time that Johann Hoch was answering them. What if Hoch had answered one of her ads? Imagine the farce that could have resulted as the two tried to poison each other! It sounds like a 1940s comedy waiting to happen.[153] Chief Deputy Sheriff Charles Peters of Chicago noted it at the time. "She was a woman Hoch, and he was a man Gunness," he said. "Suppose, now, that Hoch had seen one of her advertisements, answered it, and a meeting had been arranged. She would have had in her mind Hoch's money, and Hoch would have had in mind her money. Then would have come the contest, each plotting, scheming, with all of his or her cleverness, to get the better of the other. It would have beat, I believe, any drama of villainy ever produced on the stage. Which would have outwitted the other? Would each have been able to keep his or her designs secret from the other? Would each have smiled in his or her sleeve over the dupe he or she was making of the other? In other words, which of them would now be under the ground, a victim of the other's treachery, and which enjoying the money of the other, providing, of course, that the victor was able to keep out of the clutches of the law?"[154]

In spring 1908, the farmhouse was destroyed in a fire. In the wreckage were the bodies of four people, believed to be Belle and three of her children. The house had burned for twelve full hours, leaving not a shard of wood left, and two hundred pails of water were necessary to cool the bricks enough that authorities could even get near the bodies.[155]

But the adult corpse was headless, and none could really be positively identified. As the farm was searched, the bodies of several more people, badly mutilated, were found on the property as well. Three children were found buried, along with six adult bodies that were buried in a hogs' pen.

Belle's Chicago sister, Nellie Larson, didn't seem terribly upset by the loss. "All she loved was money," said Nellie, "and we didn't have much to do with each other, because she thought she was better than I was, because she had more money, a better house, and clothes." She noted that her sister was "always wild." Belle had tried to adopt Nellie's oldest daughter, Olga, but Olga stayed with Belle for six weeks and insisted on returning home.

One of Nellie's other daughters was sent to La Porte after the fire, but said, "I never saw the body supposed to be that of my aunt when I was in La Porte last Friday, but I couldn't bear to look at it. My brother had never seen her very much, so he couldn't identify her. So far as her immediate relatives are concerned, Mrs. Gunness has been identified by none of them."[156]

Early in the investigation, even the sheriff didn't believe that the headless body was really that of Belle Gunness; like many people at the time, he thought she'd killed someone else and burned that body, hoping it would be thought of as her. He was especially contemptuous of suggestions that her having deposited $750 in the bank right before the fire was evidence that she was dead. He thought it was a ruse. "Nothing could be less convincing to me," he said. "It is my firm belief that Mrs. Gunness was worth $50,000 and that she had much of it in ready cash. I believe she took enough money with her to last the rest of her life."[157]

Another relative, Miss Minnie Olander, was the sister of Jennie Olson, whose body was found at the farm. She didn't believe Belle was dead, either. At the morgue, looking down at the headless body, she dramatically said, "That woman Bluebeard is still alive. That is not Belle. That is the body of some other woman. I am positive of that. She has fled."[158]

On May 8, the *Chicago Evening American*, ever-eager to promote a sensational rumor, published a list of seventeen reasons to believe that Belle was still alive, some of which held up to fact-checking better than others:

1. No one can cut off their own head, and fire wouldn't completely obliterate it.
2. The gold in Belle's teeth had not been found (diagrams of her teeth were published).

3. The heads of the children were not burned nearly so badly as Belle's would have been.
4. The headless body was shorter than Belle's.
5. A young woman who worked for Belle was missing.
6. Belle wrote out her will right before the fire.
7. The $700 or so dollars she put in the bank was probably nowhere near all of her money.
8. Alfred D. Levi, a Chicago druggist who ran a shop at Wabash and Harrison, swore he saw Belle days after the fire.
9. Right before the fire, a woman was seen in an automobile in LaPorte heading for Chicago (a rare enough event to count as a clue in 1908).
10. Belle's sister allegedly said the corpse was not Belle's.
11. There were blood stains on the fragments of the children's clothes. There were none on the decapitated body, and that body may have been dead for days.
12. Neighbors also said that the headless body did not look like Belle's.
13. A hired man had knocked on the door before the fire and found no one home.
14. A ring found and said to be Belle's was probably too small to have fit on her finger.
15. Belle had moved a large can of kerosene from an outhouse into the main house the day before the fire.
16. Mrs. Gunness was said to know that the brother of one of the victims was on his way to get revenge.
17. Belle did not seem like the sort who would committ suicide.[159]

The *Evening American* copied the photograph of her head and pasted it on different outfits to show what she might look like if she were disguised as a man. A Chicago woman who looked vaguely like Belle was dragged out of a train by two traveling salesmen and the conductor before being cleared. The topic of whether Belle was still alive became so controversial that one man reportedly slit his own throat to prove a point in an argument with his brother over it.

Eventually, bits of human teeth were found in the rubbish and identified as those of Belle Gunness. This laid most of the questions about the identity of the headless body to rest. And yet, doubts remained. The same day the teeth were found, a letter arrived from a New York man who was sure he'd put Belle up at his hotel, where she'd waited on a ship for Europe a few days after the fire.

The police and authorities decided that the fire had been started by Ray Lamphere, a man Gunness had often employed as an aide. He was charged with several counts of murder.

The *American's* composite of how Belle might look in disguise.

Lamphere admitted that he'd *seen* the fire hours before it was reported, but declined to alert firefighters because he assumed, correctly, that they'd suspect him of arson. As far as the law was concerned, Lamphere had poisoned Gunness and the children, then burned the house down to destroy their bodies and the evidence. The sheriff's working theory was that Gunness had refused to marry him and had threatened to frame him for all of the murders on the farm.

At Ray Lamphere's trial, his lawyers suggested that the headless body was that of a woman Belle had lured to the farm to work as a housekeeper, then murdered. According to Lamphere's defense team, she had poisoned the still-living children, dressed the adult body in her own clothes, removed her own false teeth to plant as evidence, then set the house on fire and fled. Lamphere said he had helped her do it.

Belle's dentist denied that this was possible.

"Could these teeth be removed?" the prosecutor asked.

"By only melting the gold crowns."

"Could they have been pulled?"

The dentist was emphatic in saying, "No, sir."[160]

The prosecution seemed quite intent on showing that Lamphere had committed *all* of the murders Belle was accused of; an attempt was made to make her look like a tender, loving mother. Lamphere, for his part, said that he thought Belle had killed over forty people. He was acquitted of murder, but convicted of arson, and died in prison months later.

He insisted to the end that Belle Gunness was still alive.

And rumors continued for years that the body buried in Forest Home Cemetery, just outside the Chicago city limits, was not really that of Belle Gunness. Sightings of women thought to be her persisted for decades; another supposed murderess, Esther Carlson, was even strongly rumored to be Belle in disguise years later, but died before anything could be proven.

In 2007, a century after the fire, a team of University of Indianapolis grad students led by Andrea Simmons succeeded in having the skeleton exhumed. To their surprise, the adult bones in the crumbling coffin were mixed with the bones of two children, whom no one had noted were buried with Belle at the time. The three children whose bodies were found after the fire were buried beside her. Could parts of their bodies have been mixed in with Belle's, for some reason?

The goal of the exhumation had been to attempt to match the DNA to samples taken from the saliva on an envelope Belle had licked more than a century before. While it was noted that, contrary to early reports, the body *was* about the right height to be Belle, the finding of the children's bones was a surprise.

The results of the DNA tests were inconclusive, and the true story of what became of Belle Gunness remains an open question.

Rings found in the smoldering rubble.

Whatever Happened to Conway, the One-Legged Killer Clown?

When I first took a job as a ghost tour guide, I was expected to assist on ghost hunts from time to time. My favorite place to go was the Congress Hotel. Though most of the ghost stories going around about the place are outright fiction (there is no room so haunted they blocked it off, and it certainly didn't inspire Stephen King's *1408*), there are plenty of good murder stories, historical tales, and outstanding legends about the place that need no embellishment. You can poke around the nooks and crannies of the old hotel for days and keep finding all sorts of things besides ghosts.

But there *are* lots of ghost stories that have firsthand eyewitness accounts to back them up, which is really rather rare in ghost lore. From day one, my favorite of the ghost stories was the legend of Peg-Leg Johnny, which two different security guards told me about. On my first investigation, one told me that they'd recently been getting calls from the seventh floor of the south wing that a homeless man with a peg leg was lying around on the floor. When security came to find the man, he'd vanished. Another guard told me he'd seen "the peg-leg guy" in the gold ballroom.

A guy on my crew (my boss at the time) told me that someone had found a news article about a hobo with a peg leg dying in the hotel in the 1930s, but I've never found the article, and I've come to the conclusion that he was probably just lying. He didn't make up the ghost story, though—just the backstory.

And if you're inclined to believe in ghosts, there may be a *way* better historical backstory for Peg-Leg Johnny. There was a one-legged clown who killed a woman right near the Congress in 1912 and disappeared in the 1920s, never to be seen again. Could he have crept back to Chicago, camped out in the Congress, and died while escaping from the law? Probably not, but it would sure be wonderful, in a morbid sort of way.

Charles Cramer, alias Charles Conway, alias Conway the Clown, was a high-diver and parachuter at circuses and carnivals; he lost a leg in a circus accident and used a homemade artificial foot rather than a more modern prosthetic. A peg leg, really.

His wife, Louisa, was a lion tamer. One would think that a life of working with lions and jumping off of things would be exciting enough, but the two got even more thrills by working as con artists, and, most likely, as killers. In 1908, when a woman named Frances Thompson was strangled to death in a rooming house near Michigan and Roosevelt, right near the Congress, the father of the man arrested for the crime received an anonymous tip that the *real* killer had been a one-legged clown. The man who'd been arrested was acquitted, but the clown was never sought.[161]

In 1912, Mrs. Cramer met an heiress named Sophie Singer and her husband at the train station. Masquerading as another vacationer, she struck up a friendship with her and suggested that instead of a hotel, they should just rent a small apartment together and take up "light housekeeping." Her husband, she said, would help out.

The Cramers then proceeded to mooch off the Singers for some time. When Mrs. Singer decided it was time to go home to Baltimore, the Cramers became hostile; Charles eventually tied Sophie's hands, suffocated her with his handkerchief, busted her skull with a doorknob, stole her jewelry, then stashed the body under the bed.

Cramer and his wife were eventually caught in Ohio and brought back to Chicago to stand trial. In prison, Cramer continued to be a clown.

"How did you hurt your foot?" a reporter asked.

"A steamboat ran over it," he said.

"Where?"

"In the middle of the Atlantic Ocean."[162]

To a policeman, he said, "Did you know that in this state you can't hang a man with a wooden leg?"

"Why, no, I never heard about it," said the officer. "What is there against it?"

"Why, you've gotta use a rope!" said the clown.[163]

Though any number of people convicted of a crime as brutal as Cramer's were hanged for it, Cramer somehow managed to get life in prison. (His wife was given a far lighter sentence.) But that was not the end of the story.

In 1925, a tiny item appeared in the *Tribune* stating that Charles Cramer, the one-legged man, had escaped from the honor farm in Joliet and was now at large.

Seven years later, Cramer's mother filed a petition in an Ohio probate case, asking to have her son declared dead so that she could cash in his insurance. According to the *Canton Repository*, he had last been seen in Toledo in 1925, a month after making his escape.[164]

He had never been found, and never was.

Unless that's *his* peg-legged ghost hanging around at the Congress Hotel.

The Fool Killer Submarine

In November 1915, diver William "Frenchy" Deneau was digging a trench in the bed of the Chicago River to lay down some cables for Commonwealth Edison. As he did, he stubbed his toe on a bit of metal protruding from the riverbed and found that beneath three feet of muck was the wreck of a forty-foot-long homemade submarine.

It's important to remember what was going on in the world at the time. World War I, the first major war to involve submarines, airplanes, and machine guns, was tearing Europe apart. Subs were in the news almost daily. When Deneau surfaced, he put on a show of being angry. "Why didn't somebody tell me I was working in a war zone?" he asked. "A man ought to get extra pay when he has to run the risk of submarines every time he dives, oughtn't he? It's dangerous. And are there any mines in the river?"[165]

Immediately, the press went to work trying to figure out who built the thing and when. Later on, it would be said that it had been built in 1849 by Lodner Darvontis Phillips, a submarine inventor from Indiana. Some of his designs really do resemble what Phillips had found (and this was an era when submarine design was not standard; mid-nineteenth-century submarine designs sometimes looked like fish, or tennis balls).

Such theories were years away in November 1915, though, and the press scrambled for explanations. The *Tribune* said, without elaborating much on where they got the info, that the ship was a thing called "The Fool Killer," which was built as a floating vessel around the time of the Great Chicago Fire, then sold around the time of the 1893 World's Fair to Peter Nissen, a "fantastical mariner."

Now, buying a submarine in 1893 does sound like the sort of thing Peter Nissen *would* have done. Nissen was an accountant by day who moonlighted as a daredevil inventor and sailor. He'd built two ships, *The Fool Killer* and *The Fool Killer 2*, which he used to shoot the rapids at Niagara Falls, a feat that made him a very early movie star when Edison's people filmed the second one. In 1904, he made even more news when he built *The Fool Killer 3*, which was a whole new kind of craft: a giant canvas balloon he planned to roll over land and sea on his way to discovering the North Pole. It was front-page news when he set off on a test voyage to float across Lake Michigan, but the ship disappeared from sight and contact was lost overnight. The next day, the wreck of the ship, and Nissen's dead body, washed up on the shores of Indiana. He'd made it across the lake, but hadn't survived the trip.

But, while having a submarine called *The Fool Killer does* sound like a Nissen stunt, there's really nothing to tie him to the vessel Deneau had found.

Perhaps the most plausible explanation came from E. S. Monville, the federal inspector of rivers and harbors, who was tracked down by the *Chicago Examiner*. "I have heard," he said, "that a submarine made by a naval architect was sunk in the river about fifteen years ago."[166]

Some have suggested that maybe Deneau built the thing himself and planted it there. But that would have not only been a difficult thing to do without anyone noticing, but also terribly reckless: Deneau had been involved in the recovery efforts when the *Eastland* capsized in the Chicago river four months before, killing 844 people. Investigations were still going on in November 1915, and the Department of Justice was even compelled to make a statement that the submarine had not sunk the *Eastland*. To have planted a ship right at the crime scene would have been a huge risk.

But Deneau certainly saw dollar signs when he found the thing; he was going through a costly divorce at the time, and needed a money-maker. He applied for permission from the government to raise it up for exhibition purposes.

A month after the discovery, the wrecked and rusting craft was raised up and towed out to Fullerton Street on a barge Deneau owned. A month later, in January 1916, his crew got to work, cleaning years of river crud and and debris from the inside of it. Mixed into the mud were several bones: two ribs, a bit of a spine, part of an arm, and (in some accounts) the skull of a human. A few feet away from the human bones was the skull of a dog.[167] Deneau alerted the media, and it made the papers all over the country, though no one could guess who the man would have been, or what in the world would have possessed him to take his dog out on a homemade submarine.

Deneau could not have faked finding the craft itself, but the bones were another story. Planting those to build up hype would have been easy enough, and even most researchers who think the submarine was real are inclined to doubt the part about the bones.

As hype, though, they certainly worked. The crowds were immense in February, when the ship went on display at 208 South State Street. For a dime, spectators could see the submarine and the bones, and were invited to inspect the interior at their own risk. Deneau[168] himself was on hand to give a talk on the discovery and the history of submarine vessels. At the time, he was promoting it as the first submarine ever built in the United States. According to newspaper ads, he'd even attracted the sponsorship of the Skee Ball company. Come for the submarine, stay for the Skee Ball.

Ad for the *Fool Killer*.

From there, the submarine's trail becomes strange. In May, it was on display for a week in Oelwein, Iowa, as part of a traveling carnival. It made the news every day, but one can imagine that it didn't take much to make the news in Oelwein in 1916.

The next month, it was back in Chicago on display at Riverview, the old amusement park on Western Avenue (where the Riverview shopping center now stands, naturally, in the grand fashion of naming subdivisions and strip malls after whatever was removed to make room for them). This is its last known location.

Deneau continued to talk about the craft over the years. In 1917, when Deneau joined the army and was being shipped off to fight, he lamented to the press that he was being made to serve on dry land as a doughboy. "Me, with my aquatic experience!" he said. "Can you beat it?

Me! Why, I'm a hound in the water. Look at what I've done. Remember the submarine—the Fool Killer? I found it near the Madison Street Bridge!"[169]

And, far later still, his grandchilden accompanied him to the Museum of Science and Industry, where the U-505, a captured German sub from World War II, was being displayed. He chuckled and called it a "Fool Killer."[170]

There are numerous unanswered questions that haunt researchers. One of the stranger ones is the mystery of where, exactly, the thing was found. Depending on which 1915 article you're reading, Deneau either found it near the Madison Street Bridge, the Rush Street Bridge, or the Wells Street Bridge.

And no one ever adequately explained where it came from. Phillips family lore has always insisted that it was one of Lodner Phillips's crafts, but evidence isn't totally convincing, and it doesn't look much like the sort he was building at the time.

A more likely explanation, perhaps, is that it was built by George C. Baker, an inventor who was working on submarines in the early 1890s and almost certainly the "naval architect" Monville was talking of. Monville's timeline is a little off, and photographs of Baker's 1892 ship look markedly different from the one that was found in the river, but records indicate that Baker planned more than one sub; he had designs ready for several when he died in 1894,[171] and a pair of Baker's patents on file show designs that look *a lot* like the Fool Killer.[172]

But by all available evidence, Baker's football-shaped craft of 1892 was the only one he ever managed to get beyond the design phase, and when he died, his wife had it filled with sand and sunk in Lake Michigan (its own current location is yet another mystery waiting to be solved). So, depending on how you look at it, Baker's designs either explain the Fool Killer, or explain away Monville's explanation that it might have been a military test vehicle that was sunk some years before.

Even if we can ever clear up the mystery of where the Fool Killer came from, we'll be left with the lingering question of what ever happened to it. Magazine ads show that Deneau (or his investors) had it up for sale by the end of 1916, but after that ad, the submarine vanishes from the record completely. Perhaps it was sold for scrap as World War I raged on. But for all anyone knows, it might be rusting away in some downstate warehouse, waiting to be rediscovered.

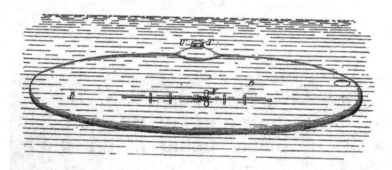

The patent diagram for one of Baker's submarines.

Who Shot Big Jim Colosimo?

From page of the *American* announcing Colosimo's murder. The photo shows him with Dale Winter.

Charlie Chaplin described the Chicago of the early twentieth century as "attractive in its ugliness, grim and begrimed, a city that still had the spirit of frontier days, a thriving, heroic metropolis of 'smoke and steel,' as Carl Sandburg says . . . it had a fierce pioneer gaiety that enlivened the senses, yet underlying it throbbed masculine loneliness."[173]

Later, the *Tribune* wrote of the bygone era of the Levee district where Chaplin and his vaudeville troupe had gone after hours in those days. In 1921, the Levee of the South Loop was already a relic of an earlier era. "The ghosts of bygone sinners flit restlessly about 22nd Street," wrote a *Tribune* columnist, "that sinister thoroughfare which once was the heart of the levee. There, in days of yesteryear, the midnight hours were clamorous with their revelry. Pianos tinkled in every bar and brothel . . . and to those frolicsome tunes which are now dead and buried, sorry little daughters of the shadows moved about in the arms of the underworld's giddy patrons. It was the profane dance of the ancient Romans, the love dance of the orient that those bygone sinners stepped in the days when the town was alive. Sex was its sole expression; lasciviousness its alpha and omega."[174]

At the time of that article, the Levee had really only been thought of as "dead" for just a bit over a year.

People still tell stories of the First Ward, the old Levee District, from the turn of the twentieth century. In the pre-Prohibition era, it was home to both the most elegant resorts in town and the seediest. As aldermen "Hinky Dink" Kenna and "Bathhouse John" Coughlin reigned over the neighborhood (wards had two aldermen in those days), brothels, gambling dens, and taverns sat right alongside elegant theaters. On South Dearborn stood the most famous brothel, the lavish Everleigh Club, which existed right near places with names like the Pervert Hotel, the Bucket of Blood, and Bed Bug Row. There was a tobacco shop where, according to legend, you got half an hour with one of the proprietesses with every two-dollar purchase. At the House of All Nations at Archer and Cullerton, there was both a two-dollar entrance and a five-dollar entrance, both of which led to the same girls.

And at the heart of it all, at 2126 South Wabash, stood Colosimo's, where gangsters, politicians, and artists rubbed elbows and enjoyed the performances of some of the top opera singers in the country. Proprietor Big Jim Colosimo was the neighborhood's precinct captain and was the controller of much of the vice operations in the area. John Torrio and his young lieutenant, Al Capone, served under him. Big Jim wore flashy clothes and was especially fond of diamonds; he was said to wear diamond-studded garters.

But 1920 marked a sea of change in the world of vice, as Prohibition went into effect. Banning liquor wasn't going to stop the demand for it, and now the price would skyrocket. Setting up a still would be like brewing your own money. A galloon of booze could be distilled fairly cheaply, then sold for many, many times the cost of production. Gangsters could sell as much as they could produce, and the seedy resorts that had made vice lords a good living now stood to make them rich beyond their wildest dreams.

Legend has it, though, that Big Jim Colosimo, who was then newly married and looking not to get involved in any more vice than he already was, informed the Chicago underworld that there'd be no boot-legging in town.

But the "ambitious vicelords" theory was only one explanation that went around after Big Jim was shot to death on the floor of his cafe in May 1920.

There had been signs around Colosimo's that something was amiss that May, though nothing that would have turned heads. A man who looked to be in his late twenties had been seen lurking around the cafe for a couple of days, described as "fat-faced, dark-complexioned, wearing a black derby hat, black overcoat, patent leather shoes, and white standup collar." No one knew him.[175] That wouldn't seem suspicious until later.

On the fatal night, May 11, there were only a few customers in the restaurant. One was a stranger who sat alone sipping apricot brandy. Nearby sat a party of four, who left behind a sheet of paper with the phone number for the National Rubber Products company, the name Samel Lavine, and the phrase, "So long, vampire," jotted on it.

Big Jim came in like he would have on any normal day and walked to his office in the back, where he traded small talk with his secretary. He made a phone call or two, chatted with some employees, then pre-pared to leave on an errand. As he stepped toward the front door, a man stepped out of the cloakroom holding a handgun. Jim turned, and two shots rang out.

One of the bullets went through the phone booth and lodged in the plaster of the wall; the other went right into Colosimo's brain. He dropped to his knees and fell forward, his face landing on the floor inches away from the front door. The gun was not a loud one. Employees in the back thought they heard a noise, but thought it came from the alley and was nothing more than a blowout on an automobile. But when Antonio Caesarino, the head chef, stepped into the main floor, he was heard to shout, "My god! Jim's shot! Get a doctor and the police!"[176]

The doctors were far too late. Colosimo was dead, and the killer had fled so quickly that no one was even sure which exit he used. Perhaps he stepped right over the body, or perhaps he took a side exit.

Big Jim's funeral was one of the first underworld funerals to become a massive public affair—the sort that would become standard in the coming decade, when having mourners in the tens of thousands, multiple truckloads of flowers, and caskets that cost more than many people made in a lifetime were de rigueur. Only some two thousand mourners were estimated at Colosimo's, but that was a remarkable enough number to make national news in the pre-Prohibition days. Vicelords were not yet royalty. His bronze casket, though, was valued at thousands of dollars in 1920 money. Bathhouse John Coughlin sang "Ave Maria" and probably made a few people envy Jim's inability to hear it.

Even as Colosimo was being laid to rest in a tomb in Oak Woods Cemetery, police were trying to figure out who had pulled the trigger. They had several suspects, and first on their list was Mrs. Vittoria Moresco, whom Colosimo had divorced only a month before. Perhaps Vittoria thought she could still get his money if he died before he changed his will. Or perhaps she just wanted revenge.

Then they thought of Dale Winter, the beautiful choir girl who now mourned over her new husband's corpse. Did she have other admirers who were so pained to see her married off that they might kill her new husband?

John W. Norton, who'd headed up the Holmes "murder castle" investigations a generation before, was sent to question her. When he asked if she suspected anyone, she reportedly said, "I should say that I suspect *everyone*."[177]

Another account of her questioning, though, is a bit less dramatic. Norton asked her if he'd ever spoken of any enemies, and she said, "No—none . . . He

Big Jim and Dale Winter, courtesy of University of Illinois at Chicago.

was as good as gold to me . . . he had a heart of pure gold. And to think he has been killed!"

"Have you any idea at all who might have killed him?" Norton asked.

"No—I don't know . . . We've been so wrapped up in each other that we didn't have time to talk over business matters. And then, just when we were so happy, someone had to step in and . . ."[178] Her voice trailed off.

Meanwhile, the *Chicago Evening American* quoted her as saying that Mrs. Vittoria Colosimo, his former wife, had come into the cafe four months before and threatened to kill them both. "We tried to quiet her," she reportedly said, "and at last succeeded. She told us to forget what she had said. I didn't believe it, and neither did Jim. And that was the last."[179]

But it couldn't be denied that Colosimo had a lot of enemies, and the *Tribune* suggested that his murder was the work of the Camorra, a then-common name for what they'd later call the Mafia, "the underworld society of little Italy to whom so many crimes of a like nature can be traced."[180]

After all, Colosimo had been receiving "Black Hand" letters. In September 1919, he'd received two of them, one asking him to drop $10,000 in a package on 22nd and State at midnight. Colosimo had dropped off a package, but it was empty. When the "Black Hander" came to collect, Colosimo was waiting in the shadows with a pearl-handled revolver. But the Black Hander was shrewd enough to make the grab and run away while a street car blocked him from view. If you gave a Black Hander an empty box when you were supposed to be giving them ten grand and didn't kill him in the process, you had to expect that a reprisal was coming.

And Colosimo was right in the middle of a lawsuit in which Marie Kerrigan, a former employee, was suing him and Mike the Greek (the legal papers really refer to him as "Mike the Greek") for her treatment at the restaurant.

According to her affadavit, Kerrigan worked alongside employees who went by names such as "Scarlet the Italian" and "Napoli the Bald." The suit not only alleged that they'd tricked her, "a girl of tender years" who had "theretofore experienced by brief and limited impressions of the realities of life," into working in a place that was not of good character. As a result, one day while she was "exercising her lawful rights and proper duties" in the ladies' room (an act that took an awful lot of legalese to describe), Napoli the Bald had barged in on her. When she told him he had no right to be in the ladies' room, he punched her in the face and "accosted her in vile and abusive language." She'd informed Mike the Greek, who told her to shut her mouth. While he did, Napoli came in and beat her further while Mike the Greek looked on, then joined in, hitting her and threatening to throw her "bodily into the alley upon the stones and abandon her there in a helpless condition."[181] Colosimo wasn't present himself for the assault, but if this was how his employees were treated, and the people involved weren't fired, one can imagine any number of people wanting revenge.

But the *Evening American* tracked Kerrigan down, and she seemed not to have any issue with Colosimo himself. "I wish it clearly understood," she said, "that I have nothing in the world against Big Jim personally. He was uniformly courteous and kind to all of us girls . . . I used to make $25 or $20 after every number when the patrons would throw money at me." However, after the suit made the papers, she'd received handwritten notes from Black Handers threatening her life. She believed that the same Black Handers were the ones threatening Colosimo. If she sued and took his money, there wouldn't be enough left for *them* to steal.[182]

Then there were the rumors about Jim wanting to block vicelords in Chicago from getting involved in bootleg liquor. Even if those rumors weren't true, with the great shift in business that Prohibition was bringing, plenty of other vicelords were going to be involved in the struggle to be the man on top of this new world order. Lots of men stood to benefit from having Big Jim out of the way.

Days after the murder, it came out that one Arthur Rockhill had seen a man running up State Street, near 8th. When the man stumbled and fell against a trash can, Rockhill helped him up and a gun fell from his pocket. "That gun went off today," the man reportedly boasted. "I got that dago ___ ____ today, the dirty stiff." He was described as a short, dark-haired, and clean-shaven Italian man about twenty-five years old. Some thought it might have been a convict named Frank Razzino.[183]

Meanwhile, Colosimo's pet goat was reported to be inconsolable.[184]

In the end, there was never enough evidence against any one person for there to be a real suspect, only vague rumors. But according to one legend, the strongest rumor in the underworld was that the trigger man had been young Al Capone, then still only twenty-one years old. Such rumors wouldn't have hurt his growing reputation as a tough guy in the years before he took control of John Torrio's rapidly growing empire.

As Prohibition took hold and jazz replaced the opera singers that Colosimo had hired, the Levee changed. When the *Tribune* columnist who spoke of the ghosts of bygone sinners checked out Colosimo's restaurant a year after his death, the patrons chuckled their way through an opera singer while they waited for the jazz to start.

"The orchestra thunders into a tone whose barbarous syncopated chords hark back to the tom-tom of Tahiti and the voodoo hymns of Liberia," she wrote. "The universal embrace in devotion to the great god Jazz follows. About the floor move the votaries, their bodies undulating, wriggling, their feet scarcely moving. The area is small, but it could be smaller and still accommodate the dozen couples that dance at the sign of Jim Colosimo."[185]

The murder of Big Jim would not be the last outstanding mystery related to him. Just a few years ago, there appears to have been an attempted break-in at his tomb in Oak Woods; the door was bent all out of shape, presumably by someone who thought that a solid bronze casket could fetch a pretty penny down at the scrap metal yard (though how they intended to get it out without attracting attention is anyone's guess). They never got past the stone slab that covers the coffin, but as a result of the would-be break-in, visitors to the cemetery who were willing could look right into the tomb.

It was built large enough to hold several people, but only one slab contains a name and dates:

JAMES COLOSIMO:
1871-1919

And there lies the mystery. Big Jim died in 1920; there was never any doubt about that. How did he come to have a typo on his tomb? Is the tomb we know as Big Jim's perhaps really that of some *other* Colosimo?

Or, as one further twist, at the time of the funeral, one of the police's suspects in the murder was Tony Villiani, who allegedly had an affair with Colosimo's first wife. He was a gravestone carver by trade, and had carved the stone for Colosimo's sister-in-law. Was this typo his own little petty revenge for some unknown slight, or even a last insult to a man he'd killed?

But Mrs. Colosimo brushed off any Villiani connection as simply "a Dale Winter story," and Villiani seemed to be out of town, not working in Chicago, that week. More likely, the man carving the dates on the slab was simply the sort of guy who was still writing 1919 on his checks in May 1920 and figured that no one would ever see his mistake.

If so, the joke's on him. Nearly a century later, we're still talking about it.

. . . and the puzzling inner slab. Photos by author.

Colosimo's tomb . . .

Did Nick "The Choir Singer" Viana Rise from the Grave?

Nicholas "The Choir Singer" Viana was executed on the Chicago gallows on his nineteenth birthday. As they brought him to the "death cell," the room where the condemned traditionally spent their last nights on Earth, he sang "Miserere" in a voice one prison official said "beat any show you ever saw." Then he shouted goodbye to all of his friends.

"Goodbye to all but Sam Cardinella," he called. "May his soul be damned!"

Known around the Levee district as "Il Diavolo," Cardinella was secretive, even by gang leader standards. He didn't head to the bar behind the Alhambra Theatre, where most of the vicelords, madames, and con men rubbed elbows after hours. He didn't have a deal with Bathhouse John to keep him out of trouble, and never reported to Big Jim Colosimo. He didn't recruit punks from the Five Points district in New York, or any other known talent. Rather, he would lure regular children into his pool room on 22nd, convince them that he was their friend, then teach them to commit crimes. He'd take most of the money his teenaged crew made in hold-ups, then cheat them out of the rest with loaded dice. None of the boys dared to complain; some seemed to believe that he had supernatural powers, or something like them, and that escape from him was impossible. And it was. When Santo Orlando, a getaway car driver, was rumored to be ready to "squawk," he was shot to death and dumped into a suburban canal.

Teenage Nicholas Viana had come to the pool room on his way home from choir practice one day. Days later, he committed the first of a dozen or so murders. "I entered Cardinella's poolroom in short trousers," he later said. "A week later, I was a criminal."[186]

And yet the gang was so secretive that they operated right in the heart of the Levee, committing hundreds of hold-ups, without Big Jim Colosimo or any of the other local vicelords even realizing that they were there.

Cardinella finally went too far when he started ordering the boys to torture their victims. On telling them that a nearby carpenter had five hundred dollars hidden someplace, he held up a knife for the boys to see.

"Here's a stiletto," he said. "Take it and stick it in his stomach. He's quiet and he doesn't like to talk. But

"Il Diavolo"

if you twist the knife around, he'll talk fast enough. When he tells you where the money is, shove the knife clear in and kill him."[187]

The young men took the knife, but then came back and admitted to Cardinella that they hadn't had the heart to do it. And they later learned that Cardinella had hired two hit men to wait around in the carpenter's shop for the boys, and that the whole thing was a set-up to get rid of a couple of them.[188]

The gang began to turn on Cardinella, and information spread to the police (again, Detective John W. Norton worked on the case), and in November 1919, a raid was enacted in which the homicide squad rounded up forty-one men, including Cardinella and Viana. When news of the arrests broke, papers spoke in awed tones of the "murder clique" overseen by the devil who ran a "college of crime." Police announced that the arrest of the gang cleared up literally hundreds of crimes, and first deputy John Alcock said it was the single most important round-up in the history of Chicago.[189] Newspapers—almost without exception—compared Cardinella to Fagin, the villain from *Oliver Twist*.

The young men of the gang told the police a lot: about Cardinella's orders to torture the carpenter, about the loaded dice. Viana could have probably saved himself by giving even more evidence, but he was still afraid that if he did, his old master would take revenge on his family. Cardinella had been arrested, too, but Viana had no faith at all that the man would actually be hanged. He still believed that Cardinella could get out of anything.

On the scaffold, as they prepared his noose, Viana said, "It is no disgrace to die for my mother, father, and sisters. I forgive everyone in the world for the wrongs they have done me. I thank the jail officials for the kindness they have shown."[190] Then he prayed with his priests, and the trap door fell.

It was said that at the moment of his death, a large mirror fell to the floor and shattered in a nearby judge's courtroom.[191]

Viana's body was turned over to his friends, who put it in a basket, rather than a coffin, and brought it to an ambulance they'd hired— cheaper than a hearse, perhaps—to take it to a funeral home on the West Side.

Cardinella, meanwhile, was still in his cell, where he scared the hell out of the hardened guards. Frank McNamara, the county physician, even went so far as to say, "If I were superstitious, I would say that Cardinella himself seemed to evoke a spirit of Satanism." The brooding gang leader didn't make friends with the guards, as most convicts on murderer's row did. He refused to eat and spent hours pacing back and forth in his cell, losing so much weight that he seemed to be wasting away. He tried to escape numerous times. Days before his own scheduled execution, his friends tried to smuggle in a bottle of nitroglycerin so that he could blast his way out of prison.

But on the night before he was to hang, he was still in the cell. His wife and six children visited him one last time, and guards listened as his wife told the younger children that their father was going "on a journey." They couldn't understand what Cardinella was saying in his thick Sicilian accent, but they recognized the word "Viana."

"This was odd," McNamara later recalled. "Nicholas Viana already met the doom that Cardinella was facing. It was strange that Cardinella should want to talk about Viana, whose last words probably had an unfavorable influence on the leader's appeals for mercy."

Cardinella broke down completely on the way to the scaffold, and would not get up to his feet after collapsing; the guards eventually had to tie him to chair in order to hang him. When the trap door fell, the chair bounced grostesquely. In a short story based on the newspaper account, Ernest Hemingway wrote of the contrast in the man's psyche: here was a heartless fiend who had casually ordered the deaths of perhaps dozens of men, but when faced with his own death, he was a total coward.

What Hemingway didn't know was that Cardinella had one more trick up his sleeve.

When he was dead and untied from the chair, his friends placed the body in a wire basket and took it to an ambulance in the jail yard, just as they'd done with Viana. This time, prison officials decided to see what was going on, and found out that the ambulance was equipped with nurses and a pulminator. When they opened it up, attendants were trying to bring Sam Cardinella back to life.

All at once, Cardinella's behavior in prison made sense. By losing weight and getting himself tied to a chair for the hanging, he made sure there'd be a shorter drop with less weight on the noose, making it more likely that he'd strangle to death, rather than breaking his neck. In theory, if Cardinella's neck stayed intact, he could be brought back to life. The physician said that there was at least a slim chance that they might have pulled it off if the ambulance hadn't been held up.

And rumors went around the jail that Cardinella had been sure it would work because his friends had already tested it—successfully—on Nicholas Viana.

The way McNamara described the stories prisoners told, they had taken Viana to a funeral home where black-robed "magicians" had chanted while doctors worked on the body, succeeding in bringing the spark of life into the limp form on the slab. But when Viana began to breathe, the chanting stopped, and the young man died a second death. The traitor to the gang was never intended to be more than a guinea pig.

Cardinella's death certificate shows that his neck was broken, and it's unlikely that they could have genuinely brought him back even if he'd only choked, unless he hadn't been quite dead yet when they took him down from the rope. But it's quite likely that Cardinella *thought* Viana had been brought back from the other side, and that he would be, too.

The story reached the press two months later, in June 1921, after the next hanging in the prison. This time, Sheriff Peters, who more than a decade before had talked about the similarities between Belle Gunness and Johann Hoch, had to explain why the bodies of the two men being executed were going to be held in the prison for more than an hour, instead of being promptly delivered to an undertaker. From his comments, it's clear that the officials took the rumors about Viana seriously.

"I'm afraid attempts will be made to revive them," Peters said. "Such an effort was made after the hanging of Nick Viana last December, and a doctor with a resuscitating apparatus succeeded in getting a flicker of life back into the body, I am told, though they failed in the end."

That was the story he heard, in any case.

The assistant jailer was even more certain that the rumors were true. "We investigated the story," he said, "and we learned that not only was Viana given oxygen for more than an hour, but that his body actually showed signs of returning life. One witness whom I have heard quoted said that the heart had actually picked up, when some unforeseen circumstances halted the resuscitation."[192]

Sheriff Peters even believed it was possible that the people who'd told him the story had changed the ending, and maybe, just maybe, Viana truly *had* been resurrected and was now at large. He had consulted with physicians who agreed that if a hanged man had only strangled, not suffered a broken neck, oxygen machines might bring them back to life. Word had gone around that an electrocuted man somewhere on the East Coast had been brought back to life recently. "It is possible," said Peters, "that one or more of the eighty-two men hanged in Cook County since 1840 cheated the law in that way. We will see that such a thing does not happen in the future."[193]

It may not have been remembered then that the city of Chicago had done experiments in this line. Almost forty years earlier, doctors had hooked up murderer James Tracy's just-hanged body to electric wires and tried to bring him back to life, just to see if they could, and got at least as far as Viana's doctors were rumored to have; his heart started beating and the expression his face changed as the dotors moved the wires.

Naturally, the legal implications were astounding. If a man was hanged and brought back, would he have to be hanged again, or would he have paid his debt in the eyes of the law? Could a legally dead man even be arrested for committing a crime after being brought back? The police don't seem to have fact-checked the Viana rumors very well; they'd simply heard the story from "the underworld" and decided to take no chances. Reporters were more vigilant. They immediately tracked down Joseph Marzano, the undertaker to whose funeral parlor at 931 Polk Street Viana had been taken. Several reporters talked to Marzano, and each got a slightly different story.

He told the *Evening Journal,* "I personally had charge of Viana's body and embalmed it immediately upon its arrival here. There is absolutely nothing to reports that relatives and friends attempted to bring him back to life with the aid of a pulminator. It is possible some of his friends would have liked to have tried it, but they had no chance."[194]

To the *Herald Examiner,* however, Marzano admitted that they'd at least *discussed* trying to revive Viana. "There is no doubt but that we would have had some success," he said. "His temperature had dropped only two points when we got the body, but we were afraid of running afoul of the law."[195]

"I am satisfied that the story is true," Peters insisted. "I do not say that the undertaker had anything to do with it. But the evidence given us tends to show that this operation took place in his morgue."[196]

The Cardinella gang was soon forgotten. By 1921, Prohibition had taken effect, and hold-up gangs and Black Handers began to seem like relics of yesterday as the beer-running gangs made the city their own.

Viana's death certificate doesn't indicate any foul play, though it does show four days between death and burial; funerals and burials were often held immediately after hangings, though not always.

Whatever Happened to Tommy O'Connor?

Cook County stopped hanging people and switched to the electric chair in 1927. But the pile of lumber that made up the gallows was kept in storage in the basement of the jail for another fifty years just in case they ever caught "Terrible Tommy" O'Connor. He had been awaiting his own date with the gallows when he escaped from prison in 1921, and under the terms of his sentence, he had to be hanged, not electrocuted. Theoretically, if he were ever caught, even decades later, they would need the gallows again.

O'Connor was no criminal mastermind, or even a particularly successful crook, just a ratty Maxwell Street tough with an itchy trigger finger. He and a man named Harry Emerson were charged with murder in 1918; Emerson was convicted while O'Connor was set free. It seems that O'Connor didn't forgive him for testifying against him, though, so he asked his old friend Jimmy Cherin to have Emerson killed in prison, then shot Cherin to death when he refused. O'Connor was arrested, but the key witness disappeared before the trial for Cherin's murder could begin, and by the time he was found (alive and well, in a bit of a shocking twist), O'Connor had run away.

In March 1921, police learned that O'Connor was living on the South Side with relatives, and four officers came to arrest him. Seeing them coming from a window, O'Connor ran out the back, firing at the cops with a pistol as he tried to make a getaway, hitting Sergeant Patrick

Tommy O'Connor's mugshot.

J. O'Neill with a shot that would prove fatal. A nationwide manhunt ensued, with cops following leads all over. Chief of Detectives Hughes and Lieutenant John Norton (again, the same Norton who had investigated the Holmes castle and interviewed Colosimo's widow) said they wouldn't rest until O'Connor was captured.

He was finally found in Minnesota, where he was captured in the middle of attempting to hold up a porter on a train. On the ride back to Chicago, O'Connor told reporters that, "It wasn't my revolver that killed [Sergeant O'Neill]. O'Neill was shot down by his own pals. A mistake, of course, but they shot him. And after that mistake they ran away and put the blame on me. Yes—on me. Me that never killed anyone. Do you wonder that I ran away? What chance had I with every policeman in the city out to get me dead or alive? Me with the con— only 138 pounds. And I never shot to kill in my life."[197]

Police Chief Fitzmorris was already worried about another escape as O'Connor was being brought to Chicago to stand trial. "We know at least three of O'Connor's toughest pals have left for St. Paul with the intention of rescuing him," he said. "They will go to the limit, for they know if they fail him and he ever gets the chance, he will kill them as he did Jimmy Cherin."[198]

But O'Connor was kept in custody long enough to be brought to trial; this time he was convicted and sentenced to hang by the neck until he was dead.

But once again, the prison couldn't hold the wily O'Connor for long.

In December 1921, a prison guard was opening a cell gate to let two prisoners in. One prisoner grabbed the guard, and O'Connor held up a gun that had allegedly been smuggled to him inside a pork chop sandwich. A third man seized the jail key while the guard was bound and gagged. O'Connor and four other prisoners then took the freight elevator to the basement, locked six kitchen workers into a closet, and then headed for the roof of a shed from which they could jump over the prison wall. One man broke his ankles when he landed, and one couldn't make the jump at all, but O'Connor and three others escaped.

Law student Harry Busch was driving his car near the jail when Tommy O'Connor jumped onto his running board at the corner of Clark and Illinois. "In comes Tommy with his cannon," Busch remembered in 1993. "He said, 'Drive like hell, you SOB, or I'll blow your brains out! I'm Tommy O'Connor!' I drove!"[199] Busch eventually crashed his car into a factory wall and last saw O'Connor running toward an alley.

Busch's view of the escaping fugitive was, perhaps, the last confirmed sighting of the O'Connor. Busch, who rose to become Mayor Richard J. Daley's private attorney, was still being asked about it on the jailbreak's seventy-fifth anniversary.

From there, "Terrible Tommy" O'Connor's whereabouts became a mystery that would bother the cops for decades.

Some said he returned to his native Ireland and died in the Black and Tan war. In other versions of the story, he started a saloon in Ireland and ran it for decades until he died of natural causes. In 1959, *Tribune* reporter John Gavin said, without really naming a source, that O'Connor had stayed right in Chicago, where he worked with outlaw Pretty Boy Floyd in the Touhy gang.[200]

Every few years the papers would re-run the story, sometimes with composite drawings of what Tommy would look like by then. By the 1940s, people were wondering what the hell would happen if he were actually caught. The old jail where the hangings used to be held was a parking lot by then, and the gallows seemed like something from another century, not just a couple of decades ago. Some thought the lawyers would find a loophole to save O'Connor's life, some thought he'd just be electrocuted instead, and some truly believed that if O'Connor was caught, they'd hang him in the parking lot where the jail used to be, perhaps setting up a makeshift tent around the place of execution.

Even fifty years after the escape, it was a common trick for reporters and photographers who were under the weather, hungover, or just wanted a day off to call in and explain that they wouldn't be in the office because they'd gotten a tip about the whereabouts of O'Connor and had to follow the lead. "This," wrote the *Tribune* in 1961, "would fetch [the reporter] time to nurture and rest his hangover, and a bit of expense money with which to cure it."[201]

By the 1970s, when O'Connor would have been in his eighties if he was still among the living, Thomas Powers of the *Tribune* wrote a column trying to entice him to come out of hiding. "True, they were going to hang you when you took off," wrote Powers, "but the judge who sentenced you is dead and the gallows has rotted. If you come back, the worst that can happen to you is that you'll get nursing home care at the taxpayers' expense. And that's just the beginning! I could put you in touch with an agent, and we could write a book so nostalgic it would make Jack Mabley weep with envy . . . you have no idea how many assistant city editors have come and gone since you up and went, and I think just about all of them have assigned reporters to the Terrible Tommy story."[202]

Powers, like many longtime Chicagoans, was dying for some closure before the rapidly approaching point when everyone would have to assume that O'Connor was dead. If Tommy would just send a postcard saying he was alive, people would have least have some idea of the solution to a mystery that lingered in the city like an open wound.

In 1977, a judge ruled that O'Connor could be presumed dead, and that the old gallows that had been waiting for him in the basement of the jail could be destroyed. The owner of Donley's Wild West Town, a small theme park in Union, Illinois, arranged to purchase them for a sum in the three-figure range, then kept them on display until 2006, when they were sold at auction. The buyer, the Ripley's Believe it or Not Museum, paid $68,300 for the rotting boards,[203] despite the fact that only a few of the beams were really original, and it's quite likely that none of them were quite as old as the auction catalog described them; it said that the gallows were the very ones that had been used on the Haymarket anarchists in the 1880s. News items from the years between that hanging and O'Connor's escape indicate that new scaffolds had been built several times.

By the time the gallows left Illinois to sit in a Ripley's warehouse in Florida, even the most optimistic had to assume that O'Connor was dead. Though conflicting dates are given for his birth, by 2006 he would have probably been at least 120. But officially, he was still awaiting execution.

The old criminal court building where he was put on trial had been turned into offices by then; the lobby was decorated with photos of notable trials and people associated with the building's history. And the portrait of Tommy O'Connor was the most prominent of them all.

How Many Husbands Did Tillie Klimek Kill?

No woman was ever hanged in Chicago, but Tillie Klimek probably came the closest. The fact that she *wasn't* hanged sparked a lot of debate as to the way women who killed were treated in Chicago. Women brought to trial for murder—of their husbands, more often than not—were almost always acquitted, and those convicted were generally given far lighter sentences than would have been passed down for a man who committed the same crime. When Tillie was given a life sentence for murdering one of her four husbands, it

Tillie Klimek, source unknown.

was noted that in recent years, there had been seven women acquitted of murder in Chicago for every woman convicted. For men, the ratio was much different.

Genevieve Forbes Herrick, the *Tribune*'s ace crime reporter, joked that nearly every single woman accused of a crime claimed that she was in bed every night by nine o'clock (as though that absolved them from suspicion), and further noted that the women who were convicted were generally older, less-attractive women.

"And Tillie Klimek," she wrote, "the squat, grewsomely [sic] cruel Polish woman, who rebuffs all human emotion from others, the woman who seems to take a grotesque delight in seeing others die, establishes the precedent in Cook County. Convicted of the murder of Frank Kupeczyk, she is sentenced to spend the rest of her natural life in the penitentiary."[204]

And Frank probably wasn't even close to the only man that Tillie had killed. In fact, the *Tribune* suspected her of poisoning twenty people and at least one dog between 1914 and 1922. Again, whether she counts as a "serial killer" depends on whose definition of the term you use, but she was quite likely one the most prolific murderers in Chicago history. Given the standards of the day, when a man could be hanged just for being present when a murder took place, her life sentence *is* a bit jarring.

Tillie went down into serial killer folklore as a "psychic" killer. According to the legends written about her later, she advertised her services as a seer, predicted the deaths of her victims, then made sure the predictions came true by killing her customers. Like many serial killer tales, the "psychic" angle has very little basis in fact. The stories probably grew from Tillie's cavalier confidence—or possibly just the sick sense of humor she diesplayed—when Joseph Klimek, her fourth husband, fell sick in 1922. Sitting by his bedside, she confidently and cheerfully told him that he wouldn't live long. As he grew sicker, she greeted him with such upbeat phrases as, "You are pretty near dead now," and, "Didn't I tell you, you aren't going to live long?"

In the meantime, while Joseph was sick, two of the family's dogs died after eating table scraps.

But Joseph didn't die, as Tillie so often insisted he would. Instead, he went to the hospital, where doctors found that his stomach was full of arsenic. They also found that Tillie had been married to at least three other men, all of whom were now dead. Coroner Hoffman began proceedings to have their bodies exhumed to be checked for arsenic.

Tillie and her cousin, Nellie Koulik, were brought in for questioning. Tillie seemed quite open about the fact that she was tired of Joseph and "wanted to get rid of him," and Nellie told police that she'd given Tillie some rat poison. Police suspected both of them, and possibly all of their neighbors, of being murderers. Soon, more and more women from around the Little Poland neighborhood were being arrested or brought in for questioning. The *Tribune* wrote that the state's attorney believed Tillie was the "High Priestess of the Bluebeard Clique."[205] By all accounts, Tillie had bad luck with husbands. With her first, Joseph Mitkiewicz, she had two children in their fourteen years of marriage. "He wasn't much of a husband," Judge Kavanagh later wrote, "even as husbands go these days. He drank too much."[206] Instead of fighting him over his drinking, Tillie apparently started buying him whiskey, slowly increasing the amount of arsenic she added to each bottle over the course of three months. After he succumbed to the poison, she cashed in his life insurance.

Within weeks, she had married one John Ruszcakski. When he died after three months, Tillie received another insurance check.

Two months after that, she married Frank Kupczyk, who got sick at once. Tillie sat by his bedside, knitting what she said would be her mourning veil and joking about his impending demise. She even showed him a picture of the fantastic coffin she'd bought him at a bargain; some reports even said that she'd brought it home and was keeping it in their apartment. When he died, just as she'd said he would, Tillie got another insurance check, then married Joseph Klimek and acted just the same way when *he* took sick.

When the three bodies were exhumed, the coroner's chemist found arsenic in each of them. There were 11.2 grains of it in the organs of the now long-dead Joseph Mitkiewicz, 13.8 in Ruszkaksi, and eight grains in Frank Kupcyzk. Two grains would be enough to kill most people. Just to be sure, the soil around the graves was tested as well, and found to be arsenic free.[207]

And then more graves were dug up.

The Little Poland neighborhood, near Damen and Augusta, was full

Exhuming the grave of Tillie's first husband. *Chicago Tribune.*

of stories of women who'd said something unkind about their husbands when they died, or had seemed glad to get the insurance money, and now all of them were suspects. These were mostly middle-aged Polish women, speaking little English and living in a rather isolated community; Tillie herself had lived in the United States since she was a baby, but still spoke only broken English, which wasn't uncommon in the neighborhood. In another era, these were exactly the sort of women who would have been pointed out as possible witches. What went on in 1922 wasn't a lot different.

Though evidence against the neighbors was lacking, it kept piling up against Tillie. One of her cousins called the state's attorney and said that her sister, Rose, had died after having dinner at Tillie's house. Another cousin said the same thing about *three* of her own siblings.

Of all those brought in, only Tillie and her cousin, Nellie Koulik, ever went to trial. Nellie was discharged at one point; when they came to take her from the cell, Tillie, with her typical sense of humor, convinced her cousin that she was being taken to the gallows. Nellie shrieked and clung to a cell door for dear life until the guards managed to pry her away, while Tillie laughed. Nellie's freedom was short-lived, though, and she ended up on trial alone.

In prison, Tillie was known to be very friendly and cheerful with the other female prisoners, but if anyone asked her about the poisonings, she'd go into a rage, vacillating between English and Polish as she shouted, "I didn't rob nobody; I didn't shoot nobody; I didn't poison nobody. I didn't! Everybody pick on me. Everybody make eyes at me

Nellie and Tillie. *Chicago Tribune.*

like they going to eat me. Why do they make eyes at me like that? I tell the truth. Anything I did, I did to myself. Nobody else."[208]

At Tillie's trial, a regular parade of her neighbors told shocking stories about her. They told tales of Tillie playing dance music on the phonograph when husband number three was dying, and quite literally dancing around his corpse when he died. They revealed that between husbands number two and number three, she'd taken up with one John Guszkowski, to whom she supposedly confessed killing her two husbands. He'd naturally declined her subsequent marriage proposal, then died himself a short while later.

Tillie sat cold and unmoved throughout the proceedings. Officially, she was only being tried for the murder of her third husband, but stories of all of the others came up as well. In all cases, Tillie seems to have slowly mixed arsenic into their food and drinks.

Lieutenant William Malone of the police testified that when he first drove Tillie to the police station, she shook her finger at him and said, "The next one I want to cook a dinner for is you. You made all my trouble."[209]

A nurse at the hospital where Jospeh Klimek was still fighting for his life said that when he'd first been brought in, Mrs. Klimek had told her, "If he makes any trouble for you, take a two by four board and hit him over the head with it."

The gravedigger who'd exhumed her first husband's body happened to be a former neighbor himself. He told about an affair Tillie had had with one John Koski, to the delight of the Polish housewives in attendance.

The press made much of her frumpiness and unattractiveness, but she'd clearly never lacked for suitors. Genevieve Forbes Herrick noted, "The woman whose appeal has ensnared many men displays an almost sexless impersonality as she surveys the younger women in the jail and criticizes their indiscretions."[210] In a separate article, she described Tillie as having "a greasy complexion and a lumpy figure. [She] growls instead of murmurs, and knows a crochet needle better than a lipstick."[211]

Taking the stand in her own defense, Tillie said that she never got much insurance money from her husbands dying. She insisted that her four husbands had either died of "moonshine" or by suicide. "They just died, same as other people," she said. "I not responsible for that. I could no help if they wanted to die." She denied that she'd bought her third husband a coffin, or danced around his corpse. Her neighbors, she said, "got it in for me."[212]

Her lawyers tried to state that when she told her late husbands that they were going to die soon, that was just her sense of humor. Many of her quotes do, in fact, sound morbid and threatening on the surface, but surely most people know a couple with a similar sense of humor. And her brother said he ate with Tillie and Joseph several times, eating the same food Joseph ate, and never got sick from it. "Food was put in one large dish," he said. "If there had been arsenic in the food, I don't see why it didn't kill me."[213]

But the evidence of the arsenic in the exhumed coffins was strong enough, and Tillie was convicted.

"This is one of the most remarkable cases in the history of criminology," said Judge Kavanagh. "The books do not contain another case like it . . . If this woman was let loose today, she would kill another man. She has a desire to see those with whom she was intimate suffer. Criminologists tell us there are few such people on this earth. I venture to say there are more husbands poisoned in this community than the police or authorities realize. But the knowledge that Tillie Klimek 'has gone down' will stay their hands."[214]

Exactly how many people Tillie killed in her career can never be known; most of the murders she was accused of on the stand were never fully investigated. In March 1923, during her trial, the *Tribune* put together a list of possible victims. Three were more or less confirmed, and Joesph Klimek would have been a fourth. But perhaps her first husband was not her first victim, and one does have to wonder what she was up to between poisoning two husbands in 1914 and two in 1921.

The list of suspected victims:

Jospeh Mitkiewicz, first husband. 1914. Arsenic found in his body.
Joseph Ruskowski, second husband. 1914. Arsenic found in his body.
Joseph Grantkowski, ex-boyfriend. Died in 1914 after "jilting" Tillie.
Helen, Stanley, and Stelle Zakrewski, young cousins of Tillie who died between 1912 and 1915, each after illnesses. In each case, Tillie tended to them while they were sick.

Sophie Sturmer, daughter of Mrs. Koulik. Died 1917.

Ben Sturmer, twin brother of Sophie. Died a month after his sister.

Wojek Sturmer, first husband of Nellie Koulik. Died 1918. Arsenic found in his body.

John Sturmer, son of Mrs. Koulik. Recovered from sickness after his father died in 1918; John thought his mother poisoned him.

Mrs. Rose Chudzinski, cousin. Died in 1919 after attending Tillie and Frank's wedding party.

"Meyers," a husband or sweetheart. Was missing as of March 1923.

Miss Stelle Grantowski, a sister of John Grantowski. She fell sick after eating candy given to her by Tillie after a fight.

Mrs. Rose Splitt, a neighbor. Said that Tillie gave her poison candy, too.

Nick Micko, a cousin. Recovered from arsenic poisoning.

Dorothy Spera, granddaughter of Mrs. Koulik. Died at age two.

Mrs. Bessie Kupcyzk, sister-in-law of Frank Kupcyzk. Fell sick after eating at Tillie's, but recovered.

Miss Lillian Sturmer, a teenage daughter of Mrs. Koulik. Lived at Mrs. Klimek's home for a year at age thirteen and became deathly sick from the food.

Frank Kupszyk, third husband. 1921. Arsenic found in his body after death.

Joseph Klimek, fourth husband. Poisoned in 1921, but eventually recovered.[215]

It's entirely possible that some of these bodies could still be exhumed. The arsenic would still be there.

Writing about the case years later, Kavanagh said, "Few reported murder cases show a deeper, craftier, more hideous malignity than this one. Day by day, through weeks and months, Tillie watched her victims die. Slowly, night and day, she kept pushing them into their graves. Not once did this cold-hearted creature display one dim spark of pity. Night after night, she slept beside an unfortunate man whose life she was taking. Morning, noon, and night, her own hand held to his lips the disguised poison. Notwithstanding her lighter generosity, Tillie is a monster of cruelty. If a man were to have perpetrated her deeds, what jury would hesitate in sending him to the electric chair?"[216]

The state's attorney fought hard for the death penalty, telling the jury, "It is time that the chain of immunity for women be broken, and I hope this will be a lesson to the women that in Cook County they will be treated the same as the men."[217] But it wasn't to be: She was given a life sentence in prison, where she lived out the rest of her days. Many were shocked that she was convicted at all. Genevieve Forbes Herick confidently stated that, "Tillie went to the penitentiary because she had never gone to a beauty parlor."[218]

However, there was nothing you could say of Tillie's looks or lack of charms that couldn't also be said of her cousin, Nellie Koulik, who was tried for murder in a separate trial. She had none of Tillie's sense of humor, and spent most of her time on the stand responding only with the words "never did" in a sing-song voice. But she also showed none of Tillie's penchant for cruelty, and was eventually acquitted.

How she got on with the children who'd called her a murderer on the stand after that is not recorded.

Tillie's home on North Winchester is still standing, a rarity for the homes of our old-time murderers.

Virginia Harrison, Lillian Collier, and the Snuggle Puppies of Wind Blew Inn

It's difficult today to imagine an era when jazz music was considered dangerous or shocking, now that the average jazz club is full of people who support NPR, not violent low-lifes. Dean O'Banion, later head of the North Side mob, got his start as a singing waiter in a North Side jazz bar that was described as one of the most dangerous jazz places in the city; even through the 1950s, that area around Clark and Grand was known as the home to tough, rowdy espresso bars.

In 1921, the *Tribune* columnist who described the new scene in the Levee also spoke of the atmosphere in River North: "A cry that is half a sob issues from a side door near the intersection of Clark and Erie. It is the wail of the saxophone. Symbol of the modern dance. Symbol of the sensuous movements that have succeeded the pure grace of the waltz. Symbol of the lost souls who drift to the port of missing men!"[219]

Eat your heart out, Bruce Springsteen.

In the middle of these opening gasps of the roaring Twenties, Lillian Collier, a flapper barely out of her teens, was setting the city on fire—at least until April 1922, when someone set her tea room, the Wind Blew Inn, on fire. The fire was sometimes blamed on "puritan arsonists," but could it have really been the last act of a messy breakup with her girlfriend?

Lillian Collier moved to Chicago with her family in the late 1910s; born Lillian Lieberman, she appears to have married a man named Herbert Collier, who didn't make the move with her and was out of the picture by 1920 when the census man came by. Lillian was then nineteen years old. She'd worked for a time as a performer in the Sells-Floto circus, then worked a stint as a writer for the *Herald Examiner,* who published her work under the rather nauseating byline of "Our Little Girl Reporter."

Around 1921, she converted a former gas station at Ohio Street and Michigan Avenue into the Wind Blew Inn, a tea room with which she hoped to emulate the artsy vibe of New York's Greenwich Village. Lit only with candles, and decorated with nude statues and a futuristic painting of a silo, it quickly became ground zero for the city's bohemian, just steps away from where the *Tribune* reporter heard the saxophone calling lost souls to the port of missing men.

Lillian's place soon became a target for reformers who no longer had the Levee to kick around. Neighbors complained about the "syncopated 'blues' music" they could hear coming from the Wind Blew Inn's piano, and parents feared that their daughters were attending "petting parties" there. Rumors that the Inn might be serving liquor under the table (probably true) were the least of their concerns.

In February 1922, the police raided the place and hauled everyone present into court, where the officers described the apparently phallic "silo" painting as obscene, and the landlord of the place next door railed that "a boilermaker must play that piano." Lillian was charged with keeping a disorderly house.

"I deny that my place was disorderly," she said. "I maintain that it was the best restaurant ever made out of a gasoline station. The Wind Blew Inn was designed

Lillian at the Wind Blew Inn.

as a place where artists and writers could foregather and discuss the arts. The windows were kept gray to give that cathedral interior . . . We made it a point to search every man who came in for hip liquor. They don't do that even in most churches."[220]

Most of the forty or so patrons who'd been arrested were promptly dismissed, but Lillian and her "aide," Virginia Harrison, were eventually brought to trial that spring. In between, Lillian compromised with the order to remove the nude statues by putting overalls on them, and gave a widely circulated interview in which she claimed she'd come to Chicago to preach "the gospel of high art."[221]

At the trial, either Lillian or Virginia (sources differ on which) can be credited with one of the finest lines ever uttered in a Chicago court: "There is no snugglepupping at the Wind Blew Inn."

Judge Jacobs was reasonably impressed that the young women meant no harm, but questioned their upbringing.

"Have either of you ever read *Little Women, Flaxie Frizzle,* or Hans Christian Anderson's tales?" he asked.

"No," said Lillian. "But we read bedtime stories in the papers."

"Well, that's good," the judge told her. "All that's the matter with you is that you have a false value of things and life in general. Start on the fairytales right away."[222]

And with that, he agreed to let the Wind Blew Inn stay open, but sentenced the two to read a book of fairytales. They dutifully checked one out from the library, and promised that if they read them and decided to change their ways, they would[223] stop Chicago's bohemia.

Judge Jacobs probably wasn't being entirely serious with the sentence; a look at some of his other cases show that he had a sort of quirky sense of humor. Around the same time as Lillian's trial, a young man was brought before him after being caught trying to steal nickels from a player piano in a South Side pool hall at four o'clock in the morning. He'd been apprehended after accidentally setting off the piano, and when it broke into "Bimini Bay," one of the latest jazz hits, the neighbors woke up and alerted the police. "It's another instance," Judge Jacobs cracked, "of jazz music being responsible for a youth's downfall."[224]

In April, shortly after the trial, the Wind Blew Inn burned down. Collier was briefly taken into the police station, but released when it was learned that she had no insurance on the place. A new version of the Inn was opened briefly on La Salle Street, but didn't last long; it was a cleaner, brighter place, and lacked the bohemian charm of the original.

Two years later, Lillian was interviewed for an article entitled, "Is Today's Girl Becoming a Savage?" In it, she defended flappers as representing a new era of freedom and opportunity for women. "Our open and honest ways are too frank for the mid-Victorian critics," she explained. "They want the chicanery, subterfuge, and the sly attempts at coquetry to convince them of true femininity. Women too long have had to play the role of the underdog. That's why they have been tread upon since the days of the cave man . . . Now woman has broken the traditional bond. She has emerged from restraint that made the old time demure miss, who was a demure miss simply becaue she dared not be otherwise. The woman of yesterday was a deceit box of suppressed desires . . . The flapper of today typifies understanding. She is the product of a new age turning to the light."[225]

I became sort of obsessed when I first ran into Lillian's story, and eventually even worked her story into a novel, *Just Kill Me*. For some time, what became of Lillian herself was one of Chicago's most puzzling unsolved mysteries. After that 1924 article, she seemed to disappear from the record entirely. Several women named Lillian Collier were found—a suffragette in Texas, a poet in Canada, a socialite in New York—but none seemed to be the same Lillian whose Wind Blew Inn had been the talk of the town in 1922.

That mystery is now solved. After an article was found giving her mother's last name (Lillian's maiden name, before she married her first husband), the rest of the pieces were put together, and the story was worth the wait: After marrying one Frank Gerard in the 1920s, Lillian moved to California and worked on Cannery Row for a time before becoming a writer under the name Nellise Child (as in "Nellie's Child," after her mother, Nellie Lieberman). Under that name, she wrote two mystery novels in the 1930s, a play that was briefly produced on Broadway by the radical Group Theater in 1935, and a couple more serious novels in the 1940s. She eventually remarried and moved to New York, where she and her son saw every Broadway show produced for several years, and continued to write plays and circulate among well-known authors and actresses. She eventually moved back to Chicago with her third husband, where she died in 1981 under the name Nellise Rosenfeld.

But still outstanding is the mystery of Virginia Harrison, described in newspapers as Lillian's "aide." Many have suggested that Virginia might have been her girlfriend, and Virginia does seem to have told at least one newspaper that her name was "Virginia Collier." When

I asked Lillian's son, who is still alive and well, he told me that he didn't know anything about the two of them being a couple, but that he thought they very well could have been. Lillian didn't mind at all when her son came out in the 1970s, which at least shows that she was ahead of her time in that regard. He even suggested another woman (the wife of a then-famous playwright) with whom she might have had an affair much later.

And there may be an even wilder twist in the story: When the Wind Blew Inn burned down, Virginia seems to have been the chief suspect. When Lillian was brought in for questioning, she described Virginia as a former employee who had recently threatened to "get even." A woman thought to be Virginia had been seeing purchasing a gallon of gasoline from a nearby filling station and walking in the direction of the Wind Blew Inn.

Virginia's background, and her whereabouts after the night of the fire, remain a complete blank space in the story. The name Virginia Harrison was common enough at the time that seeking more information about her is difficult, and the search is further complicated by the fact that Virginia Harrison might not have been her real name; the *Herald Examiner* said that her real name was Jean Lawrence. That was too common a name to be easily searched, too.

Virginia Harrison.

So even though most of the questions about Lillian have been answered (and more wonderfully than we could ever have dreamed), Virginia remains an enigma. What happened between her and Lillian so soon after the trial to break up their partnership? What sort of partnership did they have, exactly? And what became of Virginia?

A number of papers reported that the police and fire department were looking for Miss Harrison after the trial, but no article has been found indicating that they caught her, or what became of her in later years. I keep hoping she'll have a great-grandchild looking her up online one day who stumbles across one of my articles on her. Otherwise, we may have to just tell ourselves that she drifted to the port of missing women. . . .

Who Killed McSwiggin (and Why Was an Assistant State's Attorney Hanging Out with Gangsters)?

As Prohibition took hold and the "gangster" era heated up, Johnny "The Fox" Torrio kept everyone in line. The city was divided into territories that Torrio insisted should be respected. There was no reason to fight. "There's gonna be plenty of money for everyone," he said.

But he failed to account for the fact that many of the gangsters were old safe crackers, pickpockets, hit men, and thieves. With the right amount of bribery, they could run the liquor business as a more-or-less legitimate operation, and driving beer trucks around felt an awful lot like a normal, everyday job. A normal, everyday job that paid a lot better than driving a milk truck, but still. Some of the men got restless. And they got greedy. Rivalries flared, and dirty tricks were pulled.

Eventually, the bullets began to fly.

Dean O'Banion, head of the North Side gang and on Torrio's last nerve, was shot to death in his State Street flower shop in November 1924. Two months later, the three North Siders who jointly took his place, Bugs Moran, Vinnie "The Schemer" Drucci, and Hymic Weiss, took their revenge by ambushing John Torrio outside of his home, shooting him in the face. Torrio only narrowly survived, and was smart enough to take his money and retire, turning everything over to his lieutenant, Al Capone.

Capone had first appeared in the Chicago press in 1922, when the *Tribune* featured a tiny article about "Alfred Caponi," a brothel owner, facing charges for drunk driving, assault with an automobile, and carrying concealed weapons. He had been driving drunk, crashed into a taxicab, then jumped out of the car, waving a stolen police badge and threatening to shoot a witness who said the crash was his fault. Brought to the station, he threatened to have all of the officers present fired, bragging of his connections. "I'll fix this thing so easy you won't know how it's done!" he sneered.[226]

It's hard to imagine that such an obnoxious punk would emerge as a master of PR just a few years later.

A few years under Torrio's wing taught Capone a lot. When he took over the empire Torrio had built, he portrayed himself to the press as a businessman, just trying to give the people what they wanted at a fair price.

And lots of people were sympathetic to him. After all, by 1925, it was fairly obvious to all interested parties that that the "noble experiment" of Prohibition was a complete disaster. It's difficult to tell whether people were really drinking more or less; fewer people died of cirrhosis, which is generally an indicator that they were drinking less, but by some accounts the number of places where one could buy a drink in Chicago roughly tripled. The difference was that liquor prices skyrocketed. People were drinking just about as *frequently* as they had before, they just couldn't afford to drink quite so *much*. Practically nobody took the law seriously.

Chicago made efforts to repeal the law very early on. In 1922, when election season rolled around, there was an item on the Illinois ballots to allow beer and light wines. The *Chicago Evening Post* featured an article on Hannah Hanley, who, at 94, was the oldest voter in town. She had come to the United States the year James Buchanan was elected president. "I remember that very well," she said. "But at that time, women didn't have the ballot. It's pretty late in life for me to be voting, but better late than never is my motto . . . While I seldom use any beer or wine myself, I believe that the workingman should have his beer if he needs it. The rich will always have their liquor, and the Volstead act discriminates against the poor. I don't believe that those who take their beer and wine in moderation should suffer for the excesses of those who drink intemperately. So I am going to vote 'Yes' on the little ballot."[227]

The measure went on to pass by a three-to-one margin, but allowing beer again required a change to the U.S. Constitution, not a new state law. So the Chicagoans who wanted booze either had to make their own or buy it from gangsters. Many police officers didn't mind taking their bribes at all.

But the gangsters had enemies as well. One was William "The Hanging Prosecutor" McSwiggin, a twenty-six-year-old assistant state's attorney who'd earned his nickname by getting the death penalty for seven men in eight months. He was one of the toughest attorneys in the state, but in 1925, he failed to get a conviction against gangsters Jim Doherty and Myles O'Donnell, two beer runners who stood accused of murdering a rival beer supplier. You can't win 'em all.

And he'd failed to get the death penalty for John Scalisi and Albert Anselmi, two of Capone's top hit men. But he tried his best, despite getting both death threats and bribe offers from the Capone gang. After a long trial, the state told the jury that the men had to be either hanged or acquitted, and on March 18, 1926, they decided to acquit. The two hit men went free. None of the Prohibition-era gangsters would ever be hanged by the state.

Just over a month after Scalisi and Anselmi went free, on April 27, 1926, Chicagoans were shocked to learn that McSwiggin had been shot to death outside of a saloon in suburban Cicero, where he was hanging out with some of the very gangsters he'd prosecuted in court the year before.

Witnesses said that he and a few members of the O'Donnell gang had just arrived at the saloon in a Lincoln sedan and were walking toward the door when another car pulled up. A hail of machine-gun fire roared from the other car, and McSwiggin and Jim Doherty were hit by seven bullets each. The other O'Donnells hauled the wounded men into a car and drove off. An hour later, their dead bodies were found beside the road in Berwyn.

Orders went out at once to round up every known gangster for questioning, with particular attention paid to those who hung around the Hawthorne Hotel, Capone's headquarters, which was not far from the murder scene. While the police worked, authorities tried to figure out what the heck McSwiggin had been doing in the company of the O'Donnell gang in the first place. The mere fact that he, of all people, had been in a saloon was a stunner and left authorities grasping for explanation.

The first theory was that the hit had been the work of Capone's men, seeking revenge for his recent prosecution of Scalisi and Anselmi. Why McSwiggin was at the saloon in the first place, though, was not covered by this theory.

The second theory was that McSwiggin had been out gathering evidence for an upcoming case and just happened to be in the wrong place at the wrong time. A combined theory was that McSwiggin had been gathering evidence, and Capone had gotten wind of it and decided to kill both some rival gangsters *and* the hanging prosecutor in one blow.

The third theory, which no one wanted to say out loud, was that McSwiggin might have been better friends with the gangsters than anyone knew. Even though he'd worked against them in court, Doherty and O'Donnell were both boyhood pals of McSwiggin and still on friendly terms with him outside of the court room.[228] Suddenly, the fact that he didn't get a conviction against them seemed suspicious. If the public couldn't trust McSwiggin to be on the side of law and order, could they trust anyone?

Leaving the question of what McSwiggin was up to aside, all witnesses early on pointed to Al Capone as the man responsible for the shooting—not just as the man who'd ordered the killing, but perhaps as the actual trigger man, which would have been very unusual by then, but not unheard of. A hardware dealer confessed to having sold Thompson submachine guns to the Capone gang (you could buy them at hardware stores in those days), and the gang's motives were obvious. The O'Donnell gang had been trying to compete with Capone, selling booze in Cicero at lower prices than he was, and McSwiggin had just tried to have his two top hit men hanged. Hence, Capone had a motive to kill everyone present that night. Why he did the dirty work himself

Al Capone, 1930.

instead of farming it out was anyone's guess; perhaps he just wanted to show how it was done.

On May 2, the *Tribune* announced that the authorities believed that "Scarface Al Brown, whose real name is Caponi," was the killer. Though Capone had left town immediately after the shooting, authorities raided one of his former hideouts on Harlem Avenue and found eighty cases of ale, over six hundred gallons of booze, and a case of champagne, along with four sticks of dynamite, several firearms, and six slot machines. Pushing a button beneath the bar, a sliding panel opened in a wall to reveal a hiding place large enough for three men. Upstairs, in the section of the building formerly used as a brothel, there were secret panels and trap doors everywhere. Witnesses had even seen Capone around the saloon where McSwiggin was shot with a machine gun that had been hidden in a panel in the restaurant wall.

Another raid at Capone's brother Ralph's house revealed a whole arsenal, including rifles disguised as curtain rods and hidden compartments full of weapons. Detective John W. Norton led the raid and posed for the *Tribune* with a stack of guns; one has to wonder if he thought of his days investigating the H. H. Holmes building as he peered into the secret passages in the castle of Ralph Capone.

On July 27, after evading authorities for three months, Capone announced that he was going to turn himself in.

"Sometime in the forenoon, I will go with Mr. Roche to the federal building," he said, exhibiting the flair for PR that he'd miraculously developed in the four years since his drunk-driving escapades. "We have been talking by long distance telephone and I think the time is ripe for me to prove my innocence of the charges that have been made against me. I'm no squawker, but I'll tell what I know about this case. All I ask is a chance to prove that I had nothing to do with the killing of my friend, Assistant State's Attorney Bill McSwiggin . . . I trust my attorneys to see that I'm treated like a human being and not pushed around by a lot of coppers with axes to grind."

This was Capone as a master spin doctor, and people ate his story up. Chicagoans were not only eager to believe that the man they'd been buying booze from wasn't really such a monster; they also loved the idea that he was actually friendly with the state's attorney who'd prosecuted his friends. It played into the old-time romantic notions of warfare as a conflict between equals who respected, even liked, one other, but happened to be doing their duties for opposite sides.

"Just ten days before he was killed, I talked with McSwiggin," Capone said. "Doherty and Duffy were my friends, too. I wasn't out to get them. Why, I used to lend Doherty money. Big-hearted Al, I was, just helping out a friend."[229]

The next day, Capone turned himself in and was locked in jail overnight. The following morning, he was set free due to a lack of evidence and left the jail guarded by the same cops who had been hunting him for months.

McSwiggin's father, a police sergeant, was furious. "They pinned a medal on him and turned him loose," he growled.[230] He was so convinced that it was Capone who killed his son that, according to a legend that circulated in the 1930s, he walked right into the Hawthorne Hotel and accused Capone face to face. The story went that Capone didn't even flinch, but took a revolver from a holster and handed it to Sergeant McSwiggin. "If you really believe that," he said, "you ought to shoot me." But the sergeant didn't shoot.[231]

Indeed, Sergeant McSwiggin had been working the case hard, and the state's attorneys were convinced that he had information proving Capone was the shooter. But for one reason or another, he refused to share it. Though several witnesses were said to have fingered Capone, along with his brother Ralph and his bodyguard, Frank Rio, in the McSwiggin killing, no one was willing to point them out in court.

And so the exact circumstances of McSwiggin's murder remain in doubt. If Capone didn't kill him, who did? Any why? And, even more cryptically, why had McSwiggin been hanging around with the O'Donnell gang? Was he really secretly in cahoots with them, just old friends who took the gloves off outside of court, or did he just have the misfortune to be gathering evidence from gangsters when their rivals came to kill them?

The investigation into his murder did yield dividends for the police: among the items confiscated was a bookkeeping ledger showing that Capone was earning money.

And not paying taxes on it.

It would be a few years before anyone put all the pieces together, but that ledger would eventually bring Capone's reign to an end.

Did the Murder of "Tony the Greek" End a Gang Truce?

"One by one, the roses fall," said a wistful bartender when given the news that Big Jim Colosimo had been slain.[232] That was 1920. The roses were just *starting* to fall.

Some time after the McSwiggin killing in 1926, Capone ordered a hit on Hymie Weiss and Vinnie "The Schemer" Drucci, two of the North Siders who had ambushed his mentor the year before. The two were shot at on Michigan Avenue, but survived.

Taking their turn for revenge, one September evening, a caravan of eight cars drove past the Hawthorne Hotel, Capone's Cicero headquarters, and sprayed it with machine gun fire. More than a thousand bullets were shot into the place; that no one was killed was nothing short of a miracle. Capone hit the deck and stayed beneath the bullets that were meant for him.

Now it was his gang's move, and they took it by shooting O'Banion ally Hymie Weiss to death outside of Holy Name Cathedral in October 1926, across the street from the old flower shop. An outstanding, but untrue, legend states that there's still a bullet hole in the cornerstone (Tommy gun shots don't leave such neat little holes; my understanding is that the hole people mistake for a bullet hole is an old plaque holder).

By this time, after something like a hundred men had been killed in the Beer Wars, there came a movement to negotiate a truce between the gangs.

The North Siders, then led by Drucci and George "Bugs" Moran, met with Al Capone, Frank "The Enforcer" Nitti, and Jack "Greasy Thumb" Guzik from the South Side and agreed to put a halt to the violence. All past killings would be thought of as closed incidents; there would be no more revenge taken. From there on, they would go back to Torrio's old rules of respecting territories, and all discipline would be taken care of internally.

The two sides celebrated the armistice at an Italian restaurant, where a neutral party later told a reporter what sort of conversation went on at this "feast of ghouls."

"Remember that night eight months ago when your car was chased by one of ours?"

"I sure do!"

"Well, we were going to kill you that night, but you had a woman with you."

"Haha!"[233]

The peace conference was a better success than anyone would have guessed. No one wanted to keep shooting. The truce would last for several months.

But in 1927, right in the middle of the armistice, the corpse of a man was found covered in snow in a lonely spot in South Chicago Heights. His body was riddled with bullet holes and had been burned almost beyond recognition. Word had it that the body was that of Tony the Greek, a Capone ally. It looked like the peace treaty had come to an end.

Theodore "Tony the Greek" Anton was a former prize fighter, and had lately been the owner of the Hawthorne Hotel, making him Capone's landlord. On a late November night in 1926, a month after the peace conference, he'd gone home carrying over a thousand dollars worth of jewelry. When a knock came to the door, he stepped outside and was never seen alive again.

Four days later, a bloody coat was found in the snow, near what appeared to be an attempt at digging a shallow grave that someone had started to dig, then abandoned when they found the frozen ground too hard to dig into. The body couldn't be found, but it appeared that Anton had been, in gang lingo, "taken for a ride."[234]

Nearly two weeks later, a burned and bullet-ridden body was found in South Chicago Heights.

Though police insisted that the body was that of the missing Anton, witnesses at the inquest cast strong doubts. A dentist said that the teeth weren't Anton's, and one of Anton's old prizefighting buddies said that the feet of the dead man lacked a deformity that Anton had. And the corpse appeared to have been wearing a brown suit; Anton had been wearing a blue one when he disappeared.

This was enough that gangsters were able to insist that the treaty was still in effect and had not been violated. Tony the Greek was still missing, but the man who'd been taken for a ride wasn't him.

In January 1927, though, three boys were wandering in the prairie near the Calumet river when they found a rope end sticking out of the snow. Playing detective, they followed it to its other end, which turned out to be around the thigh of a man who'd been buried in a shallow grave. The man, it seemed, had been tossed in the river, then fished back out by the killers before they buried him. A bullet had been fired just below his left eye.

A paper bag full of quicklime was drawn over the head, and the middle finger had been cut off, apparently in attempt to destroy the remains before they could be identified.[235] But quicklime doesn't eat away at the flesh in real life the way it does in mystery novels; in fact, it can actually slow putrefecation. The body still had visible cauliflower ears. Further, it was remembered that Anton had worn a diamond ring on the finger that was cut off. This time, no one seemed to doubt that the body was that of Tony the Greek.

Capone was devastated, but helpless. Under the terms of the peace treaty, discipline was up to Drucci and Moran.

And, in any case, it may have been that it wasn't even a gang killing. Though it was awfully brutal for a simple robbery, the killers may have simply been people out to steal Anton's rings.

No arrests were ever made, no suspects ever brought in, and the mystery of who killed Tony and why remains a cold case.

The plaque holder often said to be a bullet hole at Holy Name Cathedral.

Who Was the Chicago
Hangman?

In 1927, Harry Stanton, the gallows builder, retired. He'd built and taken apart the scaffold on which men were hanged more than seventy times. "I've had enough of this job," he said. "And I'm going out to California and take a rest."[236] His official job had been "chief plumber of the jail and Criminal Court," but in the future, the city would need an electrician, not a plumber, to assist with executions. The state of Illinois was switching to the electric chair.

As the gallows were taken down for the last time and put in storage in case they ever needed to be brought back for the still-missing Tommy O'Connor, a mystery went with them: who was the Chicago hangman?

The city went through several gallows and scaffolds over the past fifty years, but every model since the late 1870s contained a little compartment, variously known as a "penthouse" or "sentry box," at the back, ornamented only by a small black window. An occupant—the hangman—could see out, but no one could see in. When the sheriff gave a signal, the man inside would enact the mechanism that activated the trap door and sent the condemned to their death. No one ever reported seeing a man enter or leave the box, and reporters who attended hangings sometimes made a parlor game out of guessing who "Monsieur de Chicago" was.

In 1936, former jail physician Frank McNamara said that the sentry box was just a ruse. "There was nothing in the sentry box except a mechanism with a heavy knife blade, sharp as a razor, for cutting the rope," he said. "The jailer, standing on the scaffold behind one of the deputy sherifs or jail guards, sprung the drop by pulling out a knob on the side of the penthouse. So much for the mythology of 'Monsieur de Chicago.'"[237]

But was the box *always* empty? It was in use for more than fifty years, and sometimes reports of hangings make it seem as though jailer and sheriff were nowhere near the box when the trap door fell.

Certainly Chicago didn't have an official *expert* hangman who would take measurements, prepare ropes, and know exactly how far to drop convicts to ensure that their necks were broken instantly. Such scientific methods were generally unknown in American cities; the person in the sentry box would have simply been the man who activated the trap door.

Hangings in Chicago were generally a group effort. Usually the sheriff would prepare the rope, though in the case of the first hanging, back in 1840, it was prepared by "Black George" White, the town crier, and various assistant superintendents and officials took the job of tying the noose occasionally.

Stanton, or someone else in the system, would often assemble the scaffold twice per hanging, first in the alley between the court and the jail the night before (sparking the enduring myth that hangings were held in the alley), just to test it and make sure all the pieces were there. Sandbags would be often be hanged to get the "spring" out of the rope.

The sentry box was first added in 1878, when a new scaffold was built for the hanging of two murderers, Sherry and Connolly. "Back of the drop," wrote the *Inter Ocean*, "about three feet from the main wall, was the false partition, in which hidden from mortal eye was the official who, at a given signal, was to sever with a keen-edged chisel the slender cords, the parting of which would let fall the 'drop' and send two souls out into the great unknown beyond. Who went into that box is, for obvious reasons, kept secret. No one, so far as can be ascertained, saw him enter; no one saw him leave. That mysterious box was, throughout the whole time, the object of much jealous care on the part of Sheriff Kern and his confidential assistants."[238]

In that case, the press said that the Sheriff said, "All ready," and knocked on the wall of the box to give a signal to the man inside. You probably couldn't enact a mechanism simply by knocking on the wall.

The sentry box attracted national attention in 1887, when a gallows had to be built large enough to hang all five of the anarchists convicted to die for their role in the Haymarket Rally of 1886 (only four were hanged; one bit into a dynamite cap and blew his own brains out

the night before). The jail that day
was crowded with reporters from
all over the country.

"The weird effect [of seeing the
gallows] is heightened," wrote one,
"by the little sentry box, which
is located just back of the trap.
In this is stationed the man who
really is the executioner. Into this
box extends a rope, and at a given
signal the unknown man inside
cuts the ropes with a brand-new
and specially-sharpened chisel of
wide dimensions, by striking the
chisel a heavy blow with a mallet.
Down goes the trap a distance
of six feet, and at the same time
the murderers are launched into
eternity."[239]

Hanging of the Haymarket
anarchists; the "sentry box" is
visible behind the ropes. No photo
of the sentry box has been found,
and it was not present in the
gallows that were sold in the 1970s.

Of the executioner that partic-
ular day, the *Tribune* wrote, "Who was in the box was not revealed by
the officials. The unknown man had entered his hiding place before
any outsiders were allowed to enter the room and had not emerged
when, after the hanging, the visitors were requested to file out at the
other end of the corridor."[240]

In 1888, when Zephyr Davis was hanged, it was said that the drop
fell after Sheriff Matson raised his hand.[241]

Different accounts of other hangings sometimes seem to confirm
McNamara's statement, and sometimes go against it. Accounts of the
1882 hanging of James Tracy refer to the sheriff pulling a knotted rope
projecting from the compartment, which sounds like more of a way of
activating a mechanism than giving a signal. This method seems to
have stuck; when Patrick Pendergast was hanged for the assassination of
Mayor Carter Harrison in 1894, the *Tribune* noted that, "Jailer Morris
passed back to the sentry box, which occupied the rear of the scaffold,
[and] pulled a cord which gave the signal to the mean concealed inside,
whose duty it was to cut the rope, which released the trap."[242] That

same year, when George Painter
was hanged, there was a similar
note in the press; Morris pulled a
"signal rope on the executioner's
box."

But as late as the 1920s, there
are accounts of the sheriff stepping
off the scaffold before the drop fell.

It may be that the sentry box
originally did contain a hidden
executioner who made the final
move to set off the trap door, but
his job was phased out or made
optional as modifications were
added. Adjustments to the gallows

The gallows erected for George
Painter, with the sentry box
clearly visible.

were made constantly; at one point the carpenters tweaked it so that
the falling trap door wouldn't make the loud "bang" that spectators
always found disturbing. One scaffold was made that used no nails
or screws, only interlocking parts, so prisoners wouldn't have to hear
it being hammered together (many prisoners reported hearing ghostly
sounds of the scaffold being built night after night, even when no such
construction was taking place).

But backing up McNamara's claim, it seems that no one ever saw
anyone go into the box, and no one ever saw anyone come out. If there
was a Chicago hangman, his identity was successfully kept a secret.

The St. Valentine's Day Massacre

The truce between gangs lasted longer than most might have expected, but it didn't last forever. The roses kept falling.

In 1927, Vinnie "The Schemer" Drucci was shot down by a cop who said Drucci was reaching for his gun; plenty of people doubted the cop's story, but everyone was happy enough to have Drucci out of the way that no one put up much of a fuss. This left only George "Bugs" Moran left to run the old O'Banion gang on the North Side, and he and Capone went back and forth shooting at each other throughout 1927 and '28.

In February 1929, the *Chicago Tribune* began a weekly series of lengthy articles on the history of the city's gangland. Right after the second article was published came what would become Chicago's most famous gang crime: the St. Valentine's Day Massacre.

The details of what happened on that cold Valentine's Day in 1929 are hazy. Five men from the Moran gang, plus an optometrist who thought it was cool to hang around with gangsters and one mechanic who was sort of a lapsed member, had gathered in the SMC Cartage Company, on North Clark Street. It's generally assumed that they were waiting on Bugs Moran to show up. Instead of their leader, though, a police car drove up, carrying two men dressed in plain clothes and two dressed as cops. The seven men in the garage were lined up against the north wall, as though this were a regular liquor raid. All of them cooperated, without showing any signs of a struggle.

At this point, the details get a little hazy; what's known is that all seven were shot down in one quick spray of bullets. Perhaps the men dressed as cops asked something like, "Which one of you mugs is Bugs Moran?" When no one said anything, since Moran wasn't there, they simply shot all seven of them in one hail of bullets. In my own imagination, the men dressed as cops then lower their guns and say something like, "Keep the change, ya filthy animals."

At this point, the men in plain clothes were marched out at gunpoint by the men dressed as cops, so anyone walking by would have thought they were seeing an ordinary liquor raid. It wasn't until several hours later that someone heard Highball the Dog, chained to an axel, barking and went inside. He ran out screaming, "They're full of dead men in there!"

He wasn't quite correct: One man wasn't dead yet. Francis Gusenberg was still breathing, and the medics were able to get him stabilized enough to talk. Exactly what he said in the hospital is variously reported as, "Coppers did it," or perhaps, "Shot me? Why, nobody shot me."

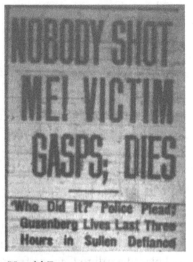

Within an hour, he was dead of having been shot at least ten times.

And so, the one eyewitness who could have possibly named the shooters passed from life, and the St. Valentine's Day Massacre became one of the city's unsolvable crimes. Many such cases went cold

Herald Examiner reports on Gusenberg's last words.

years ago, falling out of the public mind as soon as the next story came along. But when it comes to the massacre, it seems as though there's a new theory every six months. Plenty of people have claimed to have figured out exactly who was in that garage and why over the years, but no explanation has been satisfying enough to stop *more* explanations from being announced.

Early on, it was noted that the killing seemed a lot like the story "Hooch," a Charles Francis Coe short story that had just appeared in the *Saturday Evening Post*. In it, four gangsters were shot in a garage. Some theorized that these killers were wannabe gangsters acting out what they read.

That it was real cops pulling the trigger was a popular theory at first, too; it was well known that plenty of cops had gone corrupt, and rumor had it that the Moran gang had stolen $12,000 worth of liquor from one cop's personal stash. The killings, it was said, had been revenge.

Then there were theories that it was all to do with a power struggle over control of the Laundry and Dyehouse Chaueffers' Union; one of the executives of the union had been killed in November, allegedly by the Moran gang. Maybe it was revenge for *that* crime.

Naturally, police themselves initially suspected Al Capone, Moran's most famous rival. He

A *Herald Examiner* cartoon shows the reaction of crime bosses in Chicago to announcements that police would start cracking down on them.

was in Florida the day of the shooting, so there was no reason to suspect he'd pulled the trigger himself, but investigations showed that someone had placed a call to Capone from the Congress Hotel a little bit before the massacre, and again a little while afterward.

Moran himself had apparently been on the way to the garage when the shooting happened. Seeing the police car, though, he decided to lay low. After the massacre, he fled the city, but let it known that he suspected Capone; he's widely remembered as saying, "Only Capone kills guys like that."

Reached by telephone in Miami, the *Herald Examiner* allegedly quoted Capone as saying, "That fellow Moran isn't called 'Bugs' for nothing. He's crazy if he thinks I had anything to do with that killing. I don't know anything about that shooting, and I don't care. Every time anything happens in that town, I did it. But I've got a good alibi this time. I was living on the beach when it happened, getting sunburned."[243] Though the quote was reprinted in other papers, I couldn't

The crime scene.

find it in the *Herald Examiner* archives; in the edition on file in the microfilm archives, they merely reported that Capone laughed when asked if he'd ordered the massacre. The real source of the quote could be a mystery itself.

Meanwhile, rumors held that Moran was on his way to Florida to get revenge personally.

Even if Capone himself was above suspicion, his gang was not. The most high-profile arrest made in the days after the massacre was "Machine Gun" Jack McGurn, one of Capone's main hit men, who had been holed up in the Stevens Hotel for two weeks. The Gusenberg brothers had tried to kill McGurn more than once, giving him an obvious motive. But his girlfriend swore he'd been in the hotel with her at the time; he later took this "blonde alibi" across state lines to marry her, making it impossible for the state to call her to testify against him. He was eventually released on lack of evidence.

Police also suspected John Scalise and Albert Anselmi, two others Capone had used and for whom he had raised a huge legal defense to save their necks from the gallows after they were arrested for killing a cop in a shootout that followed the killing of one of the Genna Brothers gang. Not exactly the sharpest guys in the world, shooting all seven of the men in the garage, but *not* the presumed target, was exactly the sort of thing they would have done. And this might explain why the two of them were found by the side of the road in Indiana three months later, having been not only shot, but beaten to a pulp by blunt instruments. The official story of their deaths was that Capone had learned that they were trying to take over leadership of the gang and had them taken out, but perhaps they were really killed as a punishment for the botched massacre, which brought a world of heat down on Capone while failing to eliminate Moran himself.

When he himself was arrested in Philadelphia almost immediately after stepping off the train that spring and sentenced to a year in Eastern State Penitentiary, it was widely believed that he had gotten caught and imprisoned on purpose. After the massacre, a Philadelphia prison was simply a safer place to cool off.

Back in Chicago, detectives kept at work. An angry wife told police that her husband had been involved in the massacre and most other gang killings from the last several years, but several hours of questioning by Detective John W. Norton (without whom it would hardly seem like a Chicago case by this time) revealed that the man had no information at all.

Other detectives tried to figure out what Reinhardt Schwimmer, the twenty-eight-year-old optometrist who'd been among the victims, was doing in the garage that day. His mother told one group of reporters that he was only friends with the gang, not a gangster, but also told a detective that he "couldn't break away from the gang. He surely would have left them if he had been able to." In one strange side story that's generally been forgotten, Hearst's *Herald Examiner* included a rumor that Mrs. Schwimmer was a fortune teller by trade, and that she had been warning her son that "his doom was coming."[244]

Hearst, incidentally, had been publishing letters in his papers offering a $25,000 reward to anyone who came up with a good "practicable temperance substitute" for the Prohibition laws, then ran several quotes in which people talked about what a great man he was for it. Hearst papers could rarely go a full issue without talking about Hearst. Many issues contained a box of issues the Hearst papers advocated, including proportional representation in the Senate, buying lower California from Mexico, and changing to a thirteen-month calendar with four weeks per month and every holiday falling on Saturday. The thirteenth month, one assumes, would be called something like "Hearstember."

The massacre case eventually went cold, and the gang fell on hard times in the 1930s, when Capone went to Alcatraz and the repeal of Prohibition robbed the gangs of a major revenue stream. Very few gangsters of the era ended up getting rich and staying that way; nearly all of the major players ended up dead or in prison by 1935.

It was in that year that a new lead came in the case. Members of the FBI captured a lower-tier member of the Ma Barker Gang named Byron Bolton in a North Side apartment building, and, when under interrogation regarding the Barker Gang's crimes, he surprised the agents by confessing to a role in the St. Valentine's Day Massacre.

Or, anyway, the *Chicago Evening American* said that he did. Newspapers across the country published conflicting accounts of what Byron's statement said, while the FBI stated, in no uncertain terms, that Bolton had said nothing. Unaware of how the hell the reporters could have even heard, J. Edgar Hoover, head of the Bureau, issued a statement that the *American*'s report was 100 percent incorrect.[245]

Mr. Keenan   - 2 -   8-27-36

Massacre. According to Bolton, Claude Maddox of St. Louis, Tony Capezia of Chicago and a man known as "Shocker" also of St. Louis, burned the Cadillac car after the Massacre.

    Bolton has consistently denied that he personally participated in the Massacre and has expressed a willingness to confront anyone of the individuals named by him, accusing him of participation in this offense.

    In discussing this matter, Bolton has informed Special Agents of this Bureau that at the time of the St. Valentine's Day Massacre, Chief of Detectives Stege of the Chicago Police Department was on the payroll of the Capone Syndicate, receiving $5,000 per week, and kept the members of the syndicate informed as to the whereabouts of Bugs Moran.

               Respectfully,

               John Edgar Hoover,
               Director.

Excerpt from the FBI in which J. Edgar Hoover admits that Bolton spoke of the massacre (which he'd denied six months earlier).

Hoover's comments and letters preserved in the FBI file show that he was angry, paranoid that the press was tapping his phone, and ready to deny anything. When one witness wrote a letter giving information, Hoover wrote back that investigating the massacre wasn't the FBI's job and that the author should contact the Chicago police instead.

But the FBI file also shows that Hoover was lying like a rug; in a letter he wrote in August 1936, to attorney general Joseph Keenan, he not only admitted that Byron had spoken of the massacre, but summarized what he'd said.

In Bolton's version of the story, the massacre had been planned by the Capone gang simply to eliminate the Moran gang. Capone himself had met with several others in a resort at Cranberry Lake, Wisconsin. Jimmy McCrussen and Jimmy "The Swede" Moran were selected as lookouts, along with Bolton himself, and Capone went to Florida just to be above suspicion. Fred Goetz, Gus Winkler, Fred "Killer" Burke, Ray Nugent, and Bob Carey, all members of the "Purple Gang" of Detroit, were in charge of the actual shooting, and shot everyone present because they didn't know Moran on sight. Bolton also noted that John Stege, the chief of detectives in Chicago at the time, was getting about $5,000 a week from Capone.[246]

Enough of the information Bolton gave (according to Hoover) held up to fact-checking that many authorities who'd investigated the story in 1929 said that it looked about right, and matched up with several unproven assertions they'd collected, but couldn't prove, at the time. Many figured that the case had now been explained.

But new theories continue to emerge. Another story from the FBI file was later popularized in Jonathan Eig's hit 2010 book, *Get Capone*. After the Bolton confession, a man named Frank Farrell wrote to the FBI purporting to tell the real story. According to his letter, the real shooter was William "Three Finger" White. In November 1928, one William Davern, Jr., the son of a Chicago cop, had been shot to death at the C and O restaurant, a known North Side mob hangout. On his deathbed, Davern had allegedly told his cousin, WIlliam White, who the shooters were, and White had carried out the shooting in reliation, with help from Davern's father, the cop, who provided the uniforms, the car, and the means to get the police to look the other way. Capone, in this version, had nothing to do with it, just as he'd always claimed.

After *Chicago* magazine excerpted Eig's version of the story in 2010, the "It Wasn't Capone" angle briefly became one of the most popular theories about the massacre. But historians had known of the story ever since the FBI file was released and had long since brushed it off as a dead end. Three Finger White was in prison at the time of the massacre.

Bolton's confession still seems like the closest explanation to what happened, but it's beyond doubt that soon another theory will emerge that purports to tell the *real* story of the most famous morning in Chicago's gangland history, and the next year it will be (if you'll pardon the pun) shot full of holes when another theory comes along.

The whole affair has an important postscript: it was after the massacre that Herbert Hoover, newly elected president, was finally persuaded that federal attention had to be given to the gangs, as the local police were powerless against them. In 1931, Capone was finally brought in on tax-evasion charges, using the information from the bookkeeping ledger found during the raids after the 1926 slaying of William McSwiggin. John Norton, newly minted chief of detectives after decades on the force, was in charge of crowd control outside of the courthouse when Capone went to trial.

A regular parade of tailors and salespeople from Marshall Field came to testify about Capone's lavish spending. In the process, a mystery that perhaps no one thought to wonder about was solved: what kind of underwear did Al Capone wear? M. J. Oles, assistant buyer of the men's underwear department, provided the answer: He favored union suits— combination undershirts and long johns—made of ladies' hand-glove silk, custom made for him at a price of $12 a suit.[247]

Capone's income was established, and he was convicted for his failure to pay taxes on it. He did his time in Atlanta, and then in Alcatraz, before dying at his estate in Miami in 1947.

The Woman in Black
at the Drake Hotel

In the old days, it was common for well-to-do people to take up full-time residence in luxury hotels. Several gangsters—from different gangs—all lived in the Congress Hotel at the same time in the 1920s, before the gang war really heated up.

The Drake Hotel. *Photo by author.*

And in 1944, Adele Born Williams, a society matron, maintained an apartment in room 836 in the Drake Hotel, one of the jewels of the Magnificent Mile. Her husband, a Washington diplomat, was usually away from home.

In January of that year, she stepped into her apartment with her daughter. As they did, an old woman in a black Persian lamb coat stepped out of the bathroom, silently drew an antique pistol from her purse, and fired two shots at Williams's daughter. When both shots missed, she fired several more at Mrs. Williams herself, mortally wounding her before running away down the eighth-floor hall.

The mysterious woman in black made her escape, and was never found.

Mrs. Williams lived long enough to confirm that she didn't know who the woman was, or what she could have wanted. Nothing was stolen from her apartment, and no motive could be established.

Police Lieutenant Quinn initially believed that there had been no woman in black at all, and that Mrs. Williams had been shot by her daughter, who, he suspected, wanted to kill her mother before she could rewrite her will. But witnesses refuted his version of the story; a few people had seen the woman in black fleeing. "I could have tripped her," said one, "but I'm not in the habit of tripping strange women."[248]

Quinn, who would go on to help get the "stop and frisk" bill passed, kept pushing his own theory and accusing Mrs. Williams's daughter, even swearing that there wouldn't have been room in the bathroom for an old woman to hide with the ironing board down, a claim that was very easily refuted. Phone records show that just before the murder, someone in Mrs. Williams's room had made a phone call to a nearby seafood joint, further disproving the notion that there had been no third party in the room.

As police combed the building, the story only got stranger.

Detectives searched all of the stairwells immediately and found nothing. But when they searched again, they found the murder weapon on a lower floor, shattered from having been dropped from a much higher one. Either they'd missed it the first time, or someone had brought it back to the scene of the crime to dispose of it.

A spare key that was missing from the front desk turned back up on the manager's desk a few hours later.

The antique firearm was traced to one Walter Brown, who was currently in prison and certainly not a likely suspect.

But the gun also seemed to have been used in a hold-up by Brown's sister, Ellen Bennett, who just happened to be working the key desk at the Drake Hotel.

Ellen, whose name was officially Ellen Valanis-Bennett-Larksworthy-Welch, quickly became the most interesting person in the story. At fifteen, she'd married an actor nearly four times her age; a son she had with him couldn't be located. She'd enrolled at Northwestern University after assuming the identity of a friend who'd graduated high school, and had embarked on a minor life of crime, donning blonde wigs over her own red hair to mug people. She'd remarried in Milwaukee, tried to defraud an insurance company, then left her husband, who was murdered shortly thereafter in a case that remained unsolved.

By 1944, she was in her forties and going by the name of Ellen Murphy while she lived and worked in the Drake Hotel. The woman in black would presumably have gotten the spare key to Mrs. Williams's room from Ellen's desk, but Ellen claimed not to know anything about it.

Evidence connecting her to the crime was fairly strong. Two weeks before the murder, a call had been made from Ellen's room to the same seafood place that had been called from Mrs. Williams's room just before the murder. She was eventually arrested for the murder of Mrs. Williams twice, but was freed due to lack of evidence on both occasions. She passed a lie-detector test several times, as did her sister, Anna Minck, who was also briefly a suspect, and without a solid case against either of them, the police hit a dead end on the case.

In November, the authorities received a letter signed by Private D. J. Haritopulis, a young soldier stationed in Massachusetts. "I killed Mrs. Adele Born Williams," it said. "Believe me, this is the first time I killed anyone, and my conscience is driving me crazy, slow but sure." Detectives got excited for a minute, but it turned out that one of the other privates at Camp Edwards had written the letter himself and signed D. J.'s name as a prank.[249]

On the first anniversary of Mrs. Williams's death, there was still no solution. Police publicly promised that one day, the case would be solved, but it never was. For years, the newspapers retold the story every time the anniversary rolled around, speculating that some old woman could still be living in the city and harboring a terrible secret, but that woman failed to emerge.

In 1955, another society matron, Marion Thorne, was involved in hearings over her son's estate, and the attorney, surprising everyone, launched into a series of questions connecting her to the Drake Hotel murder. Apparently the attorney had found out that Williams had spoken with Mrs. Thorne's late husband the night before he died in 1938, and that Mr. Thorne had had an impressive gun collection.

"Did you ever have a Persian lamb coat?" he asked.

"No," replied Mrs. Thorne.

"Did you ever have occasion to *burn* a Persian lamb coat?"

"If I didn't have it, how could I burn it?"[250]

More than thirty years later, upon his retirement, Lieutentant Quinnn (by then Captain Quinn) looked back on the woman in black murder as "the most intriguing case I ever worked on."[251]

Looking back at this case, that Ellen Bennett was the culprit seems like the most likely explanation, even if a solid case about her could never be built. Again, one imagines that in today's world, traces of her DNA might have been found around Mrs. Williams's room and made a more scientific case against her.

What became of Ellen is a question I've never been able to answer; the periodic follow-ups on the case never mentioned her present whereabouts. I've always liked to imagine that as late as the 1990s, perhaps, when she would have been in her nineties, she was still hanging around in seedy Chicago bars, working con games on far younger men.

Was the "Lipstick Killer" Innocent?

Officially, the "Lipstick Killer" is not an unsolved mystery. The police and the state were sure they had their man. William Heirens confessed to the three "lipstick" murders in 1946, and he spent the next sixty-five years in prison.

But many people have never been satisfied that Heirens was really guilty. He recanted the confession almost immediately, and the conditions under which the police got him to make it in the first place made the old "sweat box" stories look like an amateur hour.

The first of the killings Heirens was charged with was committed in June 1945. Forty-five-year-old Josephine Ross was found stabbed to death in her apartment, her clenched fists full of dark hair that she'd ripped from the head of her assailant in the struggle. There was nothing sensational about the crime, really. It didn't even make the front page of the papers. But there were some unusual features in the case; for instance, nothing was taken from Josephine's apartment. And everyone the police could imagine as a suspect had an alibi. After investigating, police had no supsects and no motive.

Six months later, divorcee Frances Brown was found with a knife sticking out of her neck, one of several stab wounds, and a bullet hole in her head. Again, nothing had been stolen, but this time, there was a clue: Besides the bloody fingerprints found about the scene, the killer had taken a tube of lipstick and scrawled a message on the wall:

> For heavens
> sake catch me
> before I kill more
> I cannot control myself.

That was the sort of feature that made a murder marketable. Papers soon bestowed the murderer with a name: the "Lipstick Killer."

A third victim, a young girl named Suzanne Degnan, disappeared in January 1946. After several false leads, an anonymous tip led the police to search the sewers, where they found her severed head and much of her dismembered body. This time, no cryptic clue was required to bring the story to the front pages. This was one of those murders that people who were children at the time would remember as a turning point: the day their parents first began to lock their doors at night.

And this time, there were a number of witnesses who indicated that the killer had been a woman or, in some versions, a man dressed as a woman.

For some months after, the police would periodically announce that they'd captured the killer at last, but none of the arrests went anywhere. By the end of April, nearly four hundred suspects had been questioned. Everyone passed the polygraph test.

Finally, in June, the police apprehended seventeen-year-old William Heirens in the middle of a botched burglary attempt. Opinions differ as to whether Heirens tried to flee (as he claimed) or if he turned a gun on the police (as the police claimed), but in the chase, he was knocked unconcious by, of all things, an officer dropping flower pots on his head from above.

Days later, under interrogation, Heirens admitted to killing Degnan and was soon charged with the other two murders as well.

Now, whether Heirens was truly guilty or not is the subject of some debate, and both sides are currently able to make a fairly convincing case. But it is beyond doubt that the methods of interrogation used on Heirens were the sort of things that could get you put on trial for war crimes. He was cuffed to a

Heirens being booked; he collapsed seconds after this photo was taken.

hotel bed when he woke up from having flower pots dropped on his head, and for several days he was probably abused and denied food, drink, or the chance to contact his parents or a lawyer. He was pumped full of sodium penthothal, sometimes known as "truth serum," without a warrant or consent. He was given a spinal tap without anaesthesia. On his fifth day in custody, he was taken from the hospital to police headquarters, but was too broken and pained even to undergo a polygraph test at first. When he recovered sufficiently to take one, the results were inconclusive.

The full transcript of the confession he made under sodium pentathol was lost (of course), but in it he allegedly told the police of an alternate personality named "George" who had been in control of his body when he committed the murders.

At first, authorities seemed to think that the confession about the alternate personality was just Heirens setting himself up to plead insanity, but the confession began to get publicity, and theories that Heirens was not just Susan's killer, but the "Lipstick Killer" himself, began to gain traction around the city. The press, in particular, absolutely loved the idea that Heirens was a well-groomed, studious boy who had an alternate personality who killed people. Using anonymous sources and rumors reported as fact, the public was soon convinced of Heiren's guilt.

There was some hard evidence, too. A bloody fingerprint found at a crime scene seemed to match Heiren's prints, though not *quite* well enough to be considered conclusive. A scrapbook full of Nazi pictures was found in his dorm; it had been burgled from a veteran who lived near the Degnan family. A gun Heirens had in his possession was found to be linked to an unsolved shooting.

But the hard evidence was hardly noted compared to the thrilling confession. By the time the case went to trial, the Chicago papers were being criticized around the world for having tried and convicted Heirens already.

His lawyers, who believed he was guilty from the start, convinced him that his best bet was a plea bargain. If he signed a confession, he would get life in prison, but would at least save himself from the electric chair. He signed the confession, but immediateley retracted it, then again admitted that he'd committed the three murders.

At the end of his trial, he was sentenced to three consecutive life sentences, and was already back to saying that he was innocent before he was even taken from the courthouse to the prison. Once incarcerated, though, he seemed resigned to the fact that he was never getting out. Older inmates advised him to walk slowly, drink a lot of water, and take up smoking. His girlfriend promised to send a photograph, but then cut off all contact, as did the rest of his friends and everyone else in his life.

Except the reporters.

Heirens spent the rest of his life taking college courses by correspondence (he was the first prisoner in the state to earn a degree behind bars), and he eventually even worked as a sort of "jailhouse lawyer," helping prisoners with their own appeals. But his attempts at clemency for his own case were never successful; he would remain in prison until his death in 2012.

Since his arrest, nearly every piece of evidence against him has been brought into question. The fingerprint, in particular, has been proven and disproven time and again.

A reporter who visited him in prison in 2008 found him a grouchy man with an obvious distrust of reporters. At seventy-nine, he was in failing health, suffering from a fading memory, particularly of more recent years, when one day had pretty much been the same as the day before. But he remembered June 25, 1946, his last day of freedom. He'd been at a party for an uncle who'd just returned from fighting in World War II.[252]

By then, Heirens had been in and out of correctional facilities for burglary and other small raps; breaking into homes and taking whatever he could find was a habit he couldn't seem to break. On the day he was taken, he said, he had a revolver with him because he was planning on carrying an awful lot of cash; he was intending to cash in some savings bonds. When the post office was closed, he broke into a house to steal enough money to take his girlfriend on a date. It was during that burglary that he was caught.

His memories of the next several days, when he was strapped to a bed and pretending to be out cold as much as he could, were hazy. He remembered his fingerprints being taken. He remembered police hovering over him, asking how he killed Susan Degnan. And he remembered a male nurse pouring ether on his genitals while encouraging him to confess. By that time, unbeknownst to Heirens, the police had already told the press they'd caught Susan's killer. He didn't scream until the fifth day, when he was given the spinal tap. It was then that he thought about confessing to whatever they'd accused him of, just to bring the ordeal to an end.

More than six long decades later, he was still "mad as hell," but resigned to his fate. As early as 1965, the parole board had told him that "[t]here are just too damn many people that remember the case. You have to just allow time to be in your favor on this." At the time, the case was certainly well remembered in the city. It had served as the basis of Charles Einstein's 1953 novel, *The Bloody Spur*, and a 1956 Fritz Lang film, *While the City Sleeps*. Those would help keep the story alive in the public mind.

As all those who had convicted him in the first place died off, though, and the crime was overshadowed by later sensational murders, the results of Heirens's appeals remained the same. His release was ordered once in 1983, but the U.S. Court of Appeals reversed the magistrate's decision before he could set foot out of the prison.

It was not until April 1995 that a defense attorney formally presented the case for Heirens's innocence to the Prisoner Review Board. The attorney, Jed Stone, had all of the surviving evidence analyzed and found it to be very weak. Even the "bloody fingerprint" was quite possibly planted; it appeared to be a "rolled" fingerprint, the kind you'd take at the police station, not the kind a criminal would leave behind by simply touching something. The Stone team also noted that one Richard Thomas had confessed to murderering Degnan, and his handwriting was a better match for that found on Degnan's ransom note than Heirens's own.

Indeed, most[253] of the evidence against him had been discredited, the conditions of his confession were a textbook example of how to get a false confession out of someone, and it was now widely believed that it was a reporter, not the killer, who had scrawled the lipstick message on the wall in the first place. The handwriting on the wall certainly wasn't close to a match for Heirens's own, and it *does* seem a lot more like the kind of note a reporter would imagine a killer leaving than the kind a killer would actually leave.

But any means of *proving* Heirens's innocence, not just introducing a reasonable doubt to his guilt, was long lost by then. The Prisoner Review Board found him guilty again.

In 2002, an attempt was made to have him freed on the grounds that the case against him was flawed; the petition stated that his case "stands out as one of the grossest miscarriages of justice in the history of the United States. His conviction is contaminated by more sources of error—prosecutorial misconduct, police misconduct, incompetent defense counsel, unprecedented prejudicial pre-trial publicity (orchestrated by police and prosecutors), junk science, probably false confessions, and mistaken eyewitness identification—than any other case we have studied."

But the parole board turned him down again, and once again the time after that, telling him in 2007 that God may forgive him, but the state would not.

The various authorities who visited and studied Heirens in prison ended up with mixed opinion about his guilt. Robert Ressler interviewed him as part of an FBI study of serial killers, and noted that while Heirens was "kind of a pathetic old man now," he was convinced that, as a teenager, Heirens had been a psychopath. Steven Drizen of Northwestern Law School worked on Heirens's case for years, and wasn't convinced either way as to his guilt, but leaned toward thinking he was innocent.

In my own review of the case, I'm totally unsure whether or not to think Heirens was guilty. There are two possible explanations: either he became a scapegoat for a police force determined to pin a brutal murder on *somebody*, or they happened to frame a guilty man.

Was There a Shark
in Lake Michigan?

The legend of the Lake Michigan shark has driven an awful lot of people crazy. According to both legend and the Global Shark Attack File, a boy named George Lawson was bitten by a bull shark in Lake Michigan in 1955. In some accounts, Lawson lost a leg in the encounter before being rescued by one John Adler. And yet, no contemporary document has yet been found to establish that the attack really happened; the earliest reports anyone has found came two decades later. Of all the Chicago papers, only the *Tribune*'s articles from 1955 are currently searchable online, but there's no mention of Lawson or a shark attack in them. To some, this is proof positive that it never happened.

But you never know what will and won't make the newspapers. When I compare the different stories in this volume and how they were covered by various papers, it's amazing how stories that were front-page news in one paper weren't even reported in others.

The Global Shark Attack File's source on the story was not exactly academic; it was a 1975 children's book called *Man Eating Sharks* by Felix Dennis. Dennis passed away in 2014, but in 2015 WBEZ, on the trail of Lawson and the shark, got ahold of Christopher Rowley, another author who worked on the book and remembered it well. He'd spent five weeks at the library reading up on sharks for the project; thinking back forty years later, he couldn't remember exactly where he'd read that particular story (*Man Eating Sharks* was not the sort of book that cited all of its sources), but he was pretty sure that it hadn't been invented outright. Some of the stories in the book were, he admitted, less true than others, but he thought the Chicago one was based on fact. "There's too little detail there," he said.[254]

And bull sharks *are* known
to enter freshwater from time
to time. While none has
ever been found as far from
saltwater as Lake Michigan
(at least not in a confirmed
account), it's not completely
inconceivable that one found
its way up the Mississippi
River and into Lake Michigan.
Strange things are found in

A bull shark, photographed by Albert Kok.

Chicagoland waters sometimes; more than one alligator has been found
in "Bubbly Creek," near the Stockyards, over the years.

Even shark sightings aren't completely unprecedented. In 1900, the
Cleveland Leader included a tiny item saying, "Chicago has discovered
a shark in Lake Michigan. This may be simply an advertisement for the
Windy City as a summer resort."[255]

The 1900 sighting may prove just as great a wild goose chase as the
Lawson story; all of the mentions of sharks I could find in Chicago
papers from summer 1900 were about loan sharks. But expanding the
search to papers from other cities did bring up some odd stories, such
as a *Topeka Daily Capital* item saying that "[p]eople hitherto regarded
as sane declared they saw a man-eating shark devouring Andrew Fisher,
a Southern Chicago fisherman, who put out in his boat on Sunday
night and mysteriously disappeared."[256] When Fisher's body was found,
though, it was conspicuously clear of shark bites.

One would think that longtime Chicagoans would have some
memory of the Lawson story if it had been reported at all in 1955—and
perhaps a couple of them did. At the height of *Jaws*-mania in 1975 (not
coincidentally, the year *Man Eating Sharks* was published), someone
wrote to the *Tribune* saying, "I vaguely remember a shark attack in
Lake Michigan. I do believe a young lady was killed, and no one could
figure out how this shark got into the lake. Could you help me out or
did I dream this?"

The *Tribune* believed that the writer was thinking of a time in 1969
when there *were* a few shark rumors, which were eventually found to
have been started after a man who'd been keeping a dead shark in his

freezer ever since he caught it in Florida had tossed the corpse out in the lake as a joke. But, while Richard Stanberry of the Coast Guard told the paper at the time that no attacks had been reported, he *had* heard stories of people putting abandoned live pet sharks into the lake from time to time.[257]

Months later, someone wrote into the *Tribune* asking about the George Lawson story specifically, having seen it in a one-off magazine entitled *Killer Sharks: Jaws of Death*. The *Tribune* contacted the magazine's publisher in Montreal, where a staffer said, "Oh, that. A number of people have asked us about that. We put the magazine together in four days. I think we got the story from some British magazine. Personally, I don't believe it."[258] A few years later, when asked about Lawson again, the *Tribune* simply replied that it was "[p]ure myth."[259]

Seeing as how Felix Dennis was a UK-based magazine publisher, it's quite likely that whatever source the publishers in Montreal were using was either *Man-Eating Sharks* or another Dennis publication. But *Man-Eating Sharks* was a book, not a magazine, so it could be that there's another, earlier article out there someplace that might have served as the source for both *Killer Sharks* and *Man-Eating Sharks*. But it's probably still a source from 1975, not 1955. Perhaps it was a magazine that was more likely to make up stories with little details than Rowley was. This happens a lot in history books that don't insist on primary sources (which could be a lot harder to find in the days before digitization); authors would find a good story and repeat it, unaware that the source was fictional. (Nearly everything said about H. H. Holmes since 1940 has been based on this model.)

All resources in figuring out where the story of George Lawson came from, assuming it wasn't just made up for some 1975 magazine, have not yet been exhausted. There are plenty of local 1955 newspapers left to be examined. Hospital records too, perhaps. But so far, no one has felt it likely enough that anything will really be found to put in the elbow grease to comb through all the records by hand-searching for clues.

Who Killed the
Grimes Sisters?

Few unsolved cases in Chicago today continue to attract as much interest as the 1956 murder of the Grimes sisters. The case officially went
cold decades years ago, but even now groups dedicated to finding more
evidence meet regularly in the city to compare notes, examine new
data, and work toward a solution in one of mid-century Chicago's most
brutal murders.

On December 28, 1956, fifteen-year-old Barbara Grimes and her
thirteen-year-old sister, Patricia (known as "Petey"), left their South
Side home to see *Love Me Tender* at the Brighton Theater on Archer
Avenue. Both were Elvis Presley fanatics; by most accounts they'd
already seen the film fourteen times. A friend sat beside them for a
while, but left before the end.

That friend may have been the last person to see them alive, except
for their killer. When the bus came back to their stop that evening,
Barbara and Petey weren't on it.

Police initially suggested that they'd simply run away or gone off
with boyfriends, but their mother was sure that if they'd left, they
would have taken the new radio they'd gotten for Christmas days
before. Nearly a week passed before the police began to take the case
seriously.

Once the story hit the media, sightings of the girls came in from
everywhere; some reports even suggested they'd taken the bus to
Memphis trying to find Elvis. Classmates said that Petey had told
friends she'd met Elvis in Tennessee before, or was planning to do so
soon, and the rumors seemed strong enough that Chicago police asked
law enforcement in Memphis to get involved. Elvis himself, whom
papers still had to specify was "an ex-truck driver just out of his teens

who has become an idol of many teenagers by gyrating while he sings and strums a guitar,"[260] issued a statement via the press: "If you are good Presley fans, you'll go home and ease your mother's worries."

Lead after lead came in. A junk dealer said he saw the girls in a car with Tennessee plates. Another said he saw them in a car with Wisconsin plates. Soon, about 150 police officers were involved in the search. "Police searched railroad yards, garages, sheds, and almost every conceivable place in which the girls might be hiding or held prisoner," the *Tribune* wrote.[261] Something like ten thousand people were eventually questioned.

Meanwhile, Mrs. Grimes got a number of cruel prank calls, as well as calls castigating her for having let her girls go to see an Elvis movie in the first place, or letting them go out at night. But for teenagers to be out alone at the time was hardly unusual; it was what happened to the Grimes sisters that led a certain generation of Chicagoans to decide that the world had changed, just as a murder of Susan Degnan a decade earlier had. Stories of the sort of prank calls Mrs. Grimes received do a lot of damage to any notion that people were a lot more decent back in the 1950s to start with, though.

None of the leads came to anything until January 22, when a man named Leonard Prescott was driving along German Church Road to suburban Willow Springs to buy groceries. Some of the snow had melted in a thaw, exposing the ground in a wooded area along the road. Prescott saw what he thought were two "store dummies" lying on the ground, but on closer inspection, the dummies proved to be the nude bodies of Barbara and Patricia Grimes, long dead but well preserved by the cold. Exactly how they'd been killed was difficult to determine and is still not really known. Other than some "non-lethal" marks on their bodies, there was no sign of violence, or any evidence that they'd been drugged. The most likely theory was they'd been smothered to death before their bodies were discarded.

Under intense pressure to find a suspect, police initially focused on a drifter who went by the name of "Benny" Bedwell. Picked up on the flimsy tip that the owners of a restaurant where he washed dishes had seen Bedwell and a friend with two girls, he was arrested, interrogated for three days, and forced to sign a lengthy confession saying that he and a man named Frank had killed the girls on January 13.

But Benny was completely illiterate, so a written and signed confession was of little value, and the coroner was quite sure the girls had died well before January 13. Barbara's stomach contained exactly the food her mother said she had eaten just before leaving home on December 28. No traces of alcohol were found in the bodies, which went against the confession's tale of having spent several days on a drinking spree with the girls.

There are any number of stories of people being convicted based on confessions just as demonstrably false as Bedwell's, but this time the suspect was cleared and freed. There was never another meaningful arrest in the case at all.

In 1957, a young woman's naked body was found in the woods by a group of Cub Scouts; a man made a phone call to Mrs. Grimes the day after the other woman's body was found, bragging about the current case and telling what he'd done to her daughters, including personal information that had never been published. A man was convicted who fit the profile of what we would now call a "serial killer"; he was a deranged individual who felt intense sexual pleasure from torturing and killing his victims. The names and phone numbers of two girls who lived near Barbara and Patricia were found in his home, and they told of getting strange phone calls around the time the sisters had vanished from a man who said he read their numbers from the back of bus seats. This clue wasn't exactly a smoking gun; the two names were among dozens the new killer had, and most of the others were numbers of girls who lived nowhere near Barbara and Petey. But as early as 1958 officials were urged by a psychiatrist to quiz him about the slaying of the Grimes sisters. His attorneys blocked any attempts to do so.

The twenty-one-year-old man was convicted and sentenced to ninety-nine years, serving only eleven of them before being released in the 1970s. His name is presently not being published in articles on the case, as his surviving daughters may not know about their father's past as a convict. But the information is out there for researchers, and at least one Chicago historian has uncovered new information connecting him the Grimes sisters' case.

New clues are still being found, and many people hold out hope that the murder of the Grimes sisters is still a crime that can be solved once and for all.

The Kangaroo Scare of 1974

When I was a kid, I read every book on monsters, UFOs, and ghosts they had at the library. Most of them were at least fifteen years out of date and recycled the exact same stories over and over again, seldom citing any sources. Many were actually quite skeptical in tone, now that I've reread some of

Have you seen this marsupial?

them. I didn't care. I devoured them and believed everything. I spent many recesses convincing other kids that the Loch Ness Monster was real and carried out ghost hunts in my friends' houses. I sometimes think that I was less inclined to believe in conspiracies and the paranormal than many of my friends in college and beyond because I got it out of my system early, or at least learned, a bit at a time, to sort out good evidence from bad.

Many of those books contained chapters on assorted "phantom animal" sightings. From time to time, a sort of mass hysteria would break out in which a wild animal such as a mountain lion would be seen around some town far from the animal's natural habitat for a few days, then vanish, like a sort of less-exotic Bigfoot. They were sort of B-list stories, usually—there's no locale in the world where a mountain lion sighting is more interesting than a dinosaur sighting—and now and then they'd try to punch them up by throwing in some theories that perhaps the phantom animals were of supernatural or extraterrestrial origin. Even as a kid, those seemed like a stretch to me.

But nearly all of them, as I remember it, covered Chicago's phantom kangaroo of 1974. It was the most recent outbreak, and certainly the best documented.

On October 18 of that year, a 150-pound marsupial was reported to be seen hopping around Jefferson Park. Residents noticed it while taking their garbage out and informed the police; two officers cornered the animal and wound up, in the *Tribune's* term, "thoroughly kicked for their troubles."

"We were trying to grab him and put handcuffs on him," said Officer Michael Byrne. "He took off, and we chased him for a block and a half before we lost him. He was, well, he was growling at us. It scared the hell out of us, seeing him in a gangway growling."[262]

The *Tribune* thought it was the funniest thing ever, and gleefully posted that the score at the end of the day was Kangaroo - 2, Cops - 0.

The next morning, a thirteen-year-old *Tribune* paperboy came eye to eye with the kangaroo in the early hours of dawn.

"He looked at me, I looked at him, and then away he hopped," said the paperboy, Kenneth Grieshamer. "I wondered if I should tell anybody about it because they might think I was crazy or something, seeing a kangaroo on the corner of Sunnyside and Mulligan."

"Boy, was I glad to hear someone else had seen it, too," said Officer Byrne.

By the end of the day, dozens of Jefferson Parkers had reported seeing a kangaroo in the neighborhood. The nearest zoos did not report any missing kangaroos, which made the whole thing a puzzle that the police had trouble taking seriously. The most they could do was joke around, telling people that any smart kangaroo would find a wooded area to live in, since their diet was similar to that of a deer or an antelope, and "the forest preserves are just a hop, skip, and a jump away."[263]

The police seemed to have done their homework on the creatures, though. Patrolman Edward Brensberger said that if they caught him, they could immobilize him by raising his tail from the ground. "His tail is is stabilizing rod," said Brensberger, whom I imagine was also known as "Officer Science." "He can't hop forward without it."

Where the phantom hopper came from continued to be a mystery; early reports in the *Tribune* said that a woman called the police before the first sighting and told them that her kangaroo had gone missing, but they'd declined to take her number or name down, assuming that it was a prank. Later reports in the same paper said that no such call had been been made.

The *Tribune* rewriting their story that someone had called it in, though, is just one piece of evidence that the whole story was an outright fabrication on their part. The idea of police officers genuinely trying to "slap the cuffs" on a kangaroo strains the imagination, and if they had really been thoroughly kicked by one of them, they would have probably been too busy pawing around on the ground looking for their internal organs to chase it into an alley. Though "kangaroo boxing" was once a common spectacle, the kanagroos were highly trained and wore gloves. Real ones have claws, and their kicks can go right through a person's body.

But, then again, the *Chicago Daily News* said that Byrne was only kicked in the shin and suggested that maybe the animal was really a wallaby, which was smaller and less fearsome.

For a day or two, Chicago was struck by kangaroo fever. Radio stations blasted Rolf Harris's timeless classic, "Tie Me Kangaroo Down, Sport." The national press picked up on the story, and comments came in from everywhere. Sir Laurence McIntyre, the Australian ambassador to the United Nations, suggested a very large net. "I'm not an expert," he admitted, "but I do know they can be bloody dangerous, because they're big."[264]

Randy Rush, a former cowboy in Australia, suggested, apparently with a straight face, that the best way to catch it would be for a searcher to dress up in a female kangaroo skin, approach the fugitive, and perform a mating gesture. (You first, pardner.)[265]

While in town at the end of the week for the United Republican Fund dinner, even newly minted President Ford couldn't resist a wisecrack. "A colleague was telling me there's a kangaroo that's running loose on the North Side," he said. "There's a big controversy over what to do with him when they catch him. The Chicago police want to put him in the zoo and the Chicago Bears want to put him in the backfield. And, of course, the Democrats want to register him at least once."

With Ford's wisecrack, the tale reached what a later generation would call "Peak Phantom Kangaroo." The story couldn't go much further after the president got involved. But sightings continued to trickle in for the rest of the autumn. One woman called in to report that the kangaroo—or something she *thought* must be the kangaroo—was asleep on her porch in the middle of November. Police arrived, ready to grab it by the tail (though one prays that they also had a female kangaroo suit in the car, just in case), and chased the animal out of the doorway, observing that it walked on its hind legs as it scurried under the porch, where it went to sleep again. Tearing apart the porch, they successfully lassoed the intruder and found that it wasn't the kangaroo at all, but a squirrel monkey.

Why there would have been a squirrel monkey on the Northwest Side was not explained.

Eventually, the sightings dried up and the tale became a space-filler in cryptoozoology books, where it had to compete with Bigfoot, Yeti, and other "monsters" that almost every kid in the library thought were more interesting than any kangaroo, phantom or otherwise. Today, most explanations range from "mass hysteria" to a general assumption that the whole thing was a newspaper prank, though now and then someone does suggest a paranormal origin. Almost all modern theories, though, seem to take it for granted that there was no actual kangaroo hopping around. But I don't think it's completely impossible that a kangaroo escaped from someplace and ended up hopping around the Northwest Side; Chicago is no stranger to random runaway animals, after all. In 1892, Duchess the Elephant broke out of the Lincoln Park Zoo and spent the better part of a morning wandering the neighborhood.

And in summer 1897, a hyena named Jim escaped from the zoo and created something of a panic; hyenas are not exactly cuddly creatures. Children were forced to stay indoors. Jim took up residence at Graceland Cemetery for a while, where one terrified groundskeeper said that the hyena was as big as any lion he'd ever seen at the circus, "and looked twice as vicious."[266] He was cornered on the little island in the pond where Burnham is buried, but managed to escape, continuing his reign of terror for nearly a week before being shot outside of on old folks' home in Altenheim.

In 1899, an ostrich got loose from the same zoo and jumped off the high bridge in Lincoln Park, known at the time as "Suicide Bridge." The ostrich was okay.

But all of these wild animals were real, and their point of origin was well known. The same can't be said for the phantom kangaroo of 1974.

It's not the only cryptid ever reported in Chicago, either. From time to time, there used to be stories of a sea serpent in Lake Michigan;

newspapers would spend a day or two on the story every ten years or so from 1867 until 1934, its last known appearance. They never took it particularly seriously, though, and there's a good chance that most of the sightings were invented by a bored reporter, which most people now think is exactly what happened with the kangaroo.

My attempts to locate Kenneth Grieshamer, the paperboy, came to nothing, but I found a retired Chicago cop—who now plays cops on reality shows—named Michael Byrne on Facebook, and reached out to him. He confirmed not only that he was the Michael Byrne quoted in the paper all those years ago, but he also insisted that, despite a general sense today that newspapers must have made the whole thing up, it was all true.

"It was legit, believe it or not," he told me. "I got kicked all over the place!"[267]

New on the force and still in his early twenties at the time, Byrne says he and his partner, Lenny, were patrolling the neighborhood when they saw something jumping over a fence and into an alley. They followed and approached it as Byrne readied his cuffs.

"[Lenny]'s holding a gun," Byrne now laughs, "like a kangaroo is gonna say, 'Oh, he's got a gun. I better do what he says!'"

According to Byrne, several other officers saw the kangaroo, as well, but didn't report it or admit to it, fearing that people would think *they* were out of their minds, too.

"The captain was going crazy," says Byrne. "A little guy from channel two came out and asked me what I'd do if I saw it again, and I said, 'I'll box him into a corner, and take him to kangaroo court.' The cigar dropped out of the chief's mouth."

Byrne was hauled into the chief's office, where the chief roared, "What kind of bullshit is this? Kangaroo court?"

"Well, gee, boss," said Byrne. "You can't take a *kangaroo* to *regular* court."[268]

The chief insisted that Byrne start telling reporters he hadn't really seen it after all, but now, more than forty years later, Byrne is only too happy to insist that it was all true. He even entertained an offer to box a kangaroo on Canadian television recently.

He also believes he knows where the kangaroo came from. Though he isn't naming names, there was a police officer who lived in Jefferson

Park, near where the attack took place, and who also owned a Wisconsin farm on which he kept a couple of kangaroos. Why he would have brought one home is anyone's guess, as the officer didn't report his escape for obvious reasons, but Byrne suggests it was generally known around the station that "it was one of [name withheld]'s kangaroos."

This would be a simple solution to a strange mystery, and it's not an unreasonable one: farm kangaroos in Wisconsin are not exactly *common*, but certainly not unknown. In 2015, a Beaver Dam woman made headlines when she tried to bring one of her five kangaroos into a McDonald's. She, like other kangaroo owners in the state, insists that the animals are far more docile than one might think, especially those bred in captivity. The sort of attack young Officer Byrne withstood from a young, farm-raised kangaroo might have been far less deadly than a battle with a wild adult.

These days, Wisconsin gets—and grants—permits to register a new kangaroo about once every two months. Though I couldn't find records on just how many kangaroos were in Wisconsin in the 1970s, it's not unreasonable to assume that there were probably at least a few dozen, and that one might have belonged to a Chicago cop is probably a more likely answer to the puzzle than some of the ones involving UFOs.

But, as a final thought, it's probably always worth pointing out that the week the kangaroo was first reported, David Bowie performed for three nights at the Arie Crown Theater. No connection can be established, of course, but any time something strange happened and was never explained, investigators would be remiss if they failed to point out that David Bowie was in town at the time.

Was it just a coincidence?

You decide!

Was the Man Who Killed John F. Kennedy Killed on Grand Avenue?

No one has ever actually found a body wearing "cement shoes" in the Chicago River. Though one hears a lot of stories about Al Capone disposing of dead bodies in various ponds and rivers, this wasn't generally his MO; a death no one heard about sent no messages. Bodies were usually dumped someplace where they were sure to be found, or just left lying where they fell.

But few "hits," in organized crime or elsewhere, were ever quite so public as the assassination of Richard Cain, a former Chicago cop who is thought to have been a double agent working for the "outfit." In December 1976, Cain was shot to death in the middle of a Grand Avenue lunch room.

The area around Grand and Racine's days as a "Little Italy" section of Chicago have never quite come to an end. Even though most of the old-time residents and the Italian-American social club have moved on from it today, a number of Italian delis, bakeries, and restaurants still dot the area. In 1976, though, the neighborhood's Italian identity was much stronger. Sitting on the northern edge of the industrial West Loop, the area was still the turf of juvenile greaser gangs with names like the Almighty Gaylords. Mobster Joey "The Clown" Lombardo worked a day job at a neighborhood masonry shop. And the space now occupied by an upscale toffee shop, 1117 West Grand, was the home to Rose's Poor Boy, a sandwich place.

On the day Richard Cain was killed at Rose's, workers were holding down the lunch rush when forty-nine-year-old Cain, a former cop now described by the press as a "hoodlum,"[269] came in. He'd been living in

Mexico recently, but was back in town for reasons unclear; agents who were monitoring him believed he was on some sort of mission from Sam Giancana, the acting head of the outfit. Later stories claim that he was planning on becoming the new Godfather in Chicago.

Diners saw Cain conversing with four men at a table. But then two men in ski masks arrived carrying a shotgun, and the four men with Cain abruptly left. The masked men lined everyone in the restaurant up against the wall. One of them reached for a person who resembled Cain, but was redirected on orders received via walkie-talkie from a man outside.

"Someone's coming," said a voice on the walkie-talkie. Then, seconds later, "All right. It's clear now."

It looked as though the masked men were just going to rob the place, and in some reports they even asked the patrons if anyone had any money. But then Cain was pulled slightly away from the others. One of the gunmen raised his rifle and shot twice, blowing Cain's face off from point-blank range and leaving the other patrons screaming and panicking.

One of the mean reached down and fished something out of the dead man's pocket.[270] The other said, "Coast clear" into the walkie-talkie, and the shooters slipped out, casually walking away on Grand Avenue.

No one in the sandwich shop knew who Cain was; it was only later, at the morgue, that his name was found in the waistband of his trousers. Authorities then realized that the assassinated man was the former policeman who'd spent two years as the city's chief investigator a decade before; during that time, he'd used public money to make suspected mob informers take lie-detector tests. Officially, this was to protect the public. In reality, Cain was finding out who was giving away the secrets of the mob. After he'd been implicated of helping gangsters with a massive drug warehouse robbery, the city had forced his resignation, and he'd spent three years in prison.[271]

Exactly why Cain had been killed years later, though, and who pulled the trigger, would never quite be solved.

Some spread the theory that Cain had switched sides again, and had just alerted detectives that a band of professional burglars was about to pull a heist, leading to the arrest of five of them. Perhaps the killing was retaliation. Really, the quick, painless killing would have been remarkably compassionate, compared to other killings of suspected stool pigeons in those days.

But while the police believed that the killing might very well have been the work of criminals who *thought* Cain had ratted them out, they said that they would have been misinformed; the recent arrests were "the result of outstanding police work and information obtained from other law enforcement agencies." Cain hadn't told the authorities a thing. In fact, they believed he was probably meeting at the sandwich shop to discuss an upcoming burglary he would be taking part in.

Other rumors connected Cain to the April 1973 killing of Sam DeStafano, an old outfit loan shark and fixer. Irrational, sadistic, and even rumored to be a devil worshipper, DeStafano was one of the most twisted and bizarre outfit affiliates in history, which is saying something. His idea of a good time was giving his wife a gun she didn't know wasn't loaded and forcing her to put it in her mouth and pull the trigger. When the FBI came to discuss business with him, he would serve them coffee he'd urinated in. When he finally became a liability to the outfit, he was shot to death in a West Side garage. No one was ever convicted, and now some suggested Cain had been involved, or perhaps that he was simply a person whose death would be an acceptable retaliation in the eyes of DeStafano's allies.

In the 1980s, a gangster-turned-informer told the authorities that the man who shot Cain had been Joey "The Clown" Lombardo (who, in 1985, was defended in court by Harry Busch, the man whose car the still-missing "Terrible Tommy" O'Connor had hijacked more than sixty years before). But when Lombardo was finally brought to trial for other murders in 2007, the Cain accusation didn't really come up.

Other theories suggest something even bigger: According to some, Cain was shot to make sure he never told anyone that he'd fired the shot that killed President Kennedy in 1963 on Sam Giancana's orders.

In 1992, Chuck Giancana wrote a book about his brother entitled *Double Cross: The Explosive, Inside Story of the Mobster Who Controlled America*. According to the Chuck, Cain had been sent to Miami to work with Cuban exiles preparing for the Bay of Pigs invasion, during which time he'd become a full-fledged CIA operative, and it was the CIA who eventually made him second-in-command to the Chicago sheriff. After the Bay of Pigs invasion proved to be a colossal failure, the CIA worried that President Kennedy would strip it of some of its powers. "The outfit and the CIA now shared a common enemy," Giancana wrote. "The President of the United States."[272]

Chuck had heard through the "outfit grapevine" that his brother had recruited a lot of professional hit men from all over the country to assassinate John F. Kennedy and that the CIA had sent in several "soldiers" of their own, as well as Lee Harvey Oswald, the man they intended to frame. Law enforcement official J. D. Tippit would be on hand to kill Oswald under the guise of self-defense in the line of duty, though he failed in the job, leaving them to bring Jack Ruby in to do the job later, under threat of being tortured and killed himself.

According to what Giancana's brother heard, it hadn't been Oswald shooting the gun from the book depository that day in Dallas at all: It was Richard Cain.

"On November 22, 1963," Sam Giancana allegedly said, "the United States had a coup; it's that simple. The government of this country was overthrown by a handful of guys who did their job so damned well . . . not one American even knew it happened. But I know. I know I've guaranteed the outfit's future once and for all."

Even in this account, though, Cain's murder wasn't to silence the man who would have been the most-wanted assassin in American history, but a simple power struggle; Cain had been telling everyone that he was unhappy with Giancana's leadership and was planning to take over the outfit himself. With talk like that, it was only a matter of time before he was taken out. According to Chuck, the killer at Rose's Sandwich Shop had worn mismatched gloves, one white and one black, as a message to Cain that his assassination was coming from both the "white hand" of the CIA and the "black hand" of the outfit.

This is, of course, only one of dozens of theories about what really went on that day in Dallas, and the theories about Cain are far from the most popular among JFK conspiracy theorists. But a great many of them do believe that if the assassin was anyone other than Lee Harvey Oswald, Sam Giancana at least knew who it was. Sam was just about to be brought in to testify to the FBI about links between the CIA and the mafia when he himself was shot to death in his house in 1975. The real reason for *his* killing is unknown as well, but most theories revolve around him knowing too much.

Michael Cain, Richard's half-brother, found no evidence at all to support the theory that Richard had killed President Kennedy, and determined that he had, in fact, been in Chicago on November 22, 1963, testifying before a grand jury. Strangely, this testimony couldn't be confirmed; given Cain's duties in Chicago at the time, one would think that *some* document or another would verify his whereabouts on that day. But conspiracy theorists would probably just believe that the document was fake.

And so, the very public hit on Richard Cain remains the work of unknown men for unknown reasons.

Did a "Voice from Beyond" Finger Teresita Basa's Killer?

On February 21, 1977, Ruth Loeb telephoned Teresita Basa, a coworker at Edgewater Hospital. The two chatted briefly, but Teresita indicated that she had a male visitor, so Ruth didn't keep her on the phone long.

An hour later, Teresita's next-door neighbors smelled something burning and informed the janitor, who found smoke billowing from under the crack in Teresita's door.

When firefighters entered the room, after putting out the rather minor fire, they found Teresita's murdered body lying naked under a mattress that had been set on fire; a kitchen knife was embedded in her chest. The place had been ransacked by her killer, who had apparently removed her clothes to make it look as though a sex crime had taken place (though there proved to be no evidence of sexual assault) and set the place on fire to cover his tracks.

Teresita Basa was a forty-eight-year-old respiratory therapist. Born in the Phillipines, she had come to the United States in the mid-1960s after graduating from St. Scholastica, a college operated by German nuns in Manila, then earned a master's degree in music from Indiana University before studying inhalation therapy in Chicago.[273] In her spare time, she taught piano lessons in her apartment and was writing a book.

Though the story of her death made most of the papers, it didn't become a sensation, and little more was heard of the case for some time after it was first reported. Her body was shipped to the Phillipines for burial, and police seemed to hit a dead end in their investigation.

Detective Joseph Stachula was stumped by the case, but on August 5, nearly six months after the murder, he met with Dr. Jose Chua in the Skokie apartment Chua shared with his wife, Remedios, who worked at the same hospital as Teresita. Before agreeing to give Stachula any information, Chua asked him if he believed in the occult or exorcism.

"As a police investigator," said Stachula, "particularly a homicide investigator, I have come across many strange things. But I have learned from years of experience to keep an open mind."[274]

The Chuas told him a strange story: On three occasions, Remy had been "possessed" by a voice that said "I am Teresita Basa," then gave the name of the killer, as well as all of the details of the crime. The voice had pleaded with Dr. Chua to call the police.

"I was really surprised and scared," said Dr. Chua. "But she told me I had nothing to be scared of . . . she was really pleading for me to help her solve her murder."

"All I remember," Mrs. Chua would later say, "is hearing the name 'Allan.' I just felt cold and thirsty."[275]

Born in the Phillipines, just as Teresita had been, "Remy" would testify in court that she'd had three "seizures" or "possessions" in which the spirit of Teresita Basa spoke through her lips in mid-July, the first coming only hours after her own position at the hospital had been eliminated. Devout Catholics, the Chuas had gone to see two priests. One didn't want to talk about it at all, and another told them that "possessions" only happened in early biblical times. Dr. Chua said he was frightened and embarrassed, but after the third "visit," in which the voice became more insistent, he called the police.

Though Stachula couldn't have taken the tale particularly seriously, he was desperate for clues, and the name the voice had given, "Allan Showery," corresponded with a note he'd found in Teresita's diary: "Get tickets for A. S."[276] "I would not call anyone a liar," he would say. "If they said they heard a voice from God, I would listen. It would be wrong for me to cut off an informant. I talk to pimps, prostitutes, drug addicts in the Belmont area. Dr. and Mrs. Chua are educated, intelligent people who live in a $90,000 house—a distinct change for me. I wanted information on this murder. I listened and acted on what they told me."[277]

The voice, Stachula later said, spoke in Tagalog, Teresita Basa's and Jose Chua's native dialect, which Remy knew, but didn't typically speak around the home.

Allan Showery worked as a respiratory technician for $3.66 an hour at the same hospital where Teresita and Remy were respiratory therapists. According to the voice, he had gone to Teresita's apartment acting like a friend paying a visit, then murdered her to steal her jewelry. Stachula and his partner went to visit the apartment Showery shared with his pregnant common-law wife, Yanka Kalmuk, and noticed a book about ghosts on the shelf.

"Are you superstitious?" asked one of the detectives. "Do you believe in those kind of stories?"

Yanka told them she didn't.

After a discussion in which the detectives made it clear that Showery was not under arrest, they persuaded him to accompany them to headquarters to answer a few questions. Remarkably, after initially denying the accusations, Showery signed a thirteen-page confession.

On further investigation, the detectives found that Yanka had some jewelry identified as having belonged to Teresita. Before hearing about the "voice," the detectives hadn't even known that any jewelry had been taken.

Naturally, Showery's lawyers tried to get his arrest dismissed based on the strange circumstances that had led to it and claimed that the police had threatened him into confessing (which, it was well known by then, was not an unheard-of tactic). But prosecutor Thomas Organ argued that their arrest of Showery was, in the end, based on evidence and his confession. The voice, at most, had just been what led the police to ask him questions.

There was some evidence brought up in the trial that led credence to the defense's claims. Yanka Kalmuk said that Allan had confessed because the officers had threatened to arrest *her* if he didn't. They'd brought her into the station for a "brief, emotional meeting," during which Allan had said, "Honey, I am very sorry, but our relationship is over. We've had a great seven years, but I am responsible for Miss Basa's death. I don't want you to wait for me because I am not coming back. I want you to sell the furniture and make a good life for our child."[278] Showery now said he was "just kidding" when he first made that confession; the prosecuting attorney sneered at the notion, holding up the murder weapon and shouting, "Well, Allan Showery, you weren't kidding when you plunged this knife into Teresita Basa's chest!"[279]

Defense attorneys tried to suggest another narrative; that Mrs. Chua had been the real killer. She had sold Showery the rings, and invented the "psychic episode" after losing her job at the hospital where she, Showery, and Basa had all worked, which, they said, happened to be around the time Showery had been harassing her with crank phone calls. And, certainly, the killer's attempt to make the murder look like a sex crime seems strange, as though there was some motive beyond covering up a simple jewelry burglary.

But Showery and Kalmuk gave conflicting testimony as to where they were the night of the murder, and Mrs. Chua was never truly considered a suspect.

The eight-day trial in January 1979 ended in a mistrial. Before the next trial could begin, Showery shocked the court by changing his plea to guilty and was sentenced to fourteen years in prison.

The case formed the basis for a hit book, *A Voice from the Grave*, self-published by an imprint owned by Dr. O. A. Mercado that he and his wife normally used for publishing medical books. Mercado noted around the time of its late-1979 release that it often seemed as though Teresita's ghost was prodding the production along; while writing the book over ten frantic weeks, the Mercados said they occasionally received phone calls with only silence on the other end, and an editor working on the project once stepped into her office to find her notes spinning around on her desk. Mrs. Mercado also announced plans to accompany Mrs. Chua to other states to see if her "psychic powers" would solve more murders, and noted that there was interest in the film rights.

The other investigations don't seem to have happened, but the Chuas said they would not object to a movie version of their story. "All of us want to believe in life after death," Dr. Chua said. And it did become a film, *Voice from the Grave*, in 1996.

A year after the trial, in the Chuas' first press interview, Dr. Chua said that it had been almost as though *he* were possessed, as well. "I don't know what prompted me to go so near the bed when my wife was in the trance," he said. "It was as if someone pushed me. I asked questions I didn't intend to ask . . . If I knew what was happening, I would have taped her."[280]

Since he didn't, the only record of the "possession" remains Dr. Chua's own testimony. Since the event and its subsequent publicity, the case has frequently been held up as proof of life after death, psychic phenomena, telepathy, demonic possession, or, really, whatever a given person wants to believe was going on.

As evidence of the paranormal, the case would likely be a lot more compelling to skeptics if it could be proven that Remy Chua had no connection at all to Teresita or to Allan Showery, and no way of knowing some of the things that the "voice" said. But, though a few retellings of the story try to make it appear as though this was the case, it was never seriously contended that there was no connection among Teresita Basa, Remy Chua, and Allan Showery. Remy had been to a party at Teresita's apartment before, and her shifts seem to have overlapped with Teresita's more than is sometimes supposed. She was certainly acquainted with Showery on some level, even testifiying that she'd sold him a diamond ring that he'd later returned.[281] Teresita knew him as well; Showery said in his confession that he had been working with Teresita to help her obtain citizenship; the large tips she'd given him for rides to the naturalization office convinced him that she must have a lot of money in the apartment.[282]

For skeptics, it's not difficult simply to assume that Remy Chua must have learned of the murder during the six-month period between the crime and her meeting with the detectives, and that the "possession" was either a ruse of some sort, probably to protect herself, or a psychological episode, not a psychic one. Believers note that the "voice" also apparently gave phone numbers for Teresita's cousins, who identified the jewelry, but this angle doesn't appear in many contemporary accounts of the story, and such phone numbers wouldn't have been impossible to obtain.

The more cynical might even suggest that the Chuas may have seen the story as a chance to make a lot of money, but the amount of stress and risk they put themselves under seems to undermine this explanation a little. Even Stachula and his partner must have taken their story fairly seriously; they were taking a huge risk by even bringing the story up, rather than persuading the Chuas to say that they'd heard information from an unnnamed source (which would have probably worked just as well). *Tribune* reporter John O'Brien, who'd also covered the case for *Ebony* before the trial and who later wrote a book about the case, said that the detectives became the butt of a lot of jokes around the police station. "Paper clips would fly out of nowhere and land on their desks," he said, "and they would find their mail boxes at Area 6 headquarters stuffed with notes to call people who had been dead for years."[283]

The story has been rehashed dozens of times, but neither the Chuas nor Showery seem to have commented on the case since 1980. Dr. Chua, the only witness to the "voice," died in 2002.[284]

Who Was the Tylenol Killer?

You notice some interesting things about people when you work as a tour guide.

For instance, you notice that people will sit casually through stories of hundreds of people dying, but if you mention one dead dog, they get upset.

You notice that a lot of people just come to the city to talk about how crazy anyone who lives in a big city has to be.

And, in my case, I've noticed that an awful lot of people seem to think that the Tylenol murders of 1982, when seven people in Chicago died after taking pills that were laced with cyanide, were solved years ago.

The Tylenol scare has never been a regular story of mine; it's long enough ago that many people on the bus aren't old enough to remember it, but not so far in the past that I'm comfortable making wisecracks about it. Still, when the bus is going to or from the Couch Tomb or the St. Valentine's Day Massacre site, sometimes we have to re-route a little to get around traffic or construction, and we'll end up right by the Walgreens at 1601 N. Wells, where one of the victims bought her contaminated medicine. I'll point it out and summarize the case, noting that they never figured out who was tampering with the Tylenol bottles.

And, almost every time, someone will say, "Yes, they did!" Then they'll explain to me that it had turned out to be a woman trying to kill her husband, or, occasionally, a religious fanatic.

In reality, the identity of the poisoner was never discovered. There is no established motive, and no real suspect. An unknown person, for reasons entirely unclear, added cyanide to several bottles of Tylenol on store shelves around the Chicago metro area, killing seven people.

"My gut feeling," says one firefighter, Richard Keyworth, who worked on the case, "was that their purpose was to bring the United States to its knees. 'Look at the power we have. We can shut down the entire economy. We can control the world.' And for a short period of time, they did. In today's world, it would be domestic terrorism. We didn't have that terminology back then. But it was actually the first case of domestic terrorism in the country."[285]

To call it the "first case" is to overstate things a little, but that may have been the intention behind the poisonings. And it was certainly the result. The scare became international news.

The scandal began in the suburbs. Mary Kellerman, a twelve-year-old girl in Schaumburg, woke up feeling sick; her parents kept her home from school and gave her some Tylenol. She stepped into the bathroom, then dropped unconscious. Paramedics did everything they could, but nothing worked. She was dead by ten o'clock that morning. An autopsy was ordered, but no foul play was suspected at first.

Hours after Mary died, Adam Janus, an Arlington Heighs postal worker, stopped at the Jewel Grocery store to get some Tylenol. After giving his children lunch, he took two of the pills and got on to the couch to lie down. Minutes later, he stumbled into the kitchen and collapsed. He was completely unresponsive when paramedics arrived.

Half an hour after *he* died, Mary Reiner wasn't feeling well at her home in Winfield, where she'd just brought home a week-old baby. She took two Tylenol, then fell to the floor.

Back at the Janus house, where the family was still processing what had happened, Adam's brother, Stanley, was suffering from back pain. Adam's wife brought Stanley the Tylenol; both he and Mrs. Janus took a couple, and both of them collapsed minutes later.

Doctors realized when the Janus family returned to the hospital that something very unusual was happening.

That evening, in Lombard, a woman named Mary McFarland told coworkers she had a bad headache. She went to a back room, took some Tylenol, and promptly collapsed on the floor.

And that night, Paula Price, a United Airlines flight attendant, stopped at the Walgreens in Old Town, the Chicago neighborhood in between the Loop and Lincoln Park, to pick up some painkillers. She would never be seen alive again.

Investigators for the Cook County medical office noticed that the only link at the homes of victims they could find was that each had a pill bottle marked with control number MC2880. "This is a wild stab," said Keyworth, "but maybe it's the Tylenol."[286]

Investigator Nick Pishos mentioned the Tylenol link to Deputy Medical Examiner Edmund Donoghue, who told them to open the bottle and smell the inside.

"The first one smells like the second one," Pishos said. "Almonds."

A chemical apshyxiant that stops oxygen from getting into the blood, cyanide is one of the fastest, most effective poisons in the world. Not everyone can smell it at all, but an almond aroma is a telltale sign for those who can. Lab reports showed that the pills in the Tylenol bottle contained as much as one thousand times the amount necessary to kill.

Within twenty-four hours, half a dozen suburban people were dead. Paula Price would be found in Chicago shortly thereafter; she had taken the pills in a bathroom and died before she'd even left the room.

The findings were immediately announced, and a press conference was given warning people not to take Tylenol for a while. Chicago Mayor Jane Byrne met with all relevant officials and got to work, ordering the printing of fliers in several languages, making sure that the public would be notified before one more person who'd bought medicine before it could be pulled from shelves could be poisoned.

The fact that the cyanide had been in a random handful of bottles from all around the metro area indicated that the bottles had been contaminated while they were on the shelves, not on the supply line, but Johnson & Johnson, Tylenol's parent company, immediately issued a full recall, then set up a toll-free number customers could call with any concerns. Given the nightmare-level publicity the incident brought them, the fact that Tylenol stayed in business at all makes their turn-around something of a public relations miracle.

And as Johnson & Johnson worked to save their brand, officials back in Chicago got to work trying to find a suspect. As the story became an international media sensation, leads poured in—thousands of them. Assistant U.S. Attorney Jeremy Margolis later remembered that trying to make sense of them and connect the dots was "like drinking from a fire hose."

The many people working the case didn't always work together. "It was just nuts," Richard Brzeczek, the Chicago police superintendent, would say. "People will withhold information so they can be the ones to solve the case. They want their names up on the marquee . . . [There was] some cooperation among a few chosen people, but the largesse did not extend to all participants . . . There is a general feeling of antagonism among local law enforcement against the FBI. We call them the one-way street. They want you to provide information, but refuse to divulge their own."[287]

Despite the occasional conflicts, no resource was spared in the investigation, and no one involved could later think of anything they would have done differently. With so many investigators from so many agencies from different jurisdictions working on the case at once, clashes were simply inevitable.

Theories abounded. Former Johnson & Johnson employees who may have been bitter were brought in for questioning. White-collar crime syndicates who may have been trying to lower the price of Johson & Johnson stock were probed. People who'd shoplifted from the places the Tylenol was sold were brought in. Mary Kellerman's address was publicized in an attempt to lure the killer to the scene of the crime.

The best theory was, and probably remains, that the killer had bought the Tylenol fair and square, tampered with a few pills per bottle, then returned to the stores and slipped them back onto the shelves. Scanner databases at the time were not common; if they'd been paid for in cash, there was no way to trace them. But *why* they'd done it could only be guessed at.

The most promising lead came when a man named James Lewis wrote a letter to Johnson & Johnson admitting to the crimes and demanding a million dollars to stop them from happening again. Lewis was captured in December and turned out to be nothing more than a con man who saw an opportunity. Several officials, including the attorney general, continue to this day to think he was involved in the poisoning (DNA samples were collected from him as recently as 2010), but evidence could never be found to back up those beliefs. He was given a thirteen-year sentence for his attempts to extort money from Johnson & Johnson, but in a jailhouse interview, he said, "The Tylenol murderer is still dancing in the streets."

Dan Webb, the U.S. Attorney at the time, looked back on the case and said, "One of the most sensational murder cases this century has gone unsolved because the person who did it randomly killed seven people. If you have no motive, if all you're doing is killing people for no reason whatsoever, then that is likely to be the most perfect murder because there won't be any ties back to you."[288]

Now living on the East Coast, Lewis runs a website—which still looks as though it were designed in 1995, when he was first released—maintaining his innocence and promoting recent theories that the contamination really did occur at some point along the supply chain, though the accusations tend to be brushed off by others as conspiracy theories originally peddled by a former Johnson & Johnson employee who may have an axe to grind.

Eventually, when no further deaths were reported, the story began to fade back into public memory as people either forgot it altogether or thought that it had been solved and dealt with years ago. But for people of my age (that odd generation in between Generation X and the Millennials who never aquired a moniker that stuck) and younger, pill bottles coming with foil seals, tamper-proof lids, and cotton packing are simply a fact of life, all because of a series of unsolved murders from 1982.

Who Was that Masked Man?

Max Headroom was a sci-fi TV show about a future where the world was run by TV networks. The titular character was the computer-generated face of an ultra-smarmy TV host, stuttering out catch phrases and wisecracks in a distorted voice. He was at least popular enough to become a spokesperson for Coca-Cola for a while; I remember him being popular enough that people in school did impressions of him, but I was young enough that when I tried to watch the show, I had no idea what was going on.

Nearly every time people talk about the character now, though, there's a mention of the time a man in a Max Headroom mask somehow hijacked Chicago airwaves. Clips of the broadcast intrusion have been viewed far, far more times on YouTube than clips of the Max Headroom Coke commercials.

It was November 22, 1987. In the middle of the nine o'clock news on WGN, the signal flickered and blacked out. When a picture returned to people's sets, the image was that of a man in a Max Headroom mask bobbing his head around in a halfway-decent impression of how Max appeared on the show. After a few moments, an engineer switched the uplink feed, and the real broadcaster returned. "Well," said announcer Dan Rohn with a laugh, "if you're wondering what's happened, ha ha . . . so am I!"

Two hours later, the Headroom Hacker broke onto the WTTW Public Television feed, interrupting a broadcast of *Dr. Who*. This time, there was sound. "Max" held up a Pepsi can and said, "Catch a wave" (Max's Coke commercial tagline), then tossed it aside. Then he sang a bit of "Your Love Is Fading" by the Temptations and hummed a bit of the *Clutch Cargo* theme.

Then, in reference to WGN's call letters (which stand for world's greatest newspaper; the radio station was broadcast from the Tribune

Tower), he said, "Oh, I just made a giant masterpiece for all of the greatest world newspaper nerds!"

The image then cut to a new scene, in which "Max" had turned to the side and had dropped his pants, exposing a side view of his bare ass. A second person, a

The Headroom Hacker on the air.

woman, used a fly swatter to give him a remarkably wimpy spanking. And then *Doctor Who* returned, ending the Headroom Hacker's reign of soft-core terror.

The incident made the front page of the next day's *Tribune*, which called it "the work of a sophisticated video pirate with an unsophisticated sense of humor."[289] Broadcast intrusions of that sort were rare, but not unprecedented. Usually the hacker would treat it as a joke, claiming to be an alien or something. Or, if it was happening in a movie, to get the song they wrote on the air.

The Headroom Hacker, though, was content just to spout a bunch of nonsense and subject himself to the tortures of the world's laziest dominatrix. Perhaps there was something satirical in spouting a Coke slogan while holding up a Pepsi can, but calling it "performance art" would have been a stretch.

Engineers speculated that whoever this prankster was, he was operating some seriously high-end equipment; it would require a very expensive transmitter to emit the microwave signals that pushed the programs from the studios to the transmitters that topped a number of downtown skyscrapers. "This guy had to have quite a rig," said the chief engineer of an Urbana station. "Transmitters with that much power cost $400,000 to $600,000." Other engineers later said that it could have been done with the sort of gear available to amateur radio enthusiasts, though they declined to go into details. No one wanted to provide a how-to manual for copycats.

Early online message boards, a sort of nascent version of the internet, were abuzz with theories, and hackers were quite sure that the job wouldn't even have been particularly hard; the hacker would just have to aim a transmitter at the same transponder WGN was using and use a higher power. As one poster said, "It's one of those things that doesn't work out on paper. But it works."

The FCC didn't take the incident lightly, and suggested that the hacker could be facing jail time—which was better than what would have happened in the dystopian world of the *Max Headroom* TV show, where video piracy was a capital offense. But given the fact that no one was really hurt, nothing was really damaged, and the hacker hadn't threatened the world with imminent doom or anything, the FCC wasn't inclined to put too many resources into the case.

The culprit was never caught and is presumably still at large. Rumors have gone around that it was the work of a performance artist named Eric Fournier, who initially planned to use the intrusion to get his band's music video more exposure, but chickened out and instead went for the Headroom stunt. Fournier died in 2010; former bandmates say that there's no way he was responsible, but that he'd love the rumors.

New theories are suggested now and then, and I've spoken to at least one person who claims to know exactly who did it, but no one ever stepped forward and took credit for the incident—possibly because no one wanted to admit that, having gone to all the trouble to take over the airwaves, they couldn't think of a single particularly interesting thing to say.

Did Aliens Visit O'Hare Airport?

I'm fairly skeptical of stories of ghosts, aliens, psychic phenomena, and the like. I sometimes tell people that the only "supernatural" thing that I believe in is Bob Dylan. But there's an ugly, and potentially dangerous, streak in the skeptical community. I remember one time I was walking home from a concert in Union Park and saw a flickering orange light flying high in the sky.

"What the heck is that thing?" I asked out loud.

"It's a Chinese lantern," another concert-goer told me in an exasperated tone. "*Not* a UFO."

I didn't say I thought it *was* a UFO.

But even as the Chicago Transit Authority tells us to report any suspicious activity (like I'm really going to report every weirdo I see on the bus), there exists a strain in skeptical thought circles in which people assume that everyone who dares to admit they don't understand something they see must be reaching for the wildest of explanations. And this attitude discourages people from pointing out things that could be dangerous.

Similarly, I've heard people express serious disdain over the fact than an early 1990s book entitled

A newspaper image of the first (now lost) Chicago UFO photo, which was taken in 1897, when Chicago was one of several cities where a mysterious "airship" was reported.

The Fire Officer's Guide to Disaster Control included fourteen pages on what to do in the event of a UFO crash. But, hey, why *wouldn't* firefighters need some sort of protocol for something like that? Even if the "UFO" turns out to be a disused satellite, a weather balloon, or even that old standby, swamp gas, it's not unreasonable to imagine that someday, in your duties as a firefighter, you could get a call that some as-yet-unidentified object has fallen from the sky and set a bunch of trees on fire. And what if that fallen object is part of a terrorist attack? There ought to be some sort of protocol for what you do in scenarios in which you don't know the nature of what's going on.

And, while stories of alien encounters have never been sufficient to persuade the scientific community that The Truth Is Out There, enough stories *do* exist that it probably couldn't hurt anything to put together a list of Best Practices, just in case.

There is, in fact, a National Aviation Reporting Center on Anomalous Phemomena (NARCAP), which was founded to examine incidents in which pilots and other aviation professionals encounter strange lights or objects that they can't identify or explain. Though not a government organization, they're awfully thorough; in 2007, they issued a report more than 150 pages long on a strange "flying disc" that apparently came very close to landing at O'Hare airport in Chicago.

Well, where *else* would a flying saucer land? If you were piloting a spaceship, wouldn't *you* rather touch down at an airport than out in the swamp someplace?

At approximately 4:15 p.m. on November 7, 2006, a great many airport employees reported seeing a round metallic object flying approximately 1,900 feet above ground level above gate C17. The object was variously estimated as being twenty-two to eighty feet in diameter, and hovered, apparently spinning rapidly in place, for approximately fifteen minutes, then accelerated away at a steep angle, leaving a hole in the clouds above that kept its own shape (not unlike when Bugs Bunny crashes through a door) for more than ten minutes, suggesting that the object was radiating a rather impressive amount of heat.

A ramp mechanic who was assisting with the pushback of a 737 at C17 looked up and was startled to see the craft, whatever it was, hovering silently in the air, roughly five hundred feet in the sky under low-hanging clouds. He made a radio call and told the cockpit of the nearest plane what he was seeing.

Two United mechanics were about to taxi an empty plane to gate D2 when they heard a pilot from the plane at C17 talking about a disc-shaped object hovering over the gate. "At first we laughed to each other," one said, "and then the same pilot said again on the radio that it was about seven hundred feet above ground level . . . the ATC [Air Traffic Control] controller that was handling ground traffic made a few smart comments about the alleged UFO sitting above the C terminal."

But both mechanics looked up and saw the object. "It was definitely not a blimp," one would say. "I'll tell you definitely, it's not an airplane as we know it."

Meanwhile, the ATC tower didn't see the object, even though it should have been well within their field of view. "There must be hundreds of witnesses," the mechanic said. It seemed "very deliberate, given the weather conditions and the airport operations at the time. I am still in absolute wonder and amazement of what I saw that afternoon."

At 4:48, a Gateway pilot, a United taxi mechanic, and a ground controller engaged in a radio conversation:

> **Controller**: Look at your window. Do you see anything above United concourse? They actually, believe it or not, they called us and said somebody observed a flying disc about a thousand feet above the, uh . . . gate Charley 17. Do you see anything over there?
> **Gateway Pilot**: (pause) Not that I can tell. I thought *my* job was stressful. (laughter)
> **United Mechanic**: Oh, we saw it a half hour ago. A whole bunch of us over at the, uh, Charley concourse. We thought it was a balloon but we're not sure.

A phone conversation between a United Zone Controller and an FAA area supervisor in the tower was logged, as well:

> **FAA:** Tower, this is Dave.
> **United:** Hey Dave, this is Sue in the United Tower . . . Did you see a flying disc out by C17?

FAA: Oh, it starts, Sue. (laughter) Oh, we're sorry, Sue. (laughter in background) A flying . . . you're seeing flying discs?
United: Well, that's what a pilot in the ramp area at C17 told us. They saw some flying discs above them. But we can't see above us.
FAA: Come on, Sue . . . Hey, you guys been celebrating the holidays or anything, or what? You're celebrating Christmas today? I haven't seen anything, Sue, and if I did I wouldn't admit to it.
United: (laughs)
FAA: No, I have not seen any flying disc at gate C17.

Another conversation was between the FAA and the United Ramp Tower:

United: I'm sorry, there was, I told Dave, there was a flying disc outside above Charley 17, and he thought I was pretty much high. But, um, I'm not high and I'm not drinking.
FAA: Yeah.
United: So, someone got a picture of it. So, if you guys see it out there . . .
FAA: A disc, like a Frisbee?
United: Like a UFO type thing . . . he got a picture of it . . . (laughs) . . . so if you happen to see anything. (laughs)
FAA: You know, I'll keep a peeled eye for that.

An office worker stepped outside and saw it as well, though he said he wouldn't have noticed it if he hadn't known where to look. He said it was "an elliptical sphere-like dark metal object" that "rose almost instantaneously at a slight angle towards the east" (which would mean that it was heading straight for Chicago proper).

One other witness that worker spoke to had seen the object and decided it was a bird. But the pilot in the cockpit of the 737 at C17, who had logged over thirteen thousand flight hours, said that the object was "a dirty aluminum color, very stable and without any optical distortions near it. It was perfectly round and silent." Not exactly the sort of description an experienced pilot would make of a bird.

From these transcripts, it seems as though the workers involved were all sort of embarrassed even to be talking about the "disc" and tried to laugh it off, but several of them saw it, and any time there's an unidentified object in your airspace, it's a potential safety hazard, no matter the actual origin.

The incident managed to stay under wraps for a month or two, except for a couple of radio shows like *Coast to Coast AM*, until the *Chicago Tribune* picked up on it in January 2007. Once they got wind of the story, it was all over the news for a couple of days, appearing on CNN and MSNBC, and in *New Scientist, National Ledger, Stars and Stripes*, and *Newsweek*. All at once, officials had to come up with an explanation. FAA spokeswoman Elizabeth Isham Cory said, "Our theory on this is that it was a weather phenomenon. That night was a perfect atmospheric condition in terms of low [cloud] ceiling and a lot of airport lights. When the lights shine up into the clouds, sometimes you can see funny things. That's our take on it."

This was only a step or two above blaming the sighting on swamp gas in an area without swamps. After all, the sighting didn't take place at night. The ramp lights had not yet been turned on.

Craig Burzych, a union official and air traffic control specialist who was in the tower that day, brushed off the notion that it was an alien craft quite succinctly: If these were space men, either they weren't very good at their jobs, or Chicago had really let them down. "To fly seven million light years to O'Hare," he said, "and then have to turn around and go home because your gate was occupied is simply unacceptable."

But the NARCAP report took the incident a lot more seriously. "What's unacceptable," they wrote in their report, "is this extremely cavalier and trivializing attitude toward unidentified aerial phenomena that is representative of today's aviation community."

Though they were able to come up with a few possible scientific explanations for the "hole in the clouds" that could theoretically have led to the sighting (and were presumably more likely explanations than saying it was an alien spaceship), they didn't think that any of them were really the right answer. And they were strongly critical of the flip response to what might have been a serious safety issue—brash skepticism of anything not immediately identified does no one any favors. The "don't say anything" culture could lead to people being afraid to report something that turns out to be a serious safety hazard or terrorist threat.

And United's apparent orders to witnesses not to talk about what they'd seen didn't do anything to quiet conspiracy theorists; the fact that the photo mentioned in the recorded radio conversations never surfaced is a strong indication that the person who took the picture must have feared for his job.

One baggage handler shared NARCAP's frustration. "Some of us are getting angry with this being hushed up with all the terrorism and TSA idiots hanging around," they told the *Tribune*. "If we see a funny-looking bag, all damn hell breaks loose, but park a funny silver thing a few hundred feet above a busy airport and everyone tries to hush it up. It just don't make sense."[290]

Interviews and transcripts in the NARCAP report indicate that several pictures were taken. They would have been taken from a far enough distance from the object that they'd be unlikely to show much, but they're out there. Actor/UFO buff Dan Aykroyd is rumored to be in possession of several of them, including a video (though he denies it). A few that have circulated online turned out to be hoaxes. If the photos are out there, UFO buffs are still waiting.

The Puzzling Career of Vivian Maier

Vivian Maier is not a mystery, exactly; the basic facts of her life are fairly well established. "Enigma" might be a better term.

In 2007, John Maloof was a twenty-six-year-old realtor working on a book about the history of Portage Park, his Northwest Side neighborhood. At a storage auction, he noticed a footlocker full of photographic negatives that seemed as though they might be useful in his book, took a chance, and bought them for a few hundred dollars.

What he found was a photographic treasure trove. There were portraits of people on the street: drifters, businessmen, and children. Of long-vanished buildings, self portraits, and street scenes, such as one of street performer Anderson Punch, better known as the Chicken Man, attracting a small crowd as he played an accordion while his dancing chicken perched on his head outside of the Leavitt Brothers sandwich shop. Many of them were of astonishing quality. Though the photographer, Vivian Maier, was completely unknown, the portraits exhibited a sort of technical skill far beyond what anyone could call "outsider art." Indeed, they were taken with an artist's eye for detail. They contain wit, drama, political commentary, pathos, and everything else you could ask from street photography.

And, at the time, the photographer, Vivian Maier, was still alive. Some of her old nannying charges, now grown, were paying for Maier, now over eighty, to live in an apartment in Rogers Park on the North Side. She'd been living in near poverty, missing enough payments on a storage locker that her trove of negatives were auctioned off. After falling in 2008, she was brought to a nursing home in the north suburbs. Her work was starting to get recognition online—unbeknownst to her—when she passed away in April 2009.

Maloof, in the meantime, had posted some of the photos online, but they attracted little attention, and he'd done little work trying to track down the photographer; it took him some time (and equipment) to realize just what a special discovery he'd made. When he finally found the photographer's name, it was too late; she'd died only days before. Now, he began to research Vivian's story more diligently. In October 2009, months after her death, some of the photos he posted on Flickr began to receive attention.

Maloof bought other lockers from the people who'd bought them at the auction, eventually acquiring about one hundred thousand of Maier's negatives, and spent months trying to find out all he could about the mysterious photographer, even traveling to Europe to meet distant relatives. Maier, it turned out, had spent years working as a nanny around the city, keeping largely to herself and taking photographs in her spare time. So far as could be found, she'd never shown the work to anyone and lived in near-complete obscurity. She'd moved from her native France to the United States in 1951 at the age of twenty-five, then moved to Chicago in 1956, making her home there for the next several decades.

The children she looked after knew of her interest in photography; she would often take them downtown with her when she took photographs, occasionally into stockyards and rundown neighborhoods. None of them, however, knew just how many tens of thousands of photographs she'd taken with her Rolleiflex camera. Only a few people ever saw any of them, and she may have never shown more than a few of them to another adult (the prints she made herself were generally not of as fine quality as the photographic work itself). Evidence suggests that she made a few half-hearted attempts to have some of them shown in France, but for reasons of her own, she never made a concerted effort to share her work and never invested the money to make proper prints of the vast majority of the negatives.

Maloof's work made Vivian Maier posthumously famous in Chicago, and her story even became the subject of an Oscar-nominated documentary, the Maloof-directed *Finding Vivian Maier.*

Why had no one ever seen the work? By all accounts, Maier was something of a loner, loathe to attract attention to herself. Some of the families she'd boarded with said that in several years, she'd never taken a personal phone call. As such, only small anecdotes have survived. Maloof learned that she didn't cash her social security checks and didn't like to go to doctor because she knew others couldn't afford to, and that she thought Americans smiled too much.

She does seem to have been a bit of a radical. "She liked to explore urban areas especially," Maloof told *American Photographer*, "like the Maxwell Street flea market, where there's lots of stolen goods and people not paying taxes and people who don't want their photos taken. It says a lot about her that she's going to these places, oftentimes with the children."

When suggested that some of the work, and some of the stories about her, present "some underlying horror," in her background, Maloof said, "Possibly. I think that went to the grave with her, though."[291]

Some of the mystery of her work will come out in time; to date, only a fraction of the hundred thousand or so negatives have been made public, and thousands haven't yet been scanned at all. What could be among the shots? Could there be new pictures of rarely photographed buildings or of people or places once thought lost to history? With Vivian's eye and her willingness to explore, she might have documented any number of things that would otherwise have been lost.

Despite legal hassles and copyright claims by gold-diggers determined to get a slice of the pie, Maloof has continued a near-full-time career as an advocate promoting Maier's work. But Maier herself remains something of an engima—which is probably just the way she'd want it.

For More Info:

The book may be wrapped, but my research into these cases will continue. I'm in the newspaper archives regularly, and every time a new Chicago newspaper is digitized, I get to work taking advantage of text searching to see if any articles have eluded me. Some always have, and new clues to these stories are found all the time.

To keep up to date, check the Mysterious Chicago blog at www. mysteriouschicago.com.

Endnotes

Note: in most cases, older newspaper articles did not give the author's name; individual bylines would not become common until well into the twentieth century.

1 "To Show its Riches," *Chicago Tribune*, Nov. 1, 1896.
2 Joseph Kirkland, *The Chicago Massacre of 1812* (Dibble Publishing Co., Chicago 1893).
3 Andreas, *History of Chicago Vol 1*.
4 "An Old-Time Tragedy," *Chicago Daily Inter Ocean*, April 27, 1891.
5 Kirkland, *The Chicago Massacre of 1812*.
6 "Presented with a Skeleton," *Chicago Tribune*, July 22, 1891.
7 "He Paid the Penalty," *Chicago Tribune*, July 10, 1893.
8 "Old Settlers Picnic," *Chicago Tribune*, June 27, 1893.
9 *Life of the Chicago Banker Geo. W. Green, alias Oliver Gavit, Who Was Found Guilty of Poisoning His Wife* (Chicago: Mellen and Co., 1855).
10 "Local Matters," *Chicago Democratic Press*, Sept. 20, 1854.
11 *Life of the Chicago Banker Geo. W. Green.*
12 Ibid.
13 "The Daguerrotype of Green, the Murderer and Suicide," *Chicago Tribune*, Feb. 20, 1855.
14 "Doctors All Agree," *Chicago Tribune*, March 23, 1893.
15 Louise de Koven Bowen, *Growing Up with a City* (New York: The Macmillan Co., 1926).
16 "Splendid Vault," *Chicago Tribune*, Aug. 14, 1858.
17 "Not in Lincoln Park," *Chicago Evening Journal*, Feb. 21, 1892.
18 "Lincoln Park: Working Out the Assessments," *Chicago Tribune*, Feb. 18, 1877.
19 "Not in Lincoln Park."
20 Ibid.
21 "Couch Tomb Guarded," *Chicago Examiner*, May 6, 1911.
22 "Policeman Guards Sealed Couch Tomb," *Chicago Examiner*, May 6, 1911.

23 "Lincoln Park Has Tomb Riddle," Chicago Daily News, May 6, 1911.
24 Ibid.
25 "Almost a Century," *Chicago Tribune*, Jan. 10, 1875.
26 "Obituary: Ninety and Nine," *Chicago Tribune*, Oct. 24, 1876.
27 "To Honor Kennison," *Chicago Daily Inter Ocean*, Feb. 25, 1901.
28 "Who Can Tell?" *Chicago Tribune*, April 4, 1880.
29 Pamela Bannos, "Hidden Truths," http://hiddentruths.northwestern.edu.
30 "1776 Veteran," *Chicago Tribune*, July 4, 1959.
31 "Caves Hide Boys Who Rob and Ruin," *Chicago Tribune*, Aug. 31, 1910.
32 Genevieve Maher, "When the Gold Coast was a Brewery," *Chicago Tribune*, Aug 18, 1963.
33 Ibid.
34 Ibid.
35 Ibid.
36 Ibid.
37 Ibid.
38 Personal interviews.
39 "Buried in a Barrel," *National Police Gazette*, Jan. 9, 1886.
40 "An Interesting Incident," *Chicago Daily Inter Ocean*, Dec. 19, 1885.
41 "New York," *Chicago Tribune*, Dec. 30, 1885.
42 "The Late W. L. Newberry," *Chicago Daily Inter Ocean*, Dec. 29, 1885.
43 "Shocking Tragedy," *Chicago Tribune*, Oct. 7, 1871.
44 "The Last Tragedy," *Chicago Tribune*, Oct 8, 1871.
45 Ibid.
46 Ibid.
47 Ibid.
48 "The Edsall Tragedy," *Chicago Tribune*, Oct. 8, 1871.
49 "FIRE!" *Chicago Times*, Oct. 8, 1871.
50 "Chicago in Ruins," *The Leavenworth Weekly Times*, Oct 12, 1871, 1.
51 George Lippard Barclay, *The Great Fire of Chicago* (Barclay and Co., 1872).
52 Michael Ahern, "Reporter of 1871 Fire Describes Blaze of Today," *Chicago Tribune*, Oct. 8, 1911.
53 "FIRE!"
54 Ibid.
55 "How it Originated," *Chicago Tribune*, Oct. 20, 1871.
56 "Origin of the Fire," Interview with Mrs. Leary," *Chicago Journal*, Oct. 21, 1871.
57 Ibid.
58 Ibid.
59 "The Cow," *Chicago Times*, Oct. 23, 1871.
60 "A Startling Story" Chicago Times, Oct. 23, 1871.
61 Ibid.

62 "Who Burned Chicago?," *Nashville Union and American*, Oct. 27, 1871.

63 "O'Leary Defends Noted Cow," *Chicago Tribune*, Nov. 30, 1909.

64 Ibid.

65 "The Suffrage Question," *Chicago Tribune*, Nov 23, 1867.

66 Donald Miller, *City of the Century* (New York: Simon and Schuster, 1997).

67 *Chicago Evening Journal*, Oct. 7, 1871.

68 Ibid.

69 "Mrs. Victoria C. Woodhull," *Chicago Times*, Oct. 8, 1871.

70 George Francis Train, *Man of Destiny* (Self-published, 1872).

71 *Memphis Public Ledger*, Nov. 3, 1871.

72 Train, *Man of Destiny*.

73 Detroit Free Press, Sept. 9, 1864.

74 "George Francis Train and the O'Leary Cow," *Chicago Tribune*, Dec. 16, 1871.

75 "Impending Dissolution," *Chicago Times*, Dec. 31, 1862.

76 "Deed Is Done." *Chicago Times*, Jan. 1, 1863.

77 *Chicago Times*, Oct. 27, 1871.

78 "The Storey Palace," *Olean Democract*, Oct. 15, 1888.

79 "End of Storey's Folly," *Indianapolis News*, Nov. 23, 1906.

80 "Out of the Mansion," *Chicago Tribune*, Oct. 11, 1893.

81 "And Still Another Murder," *Chicago Times*, Aug. 26, 1858.

82 "Dr. Cream Interviewed," *Chicago Tribune*, Aug. 3, 1881.

83 "Suicide by Arsenic," *Chicago Daily Inter Ocean*, April 11, 1881.

84 "Alice Montgomery," *Chicago Daily News*, April 11, 1881.

85 "Alice Montgomery's Fate," *Chicago Morning News*, April 11, 1881.

86 "That Mystery Deepened," *Chicago Daily Inter Ocean*, April 25, 1881.

87 Cornelia. Joy-Dyer, *Some Records of the Dyer Family* (New York:T. Whittaker Press, 1884).

88 Michael Bell, *Food for the Dead* (Middletown, CT: Wesleyan University Press, 2001).

89 www.smithsonianmag.com/history/the-great-new-england-vampire-panic-36482878/?no-ist.

90 Moncure Conway, *Demonology and Devil-lore Volume 1* (Mich.: Chatto and Windus, 1879).

91 Charter, Rules and Regulations of the Rosehill Cemetery, 1859.

92 *Biographical Sketches of the Leading Men of Chicago* (Chicago:Wilson & St. Clair, 1868).

93 "Samuel Patton's Case," *Chicago Daily Inter Ocean*, April 12, 1888.

94 "The Lake View Vampire," *Chicago Tribune*, Sept. 30, 1888.

95 "Vampire of Lake View," *Chicago Tribune*, Nov. 4, 1894.

96 Harry Houdini, "Zanzic, Charlatan Supreme," M.U.M. Sept. 1923, courtesy of Conjuring Arts Research Center.

97 "Hid in Secret Rooms," *Chicago Tribune*, March 23, 1893.

98 "Bone Clew Weak," *Chicago Tribune,* July 30, 1895.

99 "Castle of a Modern Bluebeard," *New York World,* Aug 11, 1895.

100 "Is a Queer Assortment of Wares," *Chicago Tribune,* Sept. 27, 1896.

101 Quinlan v. Badenoch court records, 1897.

102 "George M. Shippy Made Chief," *Chicago Tribune,* April 14, 1907.

103 1124 Clark; in modern numbering this would be on Clark just below Division.

104 "Woman Accuses Black Hand," *Chicago American,* Nov. 19, 1904.

105 "Makes Dead a Detective," *Chicago Tribune,* Nov. 22, 1904.

106 Personal correspondence.

107 M. E. Konigsburg, *King News* (New York: F.A. Stokes Co., 1941).

108 "Left In His Automobile on Lonely Road," *Chicago Evening American,* Nov. 20, 1904.

109 Mary E. Holland, "Two Men Murdered in Auto, Declares Woman Detective,"*Chicago Evening American,* Nov. 21, 1904.

110 Ibid.

111 Joseph Weil and W. T. Brannon. *Yellow Kid Weil: The Autobiography of America's Master Swindler* (Chicago, Ill.: Ziff-Davis Publishing Co., 1948).

112 *Chicago Inter Ocean,* Dec. 1, 1904.

113 Ibid.

114 Ibid.

115 Now republished in ebook form in *Mistress of Mysteries: Threeby Mary E. Holland* (Chicago: Mysterious Chicago, 2016.

116 The Hoch summary comes directly from the trial transcript.

117 "Bride Murders," *Chicago Evening American,* Jan. 21, 1905.

118 "Drama in the Death House," *Chicago Tribune,* Dec. 13, 1936.

119 "Hoch Flooded with Valentines," *Chicago Daily Inter Ocean,* Feb. 14, 1904.

120 "Hoch Gives Clew to His Secret," *Chicago Tribune,* May 21, 1905.

121 *Chicago Record-Herald,* taken here from reprint: "The Secret of Johann Hoch," *Washington Post,* Nov. 2, 1913.

122 "M Field Jr. Shoots Self, Is Near Death," *Chicago Daily Inter Ocean,* Nov. 23, 1905.

123 "After 50 Years Prairie Ave Stirs Again," *Chicago Tribune,* Dec. 12, 1937.

124 Konigsburg, *King News.*

125 "'How Was I Shot?' Asks Field," *Chicago Evening American,* Nov. 28, 1905.

126 "Death By Accident, Field Jury Verdict," *Chicago Daily Inter-Ocean,* Dec. 2, 1905.

127 "Automatic Pistol Can Only Be Fired by Hand," *Chicago Evening American,* Nov. 28, 1905.

128 Ibid.

129 Widely printed, taken here from "Woman Says She Killed Marshall Field Jr," *St. Louis Post Dispatch*, Nov. 23, 1913.

130 "Jack Johnson Don't Know," *The Day Book*, Nov. 26, 1913.

131 "Husband Kills Wife and Self on Eve of Trial," *Scranton Truth*, Sept. 23, 1914.

132 Genevieve Forbes Herrick, "Stokes Tells of Underworld Search for 'Helen.'," *Chicago Tribune*, March 6, 1925.

133 Ibid.

134 "Stokes Effort to Link His Wife with Notorious Club Bared in Sleuth's Letters," *Ogden Standard*, Feb. 27, 1925.

135 Arthur Meeker, *Chicago with Love*, (Chicago: Knopf, 1955).

136 Dan Rottenberg, "Good Rumors Never Die," *Chicago Magazine*, February 1984.

137 "Brain of Murdered Woman as Evidence," *Chicago Daily Inter Ocean*, Feb. 11, 1906.

138 "Youth Confesses to Hollist Murder," *Chicago Daily Inter Ocean*, Jan. 14, 1906.

139 "Almost Avenges," *Chicago Tribune*, Jan. 14, 1906.

140 J. Sanderson Christison, *The Tragedy of Chicago*, (Self-published, 1907).

141 *Evening Journal*, date unknown, reprinted in J. Sanderson Christison, *The Tragedy of Chicago*, (Self-published, 1907).

142 Christison, *The Tragedy of Chicago*.

143 "Conviction by Confession," *Chicago Daily Inter Ocean*, April 15, 1894.

144 "Proposal for a Skyscraper for Michigan Avenue, Chicago, in the Form of Lorado Taft's Sculpture 'Death'; Pop; Creation date: 1968," http://quod .lib.umich.edu/h/hart/x-343206/05d115356, University of Michigan Library Digital Collections. Accessed February 1, 2016.

145 "Difficulties in Reaching Chicago in 1833," *Chicago Daily Inter Ocean*, Oct. 1, 1905.

146 "Plotters in a Trap," *Chicago Tribune*, April 21, 1895.

147 Henry Graves probate file.

148 "Death of Sorenson Murder, Say Police," *Chicago Daily Inter Ocean*, May 7, 1908.

149 Ibid.

150 "Schoolteacher Tells of Remarkable Incident," *Chicago Evening American*, May 8, 1908.

151 "25 Killed," *Chicago Evening American*, May 6, 1908.

152 I call dibs on this story, by the way.

153 "If Mrs. Gunness and Hoch Had Plotted Against Each Other," *Chicago Evening American*, May 8, 1908.

154 "Say Lamphere Was Gunness Aid,"*Chicago Tribune*, Nov. 13, 1908.

155 "Mania for Money Her Ruling Passion," *Chicago Daily Inter Ocean*, May 7, 1908.

156 "Woman Bluebeard's Accomplice Confesses," *Chicago Evening American,* May 7, 1908.

157 "Woman Bluebeard Is Alive," *Chicago Evening American,* May 7, 1908.

158 "Facts Gathered to Prove Widow Gunness Is Alive," *Chicago Evening American,* May 8, 1908.

159 "State Shows Death of MrsGunness," *Chicago Daily Inter Ocean,* Nov. 15, 1908.

160 "Second Slaying Laid to Cramer," *Chicago Examiner,* Feb. 27, 1913.

161 "Conway Admits Singer Murder," *Chicago Tribune,* Nov, 3, 1912.

162 "Tell of Tragedy to Jury Today," *Chicago Tribune,* Nov. 4, 1912.

163 "Wife Requests Insurance after Husband Flees Prison" *Canton Repository* (Canton, Ohio), Sept. 29, 1932.

164 "Chicago Ready for War? Look!" *Chicago Examiner,* Nov. 24, 1915.

165 Ibid.

166 "Bones Are Found in Fool Killer," *Chicago Examiner,* Jan. 14, 1916.

167 Display ad, *Chicago Tribune,* Feb. 23, 1916.

168 "Army Makes Land Lubber of Human Fish," *Chicago Tribune,* Sept. 20, 1917.

169 Comment posted on the Mysterious Chicago blog, Nov 18, 2010.

170 "New Engines of War," *Chicago Daily Inter Ocean,* Dec. 1, 1893.

171 United States Patents US533466A and US525179A.

172 Charles Chaplin, *My Autobiography* (London: The Bodley Head, 1964).

173 "Levee Is Dead, but its Idol, 'Jazz,' Reins," *Chicago Tribune,* Sept. 22, 1921.

174 "Colosimo Slain," *Chicago Tribune,* May 12, 1920.

175 Ibid.

176 Kinsley, Philip, "Famous Mystery Cases in Review," *Chicago Tribune,* June 16, 1929.

177 "Colosimo Slain."

178 "Bares Double Death Threat," *Chicago Evening American,* May 13, 1920.

179 "Colosimo Slain."

180 Kerrigan v. Colosimoand Mike the Greek court records.

181 "Letter to Girl Bares Enemies of Colosimo," *Chicago Evening American,* May 17, 1920.

182 "Saw Colosimo's Slayer," *Chicago Evening American,* May 14, 1920.

183 "Colosimo's Pet Goat Bleats with Sorrow," *Chicago Evening American,* May 14, 1920.

184 "Levee Is Dead."

185 Frederick Thrasher, *The Gang: A Study of 1313 Gangs in Chicago* (University of Chicago Press, 1936).

186 Trial testimony.

187 "Confess to Hundreds of Crimes" *Chicago American,* Nov. 26, 1919.

188 Ibid.

189 "Viana Hanged, Goes to Gibbet Without Fear," *Chicago Evening Post*, Dec. 10, 1920.

190 "Viana Hanged in Nine Minutes," *Chicago Herald-Examiner*, Dec. 11, 1920.

191 "Plot to Revive Hanged Man Bared," *Chicago Daily News*, June 24, 1921.

192 "Sheriff Bares Plot to Revive Hanged Men," *Chicago Evening Post*, June 24, 1921.

193 "Abyssinians Hanged," *Chicago Evening Journal*, June 24, 1921.

194 "Bare Plot to Revive Hanged Viana," *Herald Examiner*, June 25, 1921.

195 Ibid.

196 "Police Killed O'Neill, O'Connor Alibi in St Paul," *Chicago Tribune*, July 29, 1921.

197 "O'Connor to Be in Chicago Jail This Morning," *Chicago Tribune*, July 30, 1930.

198 1993 *Chicago Sun Times* interview, quoted in "When Harry Met Tommy, Michael Yockel," *Chicago Sun Times*, Dec. 21, 2000.

199 Gavin, John, "How Tommy O'Connor Cheated the Noose," *Chicago Tribune*, Dec. 28, 1959.

200 "A Line O' Type or Two," *Chicago Tribune*, Jan. 2, 1961.

201 Thomas Powers, "Give Up, Terrible Tom," *Chicago Tribune*, Dec. 12, 1974.

202 www.legendaryauctions.com/lot-65124.aspx#.

203 Genevieve Forbes Herrick, "'Guilty' Is Klimek Verdict," *Chicago Tribune*, March 14, 1923.

204 "Klimek Poison List Is Twenty," *Chicago Tribune*, Nov. 19, 1922.

205 Marcus A. Kavanagh, *You Be the Judge* (Chicago:Argus Books, 1929).

206 "Poison Evidence Robs Mrs. Klimek of Indifference," *Chicago Tribune*, March 11, 1923.

207 "Tillie Charges Ready for Jury," *Chicago Tribune*, Nov. 8, 1922.

208 Genevieve Forbes Herrick, "Poison Evidence Robs Mrs. Klimek of Indifference," *Chicago Tribune,*March 11, 1923.

209 Genevieve Forbes Herrick, "Killing Ladies" *Chicago Tribune,*Feb 27, 1927.

210 Herrick, "'Guilty'."

211 "Tillie Klimek is Strong Witness in Own Defense,"*Chicago Tribune,*March 13, 1923.

212 "Got Little Insurance," *Chicago Evening American*, March 13, 1922.

213 "Poison Widow Tillie Klimek Gets Life," *Chicago Tribune*, April 1, 1923.

214 "'K' Cousins' Circle Haunted by Affliction and Death," *Chicago Tribune*, March 14, 1923.

215 Kavanagh, *You Be the Judge*.

216 "'K' Cousins' Circle."

217 Herrick, "Killing Ladies."

218 "Martha Plumbs Depths of Jazz North of River," *Chicago Tribune*, Sept. 18, 1921.

219 "Wind Blew Inn Patrons Blown out of Court," *Chicago Daily News*, Feb. 14, 1922.

220 "Chicagoans are Hicks, Girl Says," *Moberly Weekly Monitor*, Feb. 16, 1922.

221 "Sentences Girls to Fairy Tales," *Greensboro Record*, March 31, 1922.

222 "Girl Sentenced to Read Fairy Tales to Smother Bohemian Fallacies," *Bay City Times*, April 11, 1922.

223 "Jazz Piano Star When Robber Invades," *Chicago Tribune*, April 5, 1922.

224 "Is Today's Girl Becoming a Savage?," *Modesto Evening News*, June 14, 1924.

225 "Alfred Caponi Arrested," *Chicago Tribune*, Aug. 31, 1922.

226 Paul T. Gilbert, "Oldest Woman Voter Interested in Public Affairs," *Chicago Evening Post*, Nov. 7, 1922.

227 "Gangsters Turn Machine Gun on William McSwiggin," *Chicago Tribune*, April 28, 1926.

228 "Al Caponi to Give Up," *Chicago Tribune*, July 28, 1926.

229 "Caponi Freed of McSwiginn Death Charge," *Chicago Tribune*, July 30, 1926.

230 Francis Zavier Busch, *Enemies of the State* (New York: Bobbs-Merrill, 1957).

231 "Colosimo Slain," *Chicago Tribune*, May 12, 1920.

232 "Chicago Gangland," *Chicago Tribune*, March 17, 1929.

233 "Blood Drenched Coat of Missing Anton is Found," *Chicago Tribune*, Dec. 4, 1926, p. 1.

234 "Lime Covered Body of Slain Anton Found," *Chicago Tribune*, Jan. 6, 1927.

235 "Builds Gallows for 65; Now He's 60 and Through," *Chicago Tribune*, Jan. 1 1927.

236 Francis McNamara, "Drama in the Death House," *Chicago Tribune*, Dec. 13, 1936.

237 "The Gallows," *Chicago Daily Inter Ocean*, June 22, 1878.

238 "Hanged Until Dead," *Macon Telegraph*, Nov. 12, 1887.

239 " . . . To Eternity," *Chicago Tribune*, Nov. 12, 1887.

240 "Zeph Was Ready to Die," *Chicago Tribune*, March 13, 1888.

241 "Assassin Is Hanged," *Chicago Tribune*, July 14, 1894.

242 Widely reprinted, and supposedly from the *Chicago Herald Examiner* of Feb. 18, 1929, though I couldn't find it in the *Examiner* microfilm on file at the Harold Washington Public Library in Chicago. Taken here from reprint in *Indianapolis News*, Feb. 19, 1929.

243 "'Always a Good Boy' Doctor's Mother Sobs," *Chicago Herald Examiner,* Feb. 15, 1929.
244 Capone FBI File.
245 Ibid.
246 "Capone's Trail of Gold," *Chicago Tribune,* Oct. 13, 1931.
247 "Woman Shot in Drake Dies," *Chicago Tribune,* Jan. 21, 1944.
248 "Murder 'Confession' Proved to Be Hoax," *Cumberland Sunday Times* (Cumberland, Maryland), Nov. 26, 1944.
249 "Drake Murder Dragged into Thorne Case," *Chicago Tribune,* April 13, 1955.
250 "Police Capt. Quinn Retiring," *Chicago Tribune,* Nov. 15, 1976.
251 Adam Higginbotham, "The Long Long Life of the Lipstick Killer," *GQ,* April 30, 2008.
252 Ammended Petititon for Executive Clemency, 2002.
253 Jesse Dukes, "Just Another Bull Shark Story," *WBEZ Curious City,* July 8, 2015.
254 *Cleveland Leader,* July 21, 1900.
255 "Lake Michiagan Freaks,"*Topeka Daily Capital,* July 28, 1900.
256 "Action Line," *Chicago Tribune,* Aug. 12, 1975.
257 "Press Hunt for 2 Missing Sisters in South," *Chicago Tribune,* Jan. 18, 1957.
258 "Action Line," *Chicago Tribune,*Oct 13, 1975.
259 "Here's the Grimes Case History," *Chicago Tribune,* Jan. 27, 1957.
260 "Press Hunt for 2 Missing Sisters in South," *Chicago Tribune,* Jan. 18, 1957.
261 "Keystone Cops Go on a Kangaroo Caper," *Chicago Tribune,* Oct. 19, 1974.
262 "Invader Still Staying Jump Ahead of Police," *Chicago Tribune,* Oct. 20, 1974.
263 "Metropolitan,"*Chicago Tribune,* Oct. 23, 1974.
264 "Kangaroo Catching Is Revealed," *El Paso Herald-Post,* Oct. 24, 1974.
265 "Hyena Yet in Graceland," *Chicago Tribune,* June 17, 1897.
266 Personal Interview, 2016.
267 Ibid.
268 Philip Wattley, "Mob Executioners Blamed for Murder of 8 Hoods," *Chicago Tribune,* May 8, 1976.
269 "Thieves Killed Cain," *Chicago Tribune,* Dec. 27, 1973.
270 "Ex Cop Cain Shot to Death," *Chicago Tribune,* Dec. 21, 1973.
271 Chuck Giancana, *Double-Cross: The Explosive, Inside Story of the Mobster Who Controlled America* (New York: Skyhorse, 2013).
272 John O'Brien, "Accused of Murder by a Voice from the Grave," *Ebony,* June 1978.

273 "Voice Trial Begins," *Chicago Tribune,* Jan. 12, 1979.

274 "Trial Told of 'Voice from the Grave' Incidents," *Chicago Sun-Times,* Jan. 18, 1978.

275 O'Brien, "Accused of Murder."

276 Maggie Daly, "Couple Describe 'Talk from the Grave'," *Chicago Tribune,* Jan. 29, 1980.

277 "Conflicting Words of Suspect," *Chicago Tribune,* Jan. 24, 1979.

278 "Voice from the Grave Case," *Chicago Tribune,* Jan. 27, 1979.

279 Daly, "Couple Describe."

280 "Trial Told of 'Voice from the Grave' Incidents," *Chicago Sun-Times,* Jan. 18, 1978.

281 O'Brien, "Accused of Murder."

282 "A Chicago Murder Solved by a Ghost," *Chicago Tribune,* April 9, 1992.

283 Chua obituary, *Chicago Tribune,* June 23, 2002.

284 "Chicago Tylenol Murders: An Oral History," *Chicago Magazine,* Sept. 21, 2012.

285 Bergman, Joy, "A Bitter Pill," *Chicago Reader,* Nov. 2, 2000.

286 Ibid.

287 Ibid.

288 "A Powerful Video Prankster Could Become Max Jailroom," *Chicago Tribune,* Nov. 24, 1987.

289 All quotes here are taken from NARCAP's report unless otherwise noted.

290 Judy Gelman Myers, "Interview: John Maloon," *American Photographer,* March 28, 2014.

Index